The international movement of women fighting their oppression and exploitation has reached a new level since the 1960s. The resolutions collected in this volume are a product of that movement. They explain the Marxist analysis of the roots of women's oppression, and the tasks facing socialists around the world.

The Fourth International, the principal organization of revolutionary socialist groups around the world, adopted the main resolution in this book in 1979. It places the oppression and exploitation of women in the context of class society. It shows that this oppression will end only when we get rid of class society.

The resolutions adopted subsequently and published here analyse the uneven advance of women in the face of the global neo-liberal offensive. They look at the position of women in the imperialist countries and in the developing world as it stands at the beginning of the 21st century. They include a major resolution on the need for the positive actions used by socialist organizations to develop and develop their feminist work and profile.

I0091194

WOMEN'S LIBERATION & SOCIALIST REVOLUTION

Women's Liberation & Socialist Revolution

About the Notebooks for Study and Research

The Notebooks for Study and Research are published by the International Institute for Research and Education. The Notebooks focus on themes of contemporary debate or historical or theoretical importance. Lectures and study materials given in sessions in our Institute, located in Amsterdam, Manila and Islamabad, are made available to the public in large part through the Notebooks.

Since 1986 we have published around fifty issues in English. Since 1998 they have been published as a book series in collaboration with publishers in London. For many years we had a parallel series in French, the *Cahiers d'étude et de recherche* (currently under review). Different issues of the Notebooks have also appeared in languages besides English and French, including German, Dutch, Arabic, Castilian, Japanese, Korean, Portuguese, Turkish, Swedish, Danish and Russian.

Women's Liberation & Socialist Revolution

Documents of the Fourth International

Edited and Introduced by Penelope Duggan

International Institute for Research & Education, Amsterdam
Resistance Books, London

Both the International Institute for Research and Education and Resistance would be glad to have readers' opinions of this book, its design and translations, and any suggestions for future publications or wider distribution.

Our books are available at special quantity discounts to educational and non-profit organizations, and to bookstores.

To contact us, please write to: Resistance, PO Box 62732 London SW2 9GQ, Britain, email contact@socialistresistance.org or visit: www.socialistresistance.org

Second edition, published by Resistance Books, October 2010
Printed in Britain by Lightning Source
ISBN 978-0-902869-79-0

Introduction © International Institute for Research and Education, 2001.
Documents © Presse-Edition-Communication, 1979-2010

Published as issue 48 of the *Notebooks for Study and Research*.
ISSN 0298-7902

Cover photograph of the World March of Women on March 6th 2010 in Brussels © Lieve Snellings.
Cover design: Claude Roelens-Dequidt

Contents

Preface

The Marxist movement has from the start addressed the question of women's place in society, both in its writing and thinking, for example in the Communist Manifesto but notably in Engels' work Origins of the Family, Private Property and the State not forgetting also August Bebel's Woman under socialism; and in its activity – notable figures include Clara Zetkin in German Social Democracy, Alexandra Kollontai in the Russian Bolshevik party and Sylvia Pankhurst in the British suffrage movement. Links between the broad labour movement and women's activity as women have also been widely present (for example women's trade unions were formed in the early days of the trade-union movement in Ireland, Britain and Denmark, there were links between the Suffragette movement and labour unions in both Britain and Ireland).

Thus it is not surprising that the Marxist left also responded – albeit different currents in different ways – to the rise of the new women's movement in the 1960s and 70s in the context of a worldwide youth radicalisation. This emergence of feminist movements was not, as is often considered, confined to Western Europe and North America. Small feminist groups began to emerge in Latin America in the early 1970s, notably in Mexico but also elsewhere, despite the military dictatorships. Women from Latin America also made important theoretical contributions to feminism (for example Ginny Vargas, Peru). The Latin American continent-wide Feminist Encuentros, the first of which was held in 1981, are still a sign of active women's movement, despite the problems that have been noted concerning the "institutionalisation" of the movement through the presence and activity of NGOs. In India the feminist movement began to develop notably after the lifting of the State of Emergency in 1976, one of its main focuses was on the violence practised against women, notably rapes and "dowry deaths". Feminist women in Iran were a component part of the movement to overthrow the Shah in the late 1970s, and are again today an active part of the pro-democracy movement.

11

But of course this mass movement was strongest in those areas where the social conditions favoured the general youth radicalisation, in the context of the post-war boom, the massification of higher education and, particularly for women, access to contraception. From this point of view it is logical that the 1979 resolution "Women's Liberation and Socialist Revolution" republished in this book was initially developed by Fourth International women from North America and Western Europe. Indeed there was some discussion as to whether such a resolution should indeed aim to have a world-wide scope or should deal with those areas where both the Fourth International had the majority of its sections, which – although in general small – were a real reflection of that upsurge of youth radicalisation, and therefore where the development of the second wave women's movement was most marked. Although the decision taken was to deal with what were known at the time as the "three sectors" of the world (advanced capitalist countries, the "third world" and Stalinised and bureaucratised countries), the sections dealing with the latter two sectors are undoubtedly the weakest of the document.

The 1991 resolution on Latin America was an important rectification to this in terms of understanding how the processes of radicalisation and movement building could take place in that specific context. It was based on a real study of the state of the movement at that time in the Latin American sub-continent undertaken notably by comrades of the Mexican PRT. Unfortunately the real implantation of the Fourth International in other parts of the world did not allow us to do similar work there. The most important point that this resolution stressed was that women moving into struggle on the basis of their social position as women, as mothers, as shanty-town dwellers fighting for water or main drains, as peasants fighting for the right to own or work the land, could also develop a gender-conscious radicalisation. We also saw this elsewhere for example as wives in solidarity with the struggles started by their husbands (see for example the 1984-85 miner's strike in Britain) or as activists in the peace movement (the Women's Peace Camp at Greenham Common also in Britain in the early 1980s) or in the nurses' movement in France in 1988

The most important theoretical and strategic gain of the 1979 document is something which we believe holds good in general. That is that the process of transformation of society on an anti-capitalist basis, uprooting the basis for all oppression and exploitation, requires the active participation of an autonomous or independent women's movement. What is meant by an autonomous women's movement is spelt out in the resolution:

"By the women's movement we mean all the women who organize themselves at one level or another to struggle against the oppression imposed on them by this society: women's liberation groups, consciousness-raising groups, neighbourhood groups, student groups, groups organized at workplaces, trade-union commissions, organizations of women of oppressed nationalities, lesbian-feminist groups, action coalitions around specific demands. The women's movement is characterized by its heterogeneity, its penetration into all layers of society, and the fact that it is not tied to any particular political organization, even though various currents are active within it. Moreover, some groups and action coalitions, though led and sustained by women, are open to men as well, such as the National Organization for Women in the United States and the National Abortion Campaign in Britain." (Our Methods of Struggle, point 2)

The basis for regarding such a movement as a strategic necessity is that:

"b. Women are both a significant component of the working class, and a potentially powerful ally of the working class in the struggle to overthrow capitalism. Without the socialist revolution, women cannot establish the preconditions for their liberation. Without the mobilization of masses of women in struggle for their own liberation, the working class cannot accomplish its historic tasks. The destruction of the bourgeois state, the eradication of capitalist property, the transformation of the economic bases and priorities of society, the consolidation of a new state power based on the democratic organization of the working class and its allies, and the continuing struggle to eliminate all forms of oppressive social relations inherited from class society – all this can ultimately be accomplished only with the conscious participation and leadership of an independent women's liberation movement." (Our Perspective 2.b.)

However the politics of such a movement are important, it is not simply women as women:

"e. While all women are affected by their oppression as women, the mass women's liberation movement we strive to build must be basically working-class in composition, orientation, and leadership. Only such a movement, with roots in the most exploited layers of working-class women, will be able to carry the struggle for women's liberation through to the end in an uncompromising way, allying itself with the social forces whose class interests parallel and intersect those of women. Only such a movement will be able to play a progressive role under conditions of sharpening class polarization." (Our Perspective 2.e.)

This position was a break with the traditions of the Marxist movement on women's organising. Although women's movements linked to the Marxist movement were frequent, they had other roles: offering the possibility for women to have political activity where mixed political activity was not allowed, organising women supporters of the party, having specific work directed at winning women to the party. They did not, on a theoretical and on a practical level, take into account the need for an autonomous women's movement in order to build a relationship of forces sufficient to impose women's demands.

As such, this was the major debate with currents inside and outside the Fourth International who, while situating themselves as revolutionary Marxists, adhered to a conception of the revolutionary process focusing on working class represented by "the" revolutionary party as the sole agency of revolutionary social change, which would at best naturally incorporate women's demands or lay the basis for the elimination of women's inequality once it achieved power. It remains a distinctive position today in relation to other international revolutionary Marxist currents such as the Morenoist current, the IST around the British SWP or the different currents developing from the British Militant tendency.

This position developed by the Fourth International should also be seen in the context of another debate that was taking place at the same time and was concluded by the adoption in 1985 of the resolution "Socialist Democracy and the Dictatorship of the Proletariat", although the main lines of the discussion had been developed in the 1970s. This debate marked an important advance in the strategic thinking of the FI by asserting that the different experiences and interests of sectors of the exploited and oppressed implied the development of different authentically revolutionary organisations, and that one single party would not synthesise all their interests in its programme. This discussion was also marked by the experience of the Nicaraguan revolution and a further discussion of the question of the revolutionary subject in the 1980s, in which a distinction was proposed between the practical-political subject that would mobilise the mass of the population able to impose its programme, and the theoretical-political subject that would contribute to the development of the political programme while not directly mobilising the mass weight of the exploited and oppressed.

This important point was accepted by an absolutely overwhelming majority of the Fourth International at its 1979 World Congress. However, this did not preclude a number of other important debates continuing, at the congress itself and subsequently.

The position taken in favour of an independent women's liberation movement was argued essentially from the position of the failure of the *leaderships* of the parties and unions of the labour movement to take up women's demands and an idealised notion of male workers attitude to women crept in:

"They often face sexist harassment and abuse which is organized and promoted by their foremen and supervisors. Even when it comes from their fellow workers, it is often the result of an atmosphere fostered by the employer." (Our Methods of Struggle 7.)

This debate also found its prolongation after the congress in the debate about "men's benefits", that is to what extent men as individuals benefit from women's oppression, and thus have an interest, or think they do, in perpetuating a situation of inequality and discrimination.

Debates around the validity of Engels' contention that women's oppression was a product of the development of class society – a continuing subject of research and discussion among feminist anthropologists and social scientists today – produced a compromise formula:

"3. The origin of women's oppression is intertwined with the transition from pre-class to class society. The exact process by which this complex transition took place is a continuing subject of research and discussion even among those who subscribe to a materialist historical view. However, the fundamental lines along which women's oppression emerged are clear. The change in women's status developed along with the growing productivity of human labour based on agriculture, the domestication of animals, and stock raising; the rise of new divisions of labour, craftsmanship, and commerce; the private appropriation of an increasing social surplus; and the development of the possibility for some humans to prosper from the exploitation of the labour of others." (Origin and Nature of Women's Oppression 3.)

There was however complete agreement that women's oppression pre-dated capitalism and therefore would not be eliminated by the overthrow of capitalism, as the experience of the Soviet Union had shown. The chapter "Thermidor in the Family" in Leon Trotsky's book *The Revolution Betrayed* was an important text in this respect.

In common with much of the current known as "socialist" or "class struggle" within the broad feminist movement, questions of sexuality and violence were less fully dealt with in our framework although demands were formulated. Early drafts of the document implying all lesbians were separatists were amended. Later, at the 2003 World Congress, a programmatic resolution on Lesbian and Gay Liberation that drew on the analytical and strategic framework of the 1979 was adopted. Certain FI organisations in the 1970s still had, lamentably, extremely backward positions on homosexuality, going so far as not permit membership arguing that it could put the organisation in danger as an illegal activity. Such a position would now obviously not be acceptable and any such organisation would not be admitted, or would be excluded from, membership of the FI. In 1991 one organisation was dropped from membership, following a decision by all the women comrades to leave the organisation because in their opinion their party had not correctly dealt with incidents of sexual violence and harassment, although the individuals responsible were expelled.

The 1979 resolution insisted on the fact that all women are oppressed, although this oppression combines with class oppression. However the only references to women of different ethnic origin are in relation to immigrant women, although in the United States Black women were among prominent leaders of the Fourth Internationalists who contributed largely to the drafting of the document. Later texts such as the 1991 resolution about women in the Western advanced capitalist countries were better on this point. The questions of violence against women were also dealt with more fully in later texts.

Particular importance was given to the impact of the women's movement on the labour movement and the forms of organisation of women as workers, notably in the women's commissions that developed in trade unions. The forms and nature of these commissions were different depending on the traditions of the labour movement – the extent to which these trade-union leaderships accepted these as legitimate union structures or pushed them to organise outside of those structures. This did not necessarily mean however that the "legitimate" structures played a less dynamic role than those forced to organise on a more independent basis. The women's commissions in the British and French trade-union movements played an important role in pushing the trade-union leaderships to organise major national demonstrations in defence of abortion rights in collaboration with the organised women's movement in 1979. The Coalition of Labour Union Women in the United States did valuable work.

The resolution of 1979 placed itself in the perspective of a continuing existence indeed development of the women's movement. By 1991 it was clear that the world-wide impact of feminism was not expressed in the continuing growth of women's movements. Despite our conviction that women's liberation was far from being achieved, the obvious questions of legislation had to a large extent been won in advanced capitalist countries and broad united-front mobilisations thus more difficult to achieve. The continuing activity of committed feminists tended to organise itself around specific themes and in particular where women were in need of support networks that were not provided elsewhere, for example women victims of sexual violence.

At the same time, the theoretical and analytical debates opened up under the impact of the women's movement itself were leading layers of women, notably in academic circles, to the conclusion that a women's liberation movement was an impossible objective because women's different experiences shaped by their social, economic, ethnic etc. place made it impossible to have any common demands. These developments fed into and were strengthened by the intellectual movement known as "postmodernism" with its emphasis on deconstruction of meta-narratives and the impossibility of universal values or demands.

Since the start, women in the feminist movement had on the one hand challenged "universal" figures, such as "the worker", pointing out that half of all workers were women and that any discussion of the working class and any movement claiming to defend its needs and interests had therefore to address itself to those experiences. In turn the movement itself was challenged by women who felt that as black, immigrant, working class or lesbian their needs and interests were not being taken on board by a movement that seemed located primarily among younger white heterosexual women in higher education or white-collar jobs.

In fact, from the start many lesbians, who did not feel their place was in the gay movement because they found it overwhelmingly masculine (and often sexist), had been key activists and initiators in the women's movement. An amendment on this very point was introduced into the 1979 resolution by women from Britain reflecting their experience that lesbian activists had been in the forefront of the women's movement and its central campaigns, notably to defend the existing liberal abortion law.

As women organised within the trade-unions to force workers' organisations to take up the demands of their women members, the women's movement saw the development of black women's groups, lesbian groups, women against racism groups that contributed to a consciousness-raising within the movement about women's different experiences.

One way in which this impact was clearly shown was how campaigns that had started around abortion rights, such as the National Abortion Campaign in Britain, took on board the experiences of the Bangladeshi women found to being used as unwitting guinea pigs for the injectable contraceptive Depo-Provera, or the West Indian women in Britain who found obligatory sterilisation too often accompanied abortions and developed its programme accordingly.

At an international level, the International Campaign for Abortion Rights (ICAR) rapidly changed its name to the International Contraception, Abortion and Sterilisation Campaign (ICASC) – today it is today the Women's Global Network for Reproductive Rights – in order to develop and expand in an inclusive way the question of women's reproductive health and women's right to control their own bodies. It is difficult to see in what way the right to decide what happens to one's own body would not be a universal demand for women, just as the demand to be free from torture or famine must be for all humans.

The emphasis on understanding women's specific experience also gave rise to different forms of difference or essentialist feminism that accepted there were essential differences between women and men and set as their goal that what are considered "feminine" values or characteristics should be given as much social value as what are traditionally considered "male" values. This approach, like those based on a notion of patriarchy as a system of male oppression running parallel to capitalism or class society, was rejected as incompatible with a Marxist approach that understood all social relations as encompassed within the relations of production and reproduction

The entry of a generation of young women radicalising under the impact of the feminist movement also led to questioning of how easily they found their place in those organisations, in relation to older male comrades but also their own contemporaries. This was not of course specific to the organisations of the Fourth International, the symbiotic relationship between mixed radical movements and the feminist radicalisation led inevitably to questioning and challenging of forms of political organisation in general. However the Fourth

International remains the only political organisation to have adopted an analytical and programmatic resolution on the question, at its World Congress in 1991, alongside proposals of many practical measures to be taken to form a "positive action plan".

In 1979 a sharp discussion had been provoked by the proposal that women comrades should have the right to meet together to discuss together the difficulties they faced in feeling at ease and accepted in the organisation, in order to identify common features and propose to the organisation as a whole measures to confront these. This proposal – labelled anti-Leninist by the reporter on the resolution – was rejected by a majority of the outgoing leadership and of delegates, particularly from the American SWP and the current associated with it. I was one of the group of young women delegates from European and Latin American countries, as well as Canada, defending the proposal. This was our first experience of working across national and linguistic boundaries to wage a common fight. However, the debate was essentially over as the practice continued where it had already been established, and the decline of the US SWP current and their eventual departure from the International meant that it was rightly seen as just one of a number of usual measures like parity or quotas for women's representation in the leadership in the resolution adopted in 1991.

Since 1991 the contributions of the Women's Commission to the international discussions have been focused on the place of women in the developing globalisation of the world economy, as in the theses of 1995 and the document on Women and the Crisis from 2010, and in reasserting the strategic importance of integrating the feminist dimension in our party-building and programmatic elaboration. These contributions were integrated in the form of amendments made to the documents both on the world situation and building the Fourth International in 1995, 2003 and 2010.

The battle for women's liberation and for revolutionary Marxist and anti-capitalist organisations to thoroughly integrate this fight into their programme, perspectives and strategy, is not over and under the impact of the developing situation we will have new tasks of analysis and elaboration. We think that these documents have created a framework that will help us fulfill those new tasks.

Penelope Duggan, September 2010.

Socialist Revolution and the Struggle for Women's Liberation (1979)

11ᵗʰ World Congress World Congress of the Fourth International

The basic Marxist positions on women's oppression are part of the programmatic foundations of the Fourth International. But this is the first full resolution on women's liberation adopted by the international[1]. Its purpose is to set down our basic analysis of the character of women's oppression, and the place the struggle against that oppression occupies in our perspectives for all three sectors of the world revolution: the advanced capitalist countries, the colonial and semi-colonial world, and the workers states.

I. The Character of Women's Oppression

The New Rise of Women's Struggles

1. Since the late 1960s a growing revolt by women against their oppression as a sex has emerged. Throughout the world, millions of women, especially young women- students, working women, housewives – are beginning to challenge some of the most fundamental features of their centuries-old oppression.

The first country in which this radicalization of women appeared as a mass phenomenon was the United States. It was announced by the blossoming of thousands of women's liberation groups and in the mobilization of tens of thousands of women in the August 26, 1970, demonstrations commemorating the fiftieth anniversary of the victorious conclusion of the American women's suffrage struggle.

But the new wave of struggles by women in North America was not an exceptional and isolated development, as the emergence of the women's liberation movement throughout the advanced capitalist countries soon demonstrated.

---

[1] *This resolution was submitted by the United Secretariat. The vote of delegates and fraternal observers was: 100 for, 0.5 against, 6 abstentions, 6.5 not voting.*

The new women's liberation movement came on the historical scene as part of a more general upsurge of the working class and all exploited and oppressed sectors of the world population. This upsurge has taken many forms, from economic strikes, to struggles against national oppression, to student demonstrations, to demands for environmental protection, to an international movement against the imperialist war in Vietnam. Although the women's movement began among students and professional women, the demands it raised, combined with the growing contradictions within the capitalist system, began to mobilize much broader layers. It began to affect the consciousness, expectations, and actions of significant sections of the working class, male and female.

In many countries the new rise of women's struggles preceded any widespread changes in the combativity of organized labor. In others, such as Spain, it was intertwined with the explosive rise of struggles by the working class on every front. But in virtually every case, the movement rose outside of, and independent from, the existing mass organizations of the working class, which were then obliged to respond to this new phenomenon. The development of the women's movement has thus become an important factor in the political and ideological battle to weaken the hold of the bourgeoisie, and its agents within the working class.

The swift growth of the women's liberation movement, and the role it has played in the deepening class struggle, both internationally and in specific countries, confirm that the fight for women's liberation must be regarded as a fundamental component of the new rise of the world revolution.

2. This radicalization of women is unprecedented in the depth of the economic, social, and political ferment it expresses and in its implications for the struggle against capitalist oppression and exploitation.

In country after country, growing numbers of women are taking part in large-scale campaigns against reactionary abortion and contraception statutes. Oppressive marriage laws, inadequate child-care facilities, and legal restrictions on equality. They are exposing and resisting the ways in which sexism is expressed in all spheres - from politics, employment, and education to the most intimate aspects of daily life, including the weight of domestic drudgery and the violence and intimidation that women are subjected to in the home and on the street.

Women are raising demands that challenge the specific forms their oppression takes under capitalism today, and are calling into question the deep-rooted traditional division of labor between men and women, from the home to the factory. More and more they are demanding affirmative action to open the doors previously closed to women in all arenas and overcome the legacy of centuries of institutionalized discrimination.

They are insisting upon the right to participate with complete equality in all forms of social, economic and cultural activity – equal education, equal access to jobs, equal pay for equal work.

In order to make this equality possible, women are searching for ways to end their domestic servitude. They are demanding that women's household chores be socialized and no longer organized as "women's work." The most conscious recognize that society, as opposed to the individual family unit, should take responsibility for the young, the old, and the sick.

At the very center of the women's liberation movement has been the fight to decriminalize abortion and make it available to all women. The right to control their own bodies, to *choose* whether to bear children, when, and how many, is recognized by millions of women as an elementary precondition for their liberation.

Such demands go to the very heart of the specific oppression of women exercised through the family and strike at the pillars of class society. They indicate the degree to which the struggle for women's liberation is a fight to transform all human social relations and place them on a new and higher plane.

3. The fact that the women's liberation movement began to emerge as an international phenomenon even prior to the exacerbation of capitalism's worldwide economic contradictions in the mid-1970s only serves to underscore the deep roots of this rebellion. It is one of the clearest symptoms of the depth of the social crisis of the bourgeois order today.

These struggles illustrate the degree to which the outmoded capitalist relations and institutions generate deepening contradictions in every sector of society and precipitate new expressions of the class struggle. The death agony of capitalism brings new layers into direct conflict with the fundamental needs and prerogatives of the bourgeoisie, bringing forth new allies, and strengthening the working class in its struggle to overthrow the capitalist system. The development of the struggle by women against their oppression has already begun to deprive the ruling class of one of the principal weapons it has long used to divide and weaken the exploited and oppressed.

4. Women's oppression has been an essential feature of class society throughout the ages. But the practical tasks of uprooting its causes, as well as combating its effects, could not be posed on a mass scale

before the era of the transition from capitalism to socialism. The fight for women's liberation is inseparable from the workers' struggle to abolish capitalism. It constitutes an integral part of the socialist revolution and the communist perspective of a classless society.

The replacement of the patriarchal family system rooted in private property by a superior organization of human relations is a prime objective of the socialist revolution. This process will accelerate and deepen as the material and ideological foundations of the new communist order are brought into being.

The development of the women's liberation movement today advances the class struggle, strengthens its forces, and enhances the prospects for socialism.

5. Women can achieve their liberation only through the victory of the world socialist revolution. This goal can be realized only by mobilizing and organizing masses of women as a powerful component of the class struggle. Therein lies the objective revolutionary dynamic of the struggle for women's liberation and the fundamental reason why the Fourth International must concern itself with, and help to provide revolutionary leadership for, women struggling to achieve their liberation.

Origin and Nature of Women's Oppression

1. The oppression of women is not determined by their biology, as many contend. Its origins are economic and social in character. Throughout the evolution of pre-class and class society, women's childbearing function has always been the same. But their social status has not always been that of a degraded domestic servant, subject to man's control and command.

2. Before the development of class society, during the historical period that Marxists have traditionally referred to as primitive communism (subsistence societies), social production was organized communally and its product shared equally. There was therefore no exploitation or oppression of one group or sex by another because no material basis for such social relations existed. Both sexes participated in social production, helping to assure the sustenance and survival of all. The social status of both women and men reflected the indispensable roles that each of them played in this productive process.

3. The origin of women's oppression is intertwined with the transition from pre-class to class society. The exact process by which this complex transition took place is a continuing subject of research and discussion even among those who subscribe to a materialist historical

view. However, the fundamental lines along which women's oppression emerged are clear. The change in women's status developed along with the growing productivity of human labor based on agriculture, the domestication of animals, and stock raising; the rise of new divisions of labor, craftsmanship, and commerce; the private appropriation of an increasing social surplus; and the development of the possibility for some humans to prosper from the exploitation of the labor of others.

In these specific socioeconomic conditions, as the exploitation of human beings became profitable for a privileged few, women, because of their biological role in production, became valuable property. Like slaves and cattle, they were a source of wealth. They alone could produce new human beings whose labor power could be exploited. Thus the purchase of women by men, along with all rights to their future offspring, arose as one of the economic and social institutions of the new order based on private property. Women's primary social role was increasingly defined as domestic servant and childbearer.

Along with the private accumulation of wealth, the patriarchal family developed as the institution by which responsibility for the unproductive members of society- especially the young- was transferred from society as a whole to an identifiable individual or small group of individuals. It was the primary socioeconomic institution for perpetuating from one generation to the next the class divisions of society- divisions between those who possessed property and lived off the wealth produced by the labor of others, and those who, owning no property, had to work for others to live. The destruction of the egalitarian and communal traditions and structures of primitive communism was essential for the rise of an exploiting class and its accelerated private accumulation of wealth.

This was the origin of the patriarchal family. In fact, the word family itself, which is still used in the Latin-based languages today, comes from the original Latin *famulus,* which means household slave, and *familia,* the totality of slaves belonging to one man.

Women ceased to have an independent place in social production. Their productive role was determined by the family to which they belonged, by the man to whom they were subordinate. This economic dependence determined the second-class social status of women, on which the cohesiveness and continuity of the patriarchal family has always depended. If women could simply take their children and leave, without suffering any economic or social hardship, the patriarchal family would not have survived through the millennia.

The patriarchal family and the subjugation of women thus came into existence along with the other institutions of emerging class society in order to buttress nascent class divisions and perpetuate the private accumulation of wealth. The state, with its police and armies, laws and courts, enforced this relationship. Ruling class ideology, including religion, arose on this basis and played a vital role in justifying the degradation of the female sex.

Women, it was said, were physically and mentally inferior to men and therefore were "naturally" or biologically the second sex. While the subjugation of women has always had different consequences for women of distinct classes, all women regardless of class were and are oppressed as part of the female sex.

4. The family system is the fundamental institution of class society that determines and maintains the specific character of the oppression of the female sex.

Throughout the history of class society, the family system has proved its value as an institution of class rule. The form of the family has evolved and adapted itself to the changing needs of the ruling classes as the modes of production and forms of private property have gone through different stages of development. The family system under classical slavery was different from the family system during feudalism (there was no real slave family). Both were quite different from what is often called the urban "nuclear family" of today.

Moreover, the family system simultaneously fulfils different social and economic requirements in reference to classes with different productive roles and property rights whose interests are diametrically opposed. For example, the "family" of the serf and the "family" of the nobleman were quite different socioeconomic formations. However, they were both part of the family *system,* an institution of class rule that has played an indispensable role at each stage in the history of class society.

In class society the family is the only place most people can turn to try to satisfy some basic human needs, such as love and companionship. However poorly the family may meet these needs for many, there is no real alternative as long as private property exists. The disintegration of the family under capitalism brings with it much misery and suffering precisely because no superior framework for human relations can yet emerge.

But providing for affection and companionship is not what defines the nature of the family system. It is an economic and social institution whose functions can be summarized as follows:

a. The family is the basic mechanism through which the ruling classes abrogate social responsibility for the economic well-being of those whose labor power they exploit – the masses of humanity. The ruling class tries, to the degree possible, to force each family to be responsible for its own, thus institutionalizing the unequal distribution of income, status and wealth.

b. The family system provides the means for passing on property ownership from one generation to the next. It is the basic social mechanism for perpetuating the division of society into classes.

c. For the ruling class, the family system provides the most inexpensive and ideologically acceptable mechanism for reproducing human labor. Making the family responsible for care of the young means that the portion of society's accumulated wealth – appropriated as private property- that is utilized to assure reproduction of the laboring classes is minimized. Furthermore, the fact that each family is an atomized unit, fighting to assure the survival of its own, hinders the most exploited and oppressed from uniting in common action.

d. The family system enforces a social division of labor in which women are fundamentally defined by their childbearing role and assigned tasks immediately associated with this reproductive function: care of the other family members. Thus the family institution rests on and reinforces a social division of labor involving the domestic subjugation and economic dependence of women.

e. The family system is a repressive and conservatizing institution that reproduces within itself the hierarchical, authoritarian relationships necessary to the maintenance of class society as a whole. It fosters the possessive, competitive, and aggressive attitudes necessary to the perpetuation of class divisions.

It molds the behavior and character structure of children from infancy through adolescence. It trains, disciplines, and polices them, teaching submission to established authority. It then curbs rebellious, nonconformist impulses. It represses and distorts all sexuality, forcing it into socially acceptable channeis of male and female sexual activity for reproductive purposes and socioeconomic roles. It inculcates all the social values and behaviorai norms that individuals must acquire in order to survive in class society and submit to its domination. It distorts all human relationships by imposing on them the framework of economic compulsion, personal dependence, and sexual repression.

5. Under capitalism, as in previous historicai epochs, the family has evolved. But the family system continues to be an indispensable institution of class rule, fulfilling all the economic and social functions outlined.

Among the bourgeoisie, the family provides for the transmission of private property from generation to generation. Marriages often assure profitable alliances or mergers of large blocs of capital, especially in the early stages of capital accumulation.

Among the classical petty bourgeoisie, such as farmers, craftsmen, or small shopkeepers, the family is also a unit of production based on the labor of family members.

For the working class, while the family provides some degree of mutual protection for its own members, in the most basic sense it is an alien class institution, one that is imposed on the working class, and serves the economic interests of the bourgeoisie not the workers. Yet working people are indoctrinated from childhood to regard it (like wage labor, private property and the state) as the most natural and imperishable of human relations.

a. With the rise of capitalism and the growth of the working class, the family unit among the workers ceases to be a petty-bourgeois unit of production although it remains the basic unit through which consumption and reproduction of labor power are organized. Each member of the family sells his or her labor power individually on the labor market. The basic economic bond that previously held together the family of the exploited and oppressed – i.e., the fact that they had to work together cooperatively in order to survive – begins to dissolve. As women are drawn into the labor market they achieve some degree of economic independence for the first time since the rise of class society. This begins to undermine the acceptance by women of their domestic subjugation. As a result, the family system is undermined.

b. Thus there is a contradiction between the increasing integration of women in the labor market and the survival of the family. As women achieve greater economic independence and more equality, the family institution begins to disintegrate. But the family system is an indispensable pillar of class rule. It must be preserved if capitalism is to survive.

c. The growing number of women in the labor market creates a deep contradiction for the capitalist class, especially during periods of accelerated expansion. They must employ more women to profit from their superexploitation. Yet the employment of women cuts across their ability to carry out the basic unpaid domestic labor of child-rearing for which women are responsible. So the state must begin to buttress the family, helping to assure and subsidize some of the economic and social functions it used to fulfill, such as education, child care, etc.

But such social services are more costly than the unpaid domestic labor of women. They absorb some of the surplus value that would otherwise by appropriated by the owners of capital. They cut into profits. Moreover, social programs of this kind foster the idea that society, not the family, should be responsible for the welfare of its nonproductive members. They raise the social expectations of the working class.

d. Unpaid work by women in the home – cooking, cleaning, washing, caring for children – plays a specific role under capitalism. This household work is a necessary element in the reproduction of labor power soid to the capitalists (either a woman's own labor power, her husband's, or her children's, or that of any other member of the family).

Other things being equal, if women did not perform unpaid labor inside the families of the working class, the general wage level would have to rise. Real wages would have to be high enough to purchase the goods and services which are now produced within the family. (Of course, the general standard of living necessary for the reproduction of labor power is a historically determined given at any time in any country. It cannot be drastically reduced without a crushing defeat of the working class.) Any general decrease of unpaid domestic labor by women would thus cut into total profits, changing the proportion between profits and wages in favor of the proletariat.

However useful it may be, a woman's household work produces no commodities for the market and thus produces no value or surplus value. Nor does it directly enter into the process of capitalist exploitation. In value terms, unpaid domestic work in the family affects the *rate* of surplus value. Indirectly, it increases the total mass of social surplus value. This holds true whether such labor is performed by women, or shared by men.

It is the capitalist class, not men in general, and certainly not male wage earners, which profits from, women's unpaid labor in the household. This "exploitation" of the family of the toilers, the burden of which falls overwhelmingly on women, can be eradicated only by overthrowing capitalism and socializing domestic chores in the process of socialist reconstruction.

e. The indispensable role of the family and the dilemma that the growing employment of women creates for the ruling class becomes clearest in periods of economic crisis. The rulers must accomplish two goals.

They must drive a significant number of women from the work force to reestablish the reserve labor pool and lower wage levels.

They must cut the growing costs of social services provided by the state and transfer the economic burden and responsibility for these services back onto the individual family of the worker.

In order to accomplish both of these objectives, they must launch an ideological offensive against the very concept of women's equality and independence, and reinforce the responsibility of the individual family for its own children, its elderly, its sick. They must reinforce the image of the family as the only "natural" form of human relations, and convince women who have begun to rebel against their subordinate status that true happiness comes only through fulfilling their "natural" and primary role as wife-mother- housekeeper. To their dismay, the capitalists are now discovering that despite appeals to austerity and dire warnings of crisis, the more thoroughly women are integrated into the work force, the more difficult it is to push sufficient numbers back into the home.

f. In the early stages of industrialization the unregulated, unbridled, brutal exploitation of women and children often goes so far as to seriously erode the family structure in the working class and threaten its usefulness as a system for organizing, controlling, and reproducing the work force.

This was the trend that Marx and Engels drew attention to in nineteenth century England. They predicted the rapid disappearance of the family in the working class. They were correct in their basic insight and understanding of the role of the family in capitalist society, but they misestimated the latent capacity of capitalism to slow down the pace of development of its inherent contradictions. They underestimated the ability of the ruling class to step in to regulate the employment of women and children and shore up the family in order to preserve the capitalist system itself. Under strong pressure from the labor movement to ameliorate the brutal exploitation of women and children the state intervened in the long-term interests of the capitalist class – even though this cut across the aim of individual capitalists to squeeze every drop of blood out of each worker for sixteen hours a day and let them die at thirty.

g. Capitalist politicians responsible for shaping policies to protect and defend the interests of the ruling class are extremely conscious of the indispensable economic, social, and political role of the family and the need to maintain it as the basic social nucleus under capitalism. "Defense of the family" is not only some peculiar demagogic shibboleth of the ultraright. Maintenance of the family system is the basic political policy of every capitalist state, dictated by the social and economic needs of capitalism itself.

6. Under capitalism, the family system also provides the mechanism for the superexploitation of women as wage workers.

a. It provides capitalism with an exceptionally flexible reservoir of labor power that can be drawn into the labor force or sent back into the home with fewer social consequences than any other component of the reserve army of labor.

Because the entire ideological superstructure reinforces the fiction that women's place is in the home, high unemployment rates for women cause relatively less social protest. After all, it is said, women work only to supplement an already existing source of income for the family. When they are unemployed, they are occupied with their household chores, and are not so obviously "out of work". The anger and resentment they feel is often dissipated as a serious social threat by the general isolation and atomization of women in separate, individual households. Thus in any period of economic crisis, the austerity measures of the ruling class always include attacks on women's right to work, including increased pressure on women to accept part-time employment, cutbacks in unemployment benefits for "housewives", and the reduction of social services such as child-care facilities.

b. Because women's "natural" place is supposed to be in the home, capitalism has a widely accepted rationalization for perpetuating:

1) the employment of women in low- paying, unskilled jobs. "They aren't worth training because they'll only get pregnant or married and quit."

2) unequal pay rates and low pay. They're only working to buy gadgets and luxuries anyway."

3) deep divisions within the working class itself. "She's taking a job a man should have."

4) the fact that women workers are not proportionally integrated in the trade unions and other organizations of the working class. "She shouldn't be running around going to meetings. She should be home taking care of the kids."

c. Since all wage structures are built from the bottom up, this superexploitation of women as a reserve work force plays an irreplaceable role in holding down men's wages as well.

d. The subjugation of women within the family system provides the economic, social, and ideological foundations that make their superexploitation possible. Women workers are exploited not only as wage labor but also as a pariah labor pool defined by sex.

7. Because the oppression of women is historically intertwined with the division of society into classes and with the role of the family as the basic unit of class society, this oppression can only be eradicated with the abolition of private ownership of the means of production. Today it is these class relations of production – not the productive capacities of humanity- which constitute the obstacle to transferring to society as a whole the social and economic functions borne under capitalism by the individual family.

8. The materialist analysis of the historical origin and economic roots of women's oppression is essential to developing a program and perspective capable of winning women's liberation. To reject this scientific explanation inevitably leads to one of two errors:

a. One error, made by many who claim to follow the Marxist method, is to deny, or at least downplay the oppression of women as a sex throughout the entire history of class society. They see the oppression of women purely and simply as an aspect of the exploitation of the working class. This view gives weight and importance to struggles by women only in their capacity as wage workers on the job. It says women will be liberated, in passing, by the socialist revolution, so there is no special need for them to organize as women fighting for their own demands.

In rejecting the need for women to organize against their oppression, they only reinforce divisions within the working class, and retard the development of class consciousness among women who begin to rebel against their subordinate status.

b. A symmetrical error is made by those who argue that male domination of women existed before class society began to emerge. This was concretized, they hold, through a sexual division of labor. Thus, patriarchal oppression must be explained by reasons other than the development of private property and class society. They see patriarchy as a set of oppressive relations parallel to but independent of class relations.

Those who have developed this analysis in a systematic way usually isolate the fact of women's role in reproduction and concentrate on it alone. They largely ignore the primacy of cooperative labor, the essence of human society, and place little weight on women's place in the process of production at each historical stage. Some even go so far as to theorize a timeless patriarchal mode of reproduction with male control over the means of reproduction (women). They often put forward psychoanalytical explanations which readily fall into ahistorical idealism, rooting oppression in biological and/or psychological drives torn out of the materialist framework of social relations.

This current, sometimes organized as 'radical feminists', contains both conscious anti-Marxists and others who consider themselves to be making a "feminist redefinition of Marxism." But the view that women's oppression is parallel to, not rooted in, the emergence and development of class exploitation leads the most consistent to pose the need for a political party of women based on a "feminist" program that pretends to be independent of the class struggle. They are hostile to and reject the need for women and men to organize together on the basis of a revolutionary working-class program to end both class exploitation and sexual oppression. They see little need for alliances in struggle with others who are oppressed and exploited.

Both of these one-sided approaches deny the revolutionary dynamic of the struggle for women's liberation as a form of the class struggle. Both fail to recognize that the struggle for women's liberation, to be successful, must go beyond the bounds of capitalist property relations. Both reject the implications this fact has for the working class and its revolutionary Marxist leadership.

Roots of the New Radicalization of Women

1. The women's liberation movement of today stands on the shoulders of the earlier struggles by women at the turn of the century.

With the consolidation of industrial capitalism throughout the nineteenth century, increasing numbers of women were integrated into the labor market. The gap between the social and legal status of women inherited from feudalism and their new economic status as wage workers selling their labor power in the market produced glaring contradictions. For women of the ruling class, too, capitalism opened the door to economic independence. Out of these contradictions arose the first wave of women's struggles aimed at winning full legal equality with men.

Among those fighting for women's rights were different political currents. Many of the suffragist leaders were women who believed the vote should be won by showing the ruling class that they were loyal defenders of the capitalist system. Some linked the suffragist struggle to support for imperialism in World War I and often opposed the right to vote for propertyless men and women, immigrants, Blacks.

But there was also a strong current of socialist women in a number of countries who saw the fight for women's rights as part of the working-class struggle and mobilized support from working-class women and men on that basis. They fought for the right to vote and played a decisive role in the suffrage struggle in countries like the United States. They also raised and fought for other demands such as equal pay, and contraception services.

Even some of the semicolonial countries such as Chile, Argentina, and Mexico saw the emergence of feminist groups during this same period.

Through struggle the women of the most advanced capitalist countries won, to varying degrees, several important democratic rights: the right to higher education, the right to engage in trades and professions, the right to receive and dispose of their own wages (which had been considered the right of the husband or father), the right to own property, the right to divorce, the right to participate in political organizations. In several countries this first upsurge culminated in mass struggles for the right to vote.

2. Women's suffrage, following or sometimes accompanying universal male suffrage, was an important objective gain for the working class. It reflected, and in turn helped advance, the changing social status of women. For the first time in class society, women were legally considered citizens fit to participate in public affairs, with the right to a voice on major political questions, not just private household matters.

Even though the underlying cause of the subordinate status of women lies in the very foundations of class society itself and women's special role within the family, not in the formal denial of equality under the law, the extension of democratic rights to women gave them greater latitude for action and helped later generations see that the sources of women's oppression lay deeper.

3. The roots of the new radicalization of women are to be found in the economic and social changes of the post-World War II years, which have effected deepening contradictions in the capitalist economy, in the status of women, and in the patriarchal family system. To varying degrees the same factors were at work in every country that remained within the world capitalist market. But it is not surprising that the resurgence of the women's movement today first came about in the most advanced capitalist countries – such as the United States, Canada, and Britain – where these changes and contradictions had developed the furthest.

a. Advances in medical science and technology in the field of birth control and abortion have created the means by which masses of women can have greater control over their reproductive functions. Control by women over their own bodies is a precondition for women's liberation.

While such medical techniques are more widely available, reactionary laws, reinforced by bourgeois customs, religious bigotry, and the entire ideological superstructure of class society, often stand in the way of women exercising control over their own reproductive functions. Financial, legal, psychological, and "moral" barriers are fabricated to try to prevent women from demanding the right to choose whether and when to bear children. In addition, the limits placed on research due to capitalist profit considerations and sexist disregard for the lives of women have meant continuing health hazards for women using the most convenient methods of birth control.

This contradiction between what is possible and what actually exists affects the lives of all women. It has given rise to the powerful abortion rights struggles, which have been at the center of the women's movement on an international scale.

b. The prolonged boom conditions of the postwar expansion significantly increased the percentage of women in the labor force.

To take the United States as an example, in 1950, 33.9 percent of all women 18 to 64 years of age were in the labor force. By 1975 this had risen to 54 percent. Between 1960 and 1975, nearly two-thirds of all new jobs created were taken by women. Working women accounted for 29.1 percent by 1978.

Equally important, the percentage of working women with children increased dramatically, as did the percentage of working women who were heads of households.

In Spain, three times as many women are working today as in 1930.

In Britain, between 1881 and 1951 the proportion of women in employment was fairly stable, remaining at about 25 to 27 percent. By 1965, 34 percent of all women between 16 and 64 were in part-time employment, and a total of 54.3 percent came within the category of "economically active." Nearly two-thirds of the working women were married.

Only some countries that still had a high percentage of agricultural workers after the Second World War have experienced a decline in female employment over the postwar period. This was due to the fact that with the migration to the cities, many women were not reintegrated into the so-called active population. In Italy, for example, where this factor was combined with the development in small enterprises of the "typically female" sector, there has been a decline in the female percentage of the workforce.

In extremely depressed regions such as southern Italy and northern Portugal, this retrogression has actually been coupled with the resurgence of cottage industry on a significant scale. Women are induced to do piecework on their sewing machines at home, thus saving the bosses the costs of factory maintenance, health and social security payments, strikes and other "problems" caused by an organized work force.

As the influx of women into the labor force has taken place, there has been no substantial change in the degree of wage discrimination against women. In many countries this differential between the sexes has actually widened.

This is primarily because the increased employment of women has not been spread evenly over all job categories. In nearly all countries women represent from 70 to 90 percent of the work force employed in textiles, shoes, ready-to-wear clothing, tobacco, and other light industry – that is, sectors in which wages are lowest. Women also account for 70 percent or more of people employed in the service sector, with the greatest majority of women occupying the least remunerative positions: secretaries, file clerks, health workers, teachers in primary schools, keypunch operators.

Discrimination in sectors of employment – exacerbated by unequal pay for the same work in many cases – is the fundamental reason why, even in those countries where the labor movement has fought the hardest on this question, the average wage for women barely exceeds 75 percent of the average wage for men. This also explains why the differential may even widen with the massive entry of women into the lowest-paid sectors of the economy. This is the case in the United States, where the median income of fulltime, year-round women workers was 64 percent of that of men in 1955 but dropped to 59 percent in 1977.

Despite their growing place in the work force, women are still forced to assume the majority, if not the totality, of domestic tasks in addition to their wage labor. As a consequence, they often quit working temporarily when they have children, especially when they are faced with many hours of forced overtime, and then have difficulty finding new jobs later. If they continue to work they are obliged to stay home when a child is sick.

This has led to a significant increase in part-time work by women – either because they cannot find fulltime employment, or because they cannot otherwise cope with their domestic chores. But part-time work invariably brings with it lower wages, less job security, few social security benefits, and less likelihood of unionization.

The growing weight of women in the work force has had a strong impact on the attitudes of their male fellow workers. This is especially true where women have begun to fight their way into jobs in basic industry from which women were previously excluded.

But women workers still face many forms of discrimination and sexist abuse, promoted, organized and maintained by the bosses. Their fellow workers are often not aware of them, and sometimes express the same backward attitudes. And the labor bureaucracy blocks the use of union power to overcome the special obstacles women face-such as the refusal to give paid time off for maternity leaves, health hazards that are doubly dangerous for pregnant women, and harassment by foremen and supervisors who use their control over jobs to try to pressure women into sexual relations.

c. The rise in the average educational level of women has further heightened the contradictions. As labor productivity increases and the general cultural level of the working class rises, more women finish their years of secondary education. Women are also accepted into institutions of higher education on a qualitatively larger scale than ever before.

Yet, as the employment statistics indicate, the percentage of women holding jobs commensurate with their educational level has not kept pace. In all areas of the job market, from industry to the professions, women with higher educational qualifications are usually bypassed by men with less education. Moreover, throughout primary and secondary school, girls continue to be pushed-through required courses of study or through more indirect pressures – into what are considered women's jobs and roles.

As they receive more education and as social struggles raise their individual expectations, the stifling and mind-deadening drudgery of household chores and the constrictions of family life become increasingly unbearable. Thus the heightened educational level of women, combined with an intensification of the class struggle, has deepened the contradiction between women's demonstrated abilities and broadened aspirations, and their actual social and economic status.

d. The functions of the family unit in advanced capitalist society have continually contracted. It has become less and less a unit of petty production – either agricultural or domestic (canning, weaving, sewing, baking, etc.). The urban nuclear family of today has come a long way from the productive farm family of previous centuries. At the same time, in their search for profits, consumer-oriented capitalist industry and advertising seek to maximize the atomization and duplication of domestic work in order to sell each household its own washer, dryer, dishwasher, vacuum cleaner, etc.

As the standard of living rises, the average number of children per family declines sharply. Industrially prepared foods and other conveniences become increasingly available. Yet, in spite of the technological advances, surveys in a number of imperialist countries have shown that women who have more than one child and a full-time job must put in 80 to 100 hours of work per week – more hours than similar surveys conducted in 1926 and 1952 revealed. While appliances have eased certain domestic tasks, the shrinking size of the average family unit has meant that women are less able to call on grandparents, aunts, or sisters to help.

With all these changes, the objective basis for confining women to the home becomes less and less compelling. Yet the needs of the ruling class dictate that the family system be preserved. Bourgeois ideology and social conditioning continue to reinforce the reactionary fiction that a woman's identity and fullfillment must come from her role as wife-mother-house-keeper. The contradiction between reality and myth becomes increasingly obvious and intolerable to growing numbers of women.

This state of affairs is frequently referred to as "the crisis of the family", which is expressed in the soaring divorce rates, increased numbers of runaway children and rising domestic violence.

4. Greater democratic rights and broader social opportunities have not "satisfied" women, or inclined them to a passive acceptance of their inferior social status and economic dependence. On the contrary, they have stimulated new struggles and more far-reaching demands.

It was generally the young, college-educated women, those who enjoyed a relatively greater freedom of choice, and those most affected by the youth radicalization of the 1960s, who first articulated the grievances of women in an organized and outspoken way. This led some who consider themselves Marxists to conclude that women's liberation is basically a middle-class or bourgeois protest movement that has no serious interest for revolutionists or the masses of working-class women. They could not be more wrong.

The initial development of the women's liberation movement served only to emphasize the depth and scope of women's oppression. Even those with many advantages in terms of education and other opportunities were and continue to be propelled into action. The most oppressed and exploited are not necessarily the first to articulate their discontent.

5. Contributing to the growth of the women's liberation movement in recent years, and increasing the involvement of working-class women, has been the drive to cut back social expenditures in most

advanced capitalist countries. After the Second World War, in a context of heightened demands by the working class that more social services be provided by the state, the bourgeoisie, especially in Europe, was forced to expand housing developments, health services, and family allowance programs. Later, as the boom of the 1950s and 1960s generated a growing need for female labor power, facilities such as child-care centers and laundromats were extended in order to encourage women to seek employment.

Today, faced with deepening economic problems, the ruling class is slashing social expenditures and trying to shift the burden back onto the individual family, with all the consequences that has for women. But resistance to being driven out of their newly acquired places in the work force, and broad female opposition to social cutbacks such as the closing of child-care centers, have created unexpectedly thorny problems for the rulers in many countries. Imbued with a growing feminist consciousness, women have been more combative and less willing than ever before to shoulder a disproportionate burden in the current economic crisis.

6. While the women's radicalization has an independent dynamic of its own, determined by the specific character of women's oppression and the objective changes that have been described, it is not isolated from the more general upsurge of the class struggle taking place today. It is not directly dependent on other social forces, subordinate to their leadership, or beholden to their initiative. At the same time, the women's movement has been and remains deeply interconnected with the rise of other social struggles, all of which have likewise affected the consciousness of the entire working class.

a. From the beginning, the new upsurge of women's struggles has been strongly affected by the international youth radicalization and the increased challenge to bourgeois values and institutions that accompanied it. Young people -both male and female – began to question religion; to reject patriotism; to challenge authoritarian hierarchies from family to school, to factory .to army; to reject the inevitability of a lifetime of alienated labor. Radicalized youth began to rebel against sexual repression and to challenge the traditional morality equating sex with reproduction. For women, this involved a challenge to the time-honored education of females to be sexually passive, sentimental, fearful, and timid. Masses of youth, including young women, became more conscious of their sexual misery and tried to search for more fulfilling types of personal relationships.

b. One of the factors contributing to the international youth radicalization has been the role played by the liberation struggles of oppressed nations and nationalities, both in the colonial world and in the advanced capitalist countries. Moreover, these have had a powerful impact on the consciousness concerning women's oppression in general. For example, the Black struggle in the United States played a crucial role in bringing about a widespread awareness and rejection of racist stereotypes. The obvious similarities between racist attitudes and sexist stereotypes of women as inferior, emotional, dependent, dumb-but-happy creatures produced an increasing sensitivity to and rejection of such caricatures.

As the feminist movement has developed in the advanced capitalist countries, women of the oppressed nationalities have begun to play an increasingly prominent role. As oppressed nationalities, as women, and frequently as superexploited workers, these women suffer a double and often triple oppression. Their objective place in society means they are in a position to play a strategically important role in the working class and among its allies.

But there has generally been a lag in the pace with which women of oppressed nationalities have become conscious of their specific oppression as women. There are several reasons for this. For many, the depth of their national oppression initially overshadows their oppression as women. Many radical nationalist movements have refused to take up the demands of women, calling them divisive to the struggle for national liberation. The organized women's movement has often failed in its obligation to address itself to the needs of the most oppressed and exploited layers of women and understand the special difficulties they face. In addition, the hold of the family is often particularly strong among women of the oppressed nationalities, since the family sometimes seems to provide a partial buffer against the devastating pressures of racism and cultural annihilation.

Nevertheless, once the radicalization begins experience has already shown it takes on an explosive character, propelling women of oppressed nationalities into the leadership of many social and political struggles including struggles on the job, in the unions, on campuses and in the communities, as well as the feminist movement. They rapidly come to understand that the struggle against their oppression as women does not weaken but strengthens the struggle against their national oppression.

c. Contributing to the rise of the women's movement has been the crisis of the traditional organized religions, especially the Catholic church. The weakening hold of the church (accompanied by a growth in occultism and mysticism) is a dramatic manifestation of the ideological crisis of bourgeois society. All organized religion, which is part of the superstructure of class society, is predicated on and reinforces the notion that women are inferior, if not the very incarnation of evil and animality. Christianity and Judaism, which mark the cultures of the advanced capitalist countries, have always upheld the inequality of women and denied them the right to separate sexuality from reproduction.

In countries where the Catholic church has had a particularly strong hold, it is often radicalizing women who are spearheading the challenge to the power and ideological hold of the church, as shown in the demonstrations of tens of thousands for the right to abortion in Italy, or the demonstrations in 1976 against the anti- adultery laws in Spain.

In Israel, too, the fight for abortion rights shook the stability of the Begin government.

In many oppressed nations such as Québec, Ireland, and Euzkadi (the Basque country), and among the Chicano people, the repressive ideology of the Catholic church has combined in a particularly oppressive way with the myth of the "woman-mother," the center of the family, as the only pole of social, emotional, and political stability, the only refuge from the ravages of national oppression. In Québec for years this amalgam was expressed in the concept of the "revenge of the cradle," suggesting the Québécois women must save the nation from assimilation by having many children.

d. The lesbian-feminist movement emerged as an interrelated but distinct aspect of the radicalization of women.

Lesbians have organized as a component of the gay rights movement, generally finding it necessary to fight within the gay movement for their specific demands as gay *women* to be recognized. But lesbians are also oppressed as women. Many radicalized as women first and felt the discrimination they suffered because of their sexual orientation was only one element of the social and economic limitations women face in trying to determine the course of their lives. Thus many lesbians were in the forefront of the feminist movement from the very beginning. They have been part of every political current within the women's liberation movement, from lesbian-separatists to revolutionary Marxists, and they have helped to make the entire movement more conscious of the specific ways in which gay women are oppressed.

Because of the lesbian movement's insistence on the right of women to live independent of men, they often become the special target of attacks by reaction. From hate propaganda to violent physical assaults, the attacks on lesbians and the lesbian movement are really aimed against the women's movement as a whole. Attempts to divide the women's movement by lesbian-baiting must be rejected in a clear and uncompromising way if the struggle for women's liberation is to move forward.

e. In many of the advanced capitalist countries immigrant women workers have also played a special role. Not only are they superexploited as part of the work force. They are the victims of special discriminatory laws. As women, they often have no right to accompany their husbands to any given country unless they have been able to secure employment for themselves prior to immigrating. If they find work, they are often obliged to give it up to follow their husbands elsewhere. Government measures adopted in recent years to reduce the number of immigrant workers in many advanced capitalist countries have made these laws even more discriminatory.

In a country like Switzerland, where immigrant workers make up nearly 30 percent of the industrial work force, and in other European countries where immigrant women are a majority in some sectors such as the hospitals, immigrant women workers have played a decisive role in raising the political consciousness of the women's movement. They have helped lead struggles in industries that employ predominantly female workers. Even more importantly, they have helped stimulate discussion in the women's movement concerning the economic and social policies of the ruling class. Discriminatory laws in relationship to immigration in general; xenophobia and racism; the resulting divisions within the working class; the ways in which immigrant women are particularly affected by these divisions; the need for the trade unions and the women's movement to fight for the interests of the most superexploited layers; the problems faced by women who are isolated both in their own homes and by the hostile environment in which they live-all these are questions posed before the women's movement, helping to raise some of the most important aspects of a class-struggle perspective.

7. The fading of the postwar boom and the deepening economic, social, and political problems of imperialism on a world scale, highlighted by the 1974-75 international recession, led to an intensification of the attacks on women's rights on all levels. This did not lead to a decline in women's struggles, or relegate them to the sidelines as more powerful social forces came to the fore. Far from diminishing as the struggles of the organized working class sharpened in recent years, feminist consciousness and struggles by women continue to spread and to become more deeply intertwined with the developing social consciousness and political combativity of working-class women and men. Women's resistance to the economic, political,

and ideological offensive of the ruling class has been stiffened by the heightened feminist awareness. Their struggles have been a powerful motor force of social protest and political radicalization.

Responses from the Bourgeoisie and from Currents in the Workers Movement

1. Divisions rapidly appeared inside the capitalist class over how best to respond to the new rise of women's struggles in order to blunt their impact and deflect their radical thrust. After initial attempts to dismiss the women's movement with ridicule and scorn, however, the prevailing view within the ruling class has been to give lip service to the idea that women have at least some just grievances. There has been an attempt to appear concerned – by setting up some special government departments, commissions, or projects to catch women's attention, while working assiduously to integrate the leadership of the women's movement into the accepted patterns of class collaboration. In most countries, the ruling class was forced to make a few concessions that seemed least harmful economically and ideologically – and then steadily tried to take them back.

In each case the aim has been the same, whatever the tactics: to contain the nascent radicalization within the framework of minimal reforms of the capitalist system.

In many European countries, there have been moves to liberalize maternity benefits by extending leaves, raising the percentage of pay women receive while on leave, or by guaranteeing work after a maternity leave without pay. In other countries, governments have ostentatiously debated the justice of promises for equal pay laws, or liberalized divorce laws. In the United States both capitalist political parties have gone on record for passage of an equal rights amendment to the constitution while in practice they sabotage each attempt to muster enough votes to make it law.

But when it comes to social programs that would have immediate and significant economic impact-such as the expansion of child-care facilities – the gains have been virtually nonexistent.

The most serious gain extracted by the international women's movement in the decade since it arose has been the significant expansion of access to legal abortion. In more than twenty countries there has been a marked liberalization of abortion laws.

In every country where women have made measurable progress toward establishing abortion as a right, it has rapidly become clear that this right is never secure under capitalism. Wherever women begin to fight for the right to control their own reproductive functions, the most reactionary defenders of the capitalist system have immediately mobilized to prevent that elementary precondition of women's liberation from being established. The right to choose is too great a challenge to the ideological underpinnings of women's oppression.

However, it is politically important to see clearly that far-right organizations such as "Laissez les vivre", "Oui a la vie," "Right to Life," and "Society for the Protection of the Unborn Child," which are linked to xenophobic, clerical, racist, or outright fascist currents, are nourished by official governmental policies. They function as fanatical protectors of the status quo, attempting to appeal to and mobilize the most backward prejudices that run deep in the working class and petty bourgeoisie and they render a valuable service to the rulers. But without the backhanded – and sometimes open – encouragement of the dominant sectors of the ruling class, their role would be far less influential.

2. The emergence of the women's liberation movement has posed a profound challenge to all political currents claiming to represent the interests of the working class.

The Stalinists and Social Democrats especially were taken aback by the rapid development of a significant radicalization that did not look to them for leadership.

The responses given by the two mass reformist currents in the working class varied from one country to another depending on numerical strength, base in the working class and in the trade-union bureaucracies, and proximity to responsibility for the government of their own capitalist state. But in every case the reflexes of both Stalinists and Social Democrats have been determined by two sometimes conflicting objectives: their commitment to the basic institutions of class rule, including the family; and their need to maintain or strengthen their influence in the working class if they are to contain working-class struggles within the bounds of capitalist property relations.

The rise of the women's liberation movement forced both the Stalinists and Social Democrats to adapt to the changing political situation. The year 1975 in particular gave rise to a flurry of position-taking, partly in response to the initiatives of the bourgeoisie in the context of International Women's Year.

3. Under pressure from part of their own rank and file, Social Democratic parties have generally responded to the rise of the feminist movement more rapidly than the Communist parties. Even though the SPs officially have been reluctant to recognize the existence of the independent women's movement, individual women

members of the SPs have often participated actively in the new organizations that have emerged.

The formal positions taken by the SPs have frequently been more progressive than those of the Stalinist parties, especially in regard to abortion as a woman's right. Wherever Socialist parties have had the opportunity to polish up their image at low cost by coming out in favor of liberalized abortion laws, they have not hesitated to do so. Kreisky in Austria and Brandt in Germany initially took such a task. Faced with a growing women's movement in Australia, the Australian Labor Party attempted to win political support by granting subsidies to numerous small projects initiated by the movement, such as women's health centers and refuges. While these moves cost the Social Democrats little in economic terms, they served to temporarily draw the attention of women away from the inadequacy of their overall policies (on abortion and child care, for example) and helped the ALP to project itself as a "pro-woman" government.

But when confronted with the first signs of reaction from sectors of the bourgeoisie, the Social Democratic parties have been quick to retreat.

While the Labour Party in Britain was on record in favor of the right to abortion on request, the party remained silent about the reactionary proposals before parliamentary aimed at rolling back abortion rights to their pre-1967 status. Initially introduced in 1975 by a Labour MP, the new proposals would restrict the period of time in which women are permitted to obtain abortions, limit access to abortions for immigrant women, and inflict stiff penalties for all violations of the law.

Only in 1977, after a massive campaign by the independent women's movement, organized through the National Abortion Campaign (NAC), and under the pressure of its own ranks, did the Labour Party conference adopt a resolution defending the 1967 law.

The Social Democrats have proved especially useful to the bosses when it comes to imposing austerity measures to reduce the standard of living of the working class. While loudly protesting their commitment to easing the burdens of working-class women, Social Democratic governments have not hesitated to make the cuts in social services demanded by the bourgeoisie. In Denmark they eliminated 5,000 child-care workers from the state payroll with one stroke of the pen.

4. From the 1930s on, after the Stalinist bureaucracy consolidated its control of the USSR and transformed the parties of the Third International into apologists for the counterrevolutionary policies of

the Kremlin, defense of the family as the ideal framework of human relations has been the line of Stalinist parties throughout the world. This not only served the needs of the bureaucratic caste in the Soviet Union itself but coincided with the need to defend the capitalist status quo elsewhere. The openly reactionary theories of the French CP on the family were first expounded when the new family code was introduced in the USSR in 1934 and abortions were prohibited in 1936.

However demagogic they may be at times concerning women's double day of work, the demands raised by the CP today are most often proposals to rearrange things so women have an easier time meeting the tasks that fall on them in the home. From better maternity leaves, to shorter hours, to improved working conditions for women, the fight is often justified by the need to free women for their household chores – rather than from them by socializing the domestic burdens women bear. The other solution, which they sometimes propose, is to demand that men share the work load more equitably at home.

But the rise of the women's movement, the attempts of the bourgeoisie to capitalize on it, the responses of other currents in the workers movement, and the pressure of their own ranks have all compelled the Communist parties to modify and adjust their line. Even the most hidebound and rigid followers of the Kremlin, like the American Communist Party, have finally been forced to abandon some of their most reactionary positions such as opposition to an equal rights amendment to the constitution.

The deeper radicalization, the more adroitly the CPs have had to maneuver by throwing themselves into the movement and adopting more radical verbiage.

The CPs have let women members engage in public discussion and develop scathing condemnations of capitalism's responsibilities for the miserable status of women. But when it comes to program and action, the CPs opposition to women's liberation duplicates their opposition to a class struggle fight for other needs of the working class. They are ready to shelve any demand or derail any struggle in the interests of consolidating or preserving whatever class-collaborationist alliance they are working for. Thus, despite the Italian CPs formal shift and decision to support liberalization of abortion laws, in 1976 the CP parliamentary deputies made a bloc with the Christian Democrats to kill abortion law reform because it was an obstacle to advancing toward the "historic compromise".

Moreover, there is often a conflict between the positions taken by the CP locally – where they sometimes express support for struggles to establish child-care centers or abortion-contraception clinics – and the actions of the CP nationally – where they support austerity measures to cut back on such social programs.

The discrepancy between the formal positions of the Communist parties and their betrayals in the class struggle, have already brought about some sharp tensions within those parties and in the trade unions they dominate. This is especially true because the absence of internal democracy deepens the frustrations of many women who begin to see the contradictions between their own personal commitment to women's liberation and the line of their party. They have no way to influence the positions of their organization. Thus, when the Spanish CP signed the class-collaborationist Moncloa pact, women formed an opposition group in the Madrid CP to fight for internal democracy.

In France, when opposition groupings began to form in the CP in 1978, women members of the party organized around the magazine *Elles Voient Rouge* (They See Red). They sought to defend their positions and fight the sectarian policies of the party which rejected united front action with other political groups on the abortion question or any other issue.

Organizationally, too, the Stalinists have been forced to adjust. In a number of countries the Stalinists formed their own women's organizations after the Second World War. Faced with the new radicalization of women, they have invariably tried to pass these organizations off in the eyes of the working class as the only real women's movement. The independent movement threatens their pretense of being the party that speaks for working-class women, and their initial reaction has been to deepen their sectarian stance.

In Spain, for example, the CP-controlled MDM (Movimiento Democrático de la Mujer-Democratic Movement of Women) declared that it alone *was* the women's movement, and the CP proclaimed itself to be the party of women's liberation. But despite the strength of the CP, the MDM was unable to dominate the radicalization of women, which was expressed through the flourishing of women's groups on all levels throughout the Spanish state. Unable to establish the MDM by fiat, the CP was forced to recognize the existence of other groups and work with them.

5. Involvement in the women's movement has brought similar contradictions for the Social Democratic parties as well. But at the same time, the ability of both the Stalinists and Social Democrats to adapt to some of the issues raised by radicalizing women has enhanced their ability to influence the general course of the movement. When these parties decide to support one or another

mass mobilization, as they have in a number of countries recently on the abortion question, their reformist positions have all the more impact on large numbers of women. It would be a mistake to underestimate their political weight.

6. The Maoists and centrist organizations have most often adopted sectarian, economist positions on the women's liberation movement, considering it to be petty bourgeois and in conflict with their concept of the workers movement. Among these organizations, however, there have been basically two types of response. Some have refused to participate in the independent organizations and activities of the women's liberation movement. Many of these sectarian groups have set up their own auxiliary women's groups, which they counterpose to the living women's movement, arguing that such a course is the only genuinely communist strategy.

Other Maoist and centrist groups have oriented toward participating in the women's movement. But they have no understanding of the relationship between the class struggle and the fight for women's liberation. They reject a policy of united-front action, and simply tail-end the women's movement. This was an important factor contributing to the crises that tore many such groups apart at the end of the 1970s.

7. The trade-union movement has also felt the impact of the radicalization of women and its bureaucracies have been obliged to respond to the pressures from women inside and outside the organized labor movement.

Like the Stalinists and Social Democrats, even in the best of cases labor officials try to limit union responsibility for women's demands to economic questions, such as equal pay or maternity leaves. As long as possible, they resist involving labor in fighting for issues such as abortion. However, the mass character of the unions, the growing number of women in their ranks, many of whom are increasingly active in women's commissions, makes such a stance by the union bureaucracies more difficult. This was clearly seen in October 1979 when the British Trades Union Congress, under growing pressure from its own ranks, called for a national demonstration in defense of abortion rights. Some 50,000 men and women turned out. Questions such as child care and the socialization of domestic work, conditions for part-time workers, and affirmative action programs for women are raised with greater frequency today in the union movement. In some cases women are explicitly posing these demands in the general framework of the need to break down the traditional division of labor between men and women.

By forcing these issues, women workers are calling into question the reformists' attempts to maintain a division between economic and political issues and otherwise limit whatever struggles develop. They are helping the working class to think in broad social terms and encouraging the ranks of the unions to turn to and use their basic class organizations to fight for all their needs.

As women try to win the union ranks and leadership to support their demands, they are obliged to take up the question of union democracy as well. They have to fight for the right to express themselves freely, to organize their own Commissions or Caucuses, to be represented in the union leaderships, and for the union to provide the kinds of facilities, such as childcare during meetings, that will permit women to be fully active in the workers organizations.

Some unions have put out special literature, reactivated moribund women's commissions, organized meetings of women unionists, or established special training courses for women union leaders. In a number of countries special inter-union committees of women have been organized by the trade-union leadership on national, regional, or local levels. Elsewhere committees have been created under the impetus of the rank and file. The radicalization of women and the deepening economic crisis have also led to an increase in the rate of unionization of women workers in some advanced capitalist countries.

By and large, the creation of women's commissions within the unions has occurred with the blessing of the union bureaucracies. They hope to contain the radicalization of women in the unions and direct their energies in a way that will not threaten the comfortable status quo on any level – from the male monopoly of union leadership posts to the understanding between the bureaucracy and the bosses that the particular needs of women workers be ignored.

But this development reflects the huge impact that the women's liberation movement has already had on the organized labor movement. Such women's commissions within the unions are today more and more products of the women's movement as well as part of the labor movement. They stand at the intersection of the two and, if properly led, can help show the way forward for both.

Women's Liberation in the Colonial and Semicolonial World

1. Women's liberation is not a matter of interest only to women of the advanced capitalist countries with their relatively high educational level and standard of living. On the contrary, it is of vital concern and

importance to the masses of women throughout the world. The colonial and semicolonial countries are no exception.

There is great diversity in the economic and social conditions and cultural traditions in the colonial and semicolonial countries. They range from extremely primitive conditions in some areas to considerable industrialization in countries such as Puerto Rico and Argentina. All semicolonial and colonial countries, however, are defined by the imperialist domination they suffer in common. This also has specific effects on women in these countries.

Imperialist domination has meant that capitalist relations of production have been superimposed on, and have combined with, archaic, precapitalist modes of production and social relations, transforming them and incorporating them into the capitalist economy. In Western Europe the rise of capitalism was punctuated by bourgeois-democratic revolutions in the more advanced countries which broke the economic and political power of the old feudal ruling classes. But in the colonial countries imperialist penetration most often reinforced the privileges, hierarchies, and reactionary traditions of the precapitalist ruling classes, which it utilized wherever possible to maintain stability and maximize imperialist exploitation.

Using torture, extermination, rape, and other forms of terror on a mass scale, and in Africa through the outright enslavement of the native peoples, expanding European capitalism brutally colonized Latin America and parts of Asia and Africa and thrust them into the world market. With the European and eventually American conquerors came Christianity as well, which was often turned to advantage as one of the central links in the chain of subjugation.

For women in the semicolonial and colonial world the penetration of the capitalist market economy has a contradictory impact: on the one hand it introduces new economic relations that begin to lay the basis for women to overcome their centuries old oppression. But on the other hand, it takes over and utilizes the archaic traditions, religious codes, and antiwoman prejudices, initially reinforcing them through new forms of discrimination and superexploitation.

In general, the situation of women is directly related to the degree of industrialization that has been achieved. But uneven and combined development in some societies can produce startling contradictions, such as relative economic independence for women who dominate very primitive agriculture in some areas of Africa.

2. In the colonial countries, the development of capitalist production proceeds according to the needs of imperialism. For this reason, industrialization takes place only slowly and in an unbalanced,

distorted way, if at all. In most semicolonial countries, the majority of the population still lives on the land and is engaged in subsistence farming, utilizing extremely backward methods. The family -which generally includes various aunts, uncles, nieces, nephews, and grandparents – is the basic unit of petty agricultural production.

Women play a decisive economic role. Not only do they work long hours in the fields and home, but they produce children to share the burden of work and provide economic security in old age. They marry at puberty and often give birth to as many children as physically possible. Their worth is generally determined by the number of children they produce. A barren woman is considered a social disgrace and an economic disaster. Infertility is often grounds for divorce.

Because of its productive role, the hold of the family on all its members, but specifically on women, is strong. Combined with a primitive level of economic development, this brings about extreme deprivation and degradation for peasant women in the rural areas. In practice, they scarcely have any legal or social rights as individuals, and are often barely considered human. They live under virtually total domination and control by male members of their family. In many cases the restricted resources of the family unit are allocated first of all to the male members of the family; it is not uncommon for female children to receive less food and care, leading to stunted growth or early death from malnutrition. Female infanticide, both direct and through deliberate neglect, is still practiced in many areas. Often illiteracy rates for women approach 100 percent.

3. The incorporation of the colonial and semicolonial countries into the world capitalist market inevitably has an impact on the rural areas, however. Inflation and the inability to compete with larger units utilizing more productive methods lead to continuous waves of migration from the countryside to the cities. Often this migration begins with the males of the family, leaving the women, children, and elderly with an even heavier burden as they try to eke out an impoverished existence from the land on their own.

The desperate search for a job eventually leads millions of workers to leave their country of birth and migrate to the advanced industrial countries, where if they are lucky enough to find a job, it will be under miserable conditions of superexploitation.

The isolation and backward traditions of the rural areas tend to be challenged and broken down not only by migration to and from the cities but also by the diffusion of the mass media, such as radio and television.

4. With migration to the cities, the new conditions of life and labor begin to challenge the traditional norms and myths about the role of women.

In the cities the petty-bourgeois family as a productive unit rapidly disappears for most. Each family member is obliged to sell his or her labor power on the market as an individual. However, due to the extremely precarious employment situation, and the financial responsibilities that the semiproletarian city dwellers often have vis-à-vis their rural relatives, the immediate family often still includes aunts, uncles, cousins, brothers and sisters and their children, besides father, mother, and children.

Among the urban middle class and the more stable sectors of the proletariat, however, the family unit begins to become more restricted.

As they migrate to the cities, women have greater opportunity for education, for broader social contact, and for economic independence. The needs of capitalism, which bring increasing numbers of women out of family isolation, come into conflict with the old ideas about the role of women in society. In taking jobs as industrial or service workers, women begin to occupy positions that were previously forbidden them by backward prejudices and traditions. Those able to secure an education that permits them to break into professions, such as teaching and nursing, also serve as examples that contradict traditional attitudes, even in the eyes of those women who don't work. The myth of women's inferiority is increasingly called into question by this reality, which challenges their time-honored subordination.

Even for women who are not able to get an education or to work outside the home, city conditions help provide the possibility of escaping the mental prison that the rural family's isolation imposes on them. This happens through the greater impact of the mass media, the proximity of political life and struggles, the visibility of modern household appliances, laundries, etc.

5. In the colonial and semicolonial countries, women generally comprise a much lower percentage of the work force than in the imperialist countries. It tends to vary between 8 and 15 percent, although sometimes as high as 20 percent, as opposed to the advanced capitalist countries, where women make up roughly 30 to 40 percent.

As would be expected, women are concentrated in jobs that are the least skilled, lowest paying, and least protected by laws on safety conditions, minimum wages, etc. This is especially true for agricultural work, piecework in the home, and work as domestics, where a high proportion of women are employed. The average wage of female workers tends to be one-third to one-half of that of male workers. When women are able to get an education and acquire some skills, they are confined even more strictly than in the advanced capitalist countries to certain "female" occupations, such as nursing and teaching.

But women are also concentrated in industries such as textile, garment, food processing, and electrical parts and often make up a majority of the labor force employed there. Given the overwhelming predominance of such light industry in the more industrialized colonial countries, this means that, although they are a low percentage of the work force as a whole, women workers can occupy a strategically important place. In Puerto Rico, for example, women are the majority of the work force in the pharmaceutical and electrical industries, which are the major industries in the country.

The employment of women in such industries is crucial for the superprofits of the imperialists, both because they are a source of cheaper labor and also because the employment of women at lower wages or in lower-paying jobs allows the capitalists to divide and weaken the working class and keep down the overall wage scale. The process of imperialist accumulation cannot be fully understood without explaining the role of the superexploitation of women workers in the semicolonial countries.

Throughout the colonial world, unemployment and underemployment are of crisis proportions and much of this burden falls on women. To help their family survive, women are often forced to resort to such desperate and precarious sources of income as selling handicrafts or home-cooked food in the streets, or taking in laundry. Prostitution is frequently the only recourse. The endemic unemployment also exacerbates alcoholism and drug addiction, which results in greater violence against women as well as even more desperate poverty.

6. In many colonial and semicolonial countries, women have not yet won some of the most elementary democratic rights secured by women in the advanced capitalist countries in the nineteenth and twentieth centuries. Numerous countries still retain laws that place women under the legal control of their male relatives. These include, for example, laws that require the husband's permission for a woman to work, laws that give the husband control over his wife's wages, and laws that give the husband automatic guardianship of his children and control over the residence of his wife. In some countries women are still sold into marriage. They can be murdered with impunity for violating the "honor" of their men.

In countries where reforms have been made in the legal code, providing women with more rights, these often remain largely formal. Women are unable to assert these rights in practice because of the crushing weight of poverty, illiteracy, malnutrition, their economic dependence, and backward traditions that circumscribe their lives. Thus imperialism in its death agony stands as an obstacle to the most elementary democratic rights for women in the colonial world.

7. The power and influence of organized religion is especially strong in the colonial and semicolonial countries, because of the prevailing economic backwardness and because of the reinforcement and protection of the religious hierarchies by imperialism. In many countries there is no separation of religious institutions and state. Even where there is official separation, religious dogma and customs retain great weight. For example, many of the most barbaric antiwomen laws are based on religious codes. In India, the misery of millions of women is accentuated by the caste system, which, though no longer sanctioned by law, is based on the Hindu religion. In Muslim countries, the tradition of the veiling of women, which is still quite prevalent, is designed to totally banish women from public life and deny them any individuality. In Catholic countries the right to divorce is often restricted or denied.

8. Violence against women, which has been inherent in their economic, social, and sexual degradation throughout all stages of development of class society, becomes accentuated by the contradictions bred under imperialist domination. The greater access of women to education and jobs, along with their broader participation in society in general, gives women the opportunities to lead a less protected, more public life, in violation of the old traditions and values. But attempts by women to take advantage of these opportunities and break out of the old roles often lead to reactions by male relatives or others, which can take the form of ostracization, beatings, mutilations, or even murder. Such barbaric violence against women is frequently sanctioned by law. Even where illegal, it is often so widely accepted in practice that it goes unpunished.

9. Educational opportunities for women in the colonial and semicolonial countries remain extremely limited by comparison with the advanced capitalist countries. This is reflected in the high female illiteracy rate. From the level of primary school to the university level, female enrollment is lower than male, and the gap generally increases the higher the educational level.

The educational system in the colonial and semicolonial countries is organized- often more blatantly than in the imperialist countries – to reinforce the exclusion of women from social life and to bolster the imposition of the role of mother-housekeeper-wife on all female children. Coeducation is notably less prevalent, with the schools for girls invariably receiving smaller budgets, fewer teachers, and worse facilities. Where coeducation exists, girls are still required to pursue separate courses of study such as cooking, sewing, and homemaking.

Within the framework of these disadvantages, however, the pressure of the world market has brought some changes in the educational opportunities open to women. The need for a layer of more highly trained technicians has opened the doors to higher education for at least a small layer of women.

10. Women in the colonial world have even less control over their reproductive functions than women in the imperialist countries. The poor educational opportunities for females, combined with the strong influence of religion over the content of education, means that women have little or no access to scientific information about reproduction or sex. Economically and socially they are under personal pressure to produce more, not fewer children. When there is access to birth control information and devices, this is almost always in the framework of racist population control programs imposed by imperialism. In some countries forced sterilization of masses of women has been carried out by the government. In Puerto Rico the forced sterilization policies promoted by the U.S. government have victimized more than one-third of the women of child-bearing age. Forced sterilization schemes are foisted on oppressed groups within these countries as well, such as the Indian population of Bolivia.

Even in countries where forced sterilization is not official policy, the racist population control propaganda permeates society and constitutes an obstacle to the fight by women to gain control of their own bodies.

Women in semicolonial and colonial countries have been widely used as unwitting guinea pigs for testing birth control devices and drugs. And access to abortion, too, is tied to coercion, not freedom of choice. Each year, millions of women throughout the colonial world are forced to seek illegal abortions under the most unsanitary and degrading conditions possible, leading to an unknown number of deaths.

In all these ways, women are denied the right to choose when and if to bear children.

Under conditions of economic crisis, population control schemes will become more widespread and there will be more cases like Puerto Rico. The so-called "population explosion" will be blamed for the economic difficulties of the colonial and semicolonial countries in order to divert attention from the responsibility of imperialism for causing and maintaining this misery.

Racism and sexism are also imposed on the colonial world through the propagation of alien cultural standards. If the cosmetics merchants, standards of "beauty" for women in Europe and North America are oppressive to women in those areas, they are even more so when these same standards are foisted on women of the colonial and semicolonial countries through advertising, movies, and other forms of mass propaganda.

11. The strong influence of religion reinforces extreme backwardness regarding sexuality, which results in a special deprivation and degradation of women. The general proscription that women are supposed to be asexual themselves, but at the same time be a satisfying sexual slave to their husbands, is imposed more brutally on women in the colonial and semicolonial countries than in the imperialist countries, through traditions, laws, and the use of violence including the sexual mutilation of female children. Women are supposed to save their virginity for their husband. In many instances, if women do not provide sexual satisfaction to their husbands, or if they are charged with not being a virgin at the time of marriage, this is ground for divorce. The dual standard of sexual conduct for men and women is more strictly enforced than in the imperialist countries. The practice of polygamy is merely an extreme example.

Another reflection of the backwardness regarding sexuality is the harsh oppression of homosexuals, both male and female.

12. The fact that capitalist development in the colonial world incorporated precapitalist economic and social relations, many of which survive in distorted forms, means that to win their liberation, women, as well as all the oppressed and exploited, are confronted with combined tasks. The struggle against imperialist domination and capitalist exploitation often begins with the unresolved problems of national independence, land reform, and other democratic tasks.

Elementary democratic demands, such as those that give women rights as individuals independent of their husband's control, will have great weight in the struggle for women's liberation in the colonial and semicolonial countries. At the same time, they will immediately pose and be combined with social and economic issues whose solution requires the reorganization of all of society along socialist lines. Among such issues are rising prices, unemployment, inadequate health and educational facilities, and housing. They also include all the general demands that have been raised by the women's movement in the advanced capitalist countries, such as child-care centers, rights and medical facilities that would assure women the ability to control their reproductive lives, access to jobs and education. But none of these demands, including the most elementary democratic ones, can be won without the mobilization and organization of the working class, which constitutes the only social force capable of leading such struggles through to a victorious conclusion.

13. Because of the relative weakness of capitalism and of the ruling capitalist classes in the colonial and semicolonial countries, civil liberties, where they exist, are in general tenuous and often shortlived. Political repression is widespread. When women begin to struggle- as when other sectors of the population begin to rebel – they are often rapidly confronted with repression and with the necessity to fight for political liberties such as the right to hold meetings, to have their own organization, to have a newspaper or other publications, and to demonstrate. The struggle for women's liberation cannot be separated from the more general struggle for political freedoms.

The increased participation of women in social and political struggles has meant that women are a growing proportion of political prisoners in the colonial and semicolonial countries. In the prisons, women face particularly humiliating and brutal forms of torture. The struggle for freedom of all political prisoners, exposing the plight of women in particular, has been and will be an important part of the fight for women's liberation in these countries.

This struggle has an especially clear international dimension. Political prisoners exist not only in the colonial world but in the imperialist countries as well. Demands for their freedom will continue to be a rallying point for international solidarity within the women's movement.

14. The struggle for women's liberation has always been intertwined with the national liberation struggle. Whatever women do, they come up against the might of imperialist control, and the need to throw off the chains of this domination is an urgent and overriding task for all the oppressed in these countries, as the examples of Iran and Nicaragua have once again clearly demonstrated. Large numbers of women become politically active for the first time through participation in national liberation movements. In the process of the developing struggle, it becomes evident that women can and must play an even greater role if victory is to be won. Women become transformed by doing things that were forbidden to them by the old

traditions and habits. They become fighters, leaders, organizers, and political thinkers. The deep contradictions they live will stimulate revolt against their oppression as a sex, as well as demands for greater equality within the revolutionary movement. In Vietnam, Algeria, Cuba, Palestine, South Africa, the Sahara, and elsewhere, struggles by women to end the most brutal forms of the oppression they suffer have been closely intertwined with unfolding anti-imperialist struggles.

In Nicaragua, women organized through AMPRONAC (Association of Women Confronting the National Problem) played a crucial role in preparing for the final insurrection against the Somoza dictatorship. And 30 percent of the FSLN's forces were composed of women who were organized in women's brigades as well as integrated in other combat and support units.

In Iran, the participation of women in the struggle to topple the Shah brought millions into social and political life for the first time, awakening in them the desire to change their own status as well. Despite the weight of reactionary religious ideas and antiwoman measures, the deepening of mass anti-imperialist consciousness and struggle in Iran can only improve the conditions under which women will fight for greater equality and freedom.

The participation of women in the national liberation struggle also begins to transform the consciousness of men about women's capacities and role. In the process of struggling against their own exploitation and oppression, men can become more sensitized to the oppression of women, more conscious of the necessity to combat it, and more aware of the importance of women as an allied fighting force.

15. There also exist oppressed national minorities within the colonial and semicolonial countries. In Iran, for example, the oppressed nationalities constitute 60 percent of the population. In Latin America, the native Indian population is an oppressed minority. The women of these minorities face a double dimension of national oppression. Once they begin to move, their struggle can develop in an explosive manner.

The demands of women and of oppressed nationalities will often be intertwined and reinforce one another. For example, the demand of all women for the right to an education will be combined with the demand of men and women of the oppressed nationalities for the right to education in their own languages.

16. Since the rise of the colonial revolution at the beginning of this century, women have participated in anti-imperialist upsurges, but there has not been a tradition of women organizing as women,

around their specific demands, as a distinct component of there struggles. However, the development of the world capitalist system since World War II has sharpened the economic, social, and political contradictions in the colonial and semicolonial countries which will more and more propel women into struggle around their own demands.

a. In the period following World War II there was a rise in industrialization in the colonial and semicolonial countries, although the extent of this industrialization varied greatly in different countries and was distorted to fit the needs of the imperialist powers. This meant increased access by women to education and jobs.

b. Technological improvements in the areas of household tasks and control of reproduction – even though much less widely available than in the advanced ountries – began to be known and showed the possibility of freeing women from domestic drudgery and allowing them to control their reproductive function.

c. The economic crisis of world capitalism which was signaled by the international depression of 1974-75 has had a magnified effect on the colonial world, as the imperialists attempted to foist the burden of this crisis onto the backs of the masses in these countries. A disproportionate weight of the economic crisis falls on women, in the form of rising prices, cutbacks in the rudimentary health and education facilities that exist, and increased misery in the countryside. Thus the gap between what is possible for women and what exists is widening.

d. The impact of this contradiction on the consciousness of women is reinforced today by the impact of the international women's liberation movement, which has inspired women around the world and popularized and legitimized their demands.

These factors point to the conclusion that struggles by women will become a more important component of the coming revolutionary struggles in the colonial and semicolonial countries.

This struggle by women can take on explosive dimensions due to the gap between the archaic norms and values and the possibilities for the liberation of women opened up by the technological advancements of capitalism. At the same time, the religious and traditional norms and values upheld by the imperialists and their servitors are in constant contradiction with the lives of growing numbers of women. This means that once women begin to challenge their oppression, even on an elementary level, it can combine with other social ferment and lead very rapidly to the mobilization of masses of women in struggles that take on a radical, anticapitalist direction.

17. Attitudes and policies concerning the demands and needs of women in colonial and semicolonial countries are one of the acid tests of the revolutionary caliber, perspective, and program of any organization aspiring to lead the struggle against imperialism. The role and importance that we ascribe to the fight for women's liberation in these countries, and the program we put forward for achieving it, separate us from nonproletarian forces contending for leadership of the national liberation struggle.

This has long been a distinguishing feature of the program of revolutionary Marxism, as was reflected in the resolutions of the Third and Fourth Congresses of the Communist International. These resolutions drew special attention to the exemplary work of the Chinese Communists in organizing and leading mobilizations of women that preceded the second Chinese revolution of 1925-27.

If the revolutionary Marxist party does not see the importance of organizing and mobilizing women and winning the leadership of the struggle for women's liberation, the field will be open for bourgeois and petty-bourgeois forces to succeed in gaining the leadership of women's movements and diverting them into reformist channels, or even into anti-working class movements.

18. Only the road of the socialist revolution can open the way to a qualitative transformation in the lives of the masses of women of the semicolonial countries. The examples of Cuba, Vietnam, and China are a powerful beacon for the women of Asia, Africa, and Latin America. These socialist revolutions offer striking proof of the rapid advances possible once the working class in alliance with the peasantry breaks the chains of imperialist domination. When the laws of capitalist accumulation are replaced by those of a planned economy based on the nationalization of the decisive sectors of production, it becomes possible even in the impoverished countries of the semicolonial world to turn massive resources toward the development of education and childcare, medical services, and housing.

Once capitalism is eliminated, unemployment and underemployment become scourges of the past. On the contrary a shortage of labor draws women out of the home and into productive labor of all kinds in massive numbers. Social mores and traditions rooted in precapitalist and capitalist modes of production progressively disappear as this transformation develops and the working class becomes larger and more powerful.

19. Because of the extreme oppression they face, and the fact that there is no perspective for improving their lives under capitalism, women in the colonial and semicolonial countries will be thrust into the vanguard of the struggle for social change. Through internal classes and similar educational activities, sections of the Fourth International must systematically prepare their own members to understand the importance of the fight for women's liberation, even if there are no mass struggles on the political horizon as yet. We must take a conscious attitude toward winning women to socialism and training and integrating the most determined as leaders of our movement.

Women in the Workers States: Liberation Betrayed

1. The October 1917 revolution in Russia and each subsequent socialist victory brought significant gains for women, including democratic rights and integration into the productive labor force. The measures enacted by the Bolsheviks under the leadership of Lenin and Trotsky demonstratively showed that the proletarian revolution meant immediate steps forward for women.

Between 1917 and 1927 the Soviet government passed a series of laws giving women legal equality with men for the first time. Marriage became a simple registration process that had to be based on mutual consent. The concept of illegitimacy was abolished. Free, legal abortion was made every woman's right. By 1927, marriages did not have to be registered, and divorce was granted on the request of either partner. Antihomosexual laws were eliminated.

Free, compulsory education to the age of 16 was established for all children of both sexes. Legislation gave women workers special maternity benefits.

The 1919 program of the Communist Party stated: "The party's task at the present moment is primarily work in the realm of ideas and education so as to destroy utterly all traces of the former inequality or prejudices, particularly among backward strata of the proletariat and peasantry. Not confining itself to formal equality of women, the party strives to liberate them from the material burdens of obsolete household work by replacing it by communal houses, public eating places, central laundries, nurseries, etc." This program was implemented to the extent possible given the economic backwardness and poverty of the new Soviet Republic, and the devastation caused by almost a decade of war and civil war.

A conscious attempt was made to begin combating the reactionary social norms and attitudes toward women, which reflected the reality of a country whose population was still overwhelmingly peasant, where women were a relatively small percentage of the work force, and in which the dead weight of feudal traditions and customs hung over all social relations. As would be expected under such conditions, backward attitudes toward women were reflected within the Bolshevik Party as well, not excepting its leadership. The party was by no means homogeneous in its understanding of the importance of carrying through the concrete and deepgoing measures necessary to fulfill its 1919 program.

2. The decimation and exhaustion of the working-class vanguard, and the crushing of the postwar revolutionary upsurges in Western Europe, laid the basis for the triumph of the counterrevolutionary bureaucratic caste, headed by Stalin, in the 1920s. While the economic foundations of the new workers state were not destroyed, a privileged social layer that appropriated for itself many of the benefits of the new economic order grew rapidly in the fertile soil of Russia's poverty. To protect and extend its new privileges, the bureaucracy revised the policies of Lenin and Trotsky in virtually every sphere, from government based on soviet democracy, to control by the workers over economic planning, to the right of oppressed nationalities to self- determination, to a proletarian internationalist foreign policy.

By the late 1930s the counterrevolution had physically annihilated the entire surviving Bolshevik leadership and established a dictatorship that to this day keeps hundreds of thousands in prison camps, psychiatric hospitals, and exile, and ruthlessly crushes every murmur of opposition.

For women, the Stalinist counterrevolution led to a policy of reviving and fortifying the family system.

Trotsky described this process as follows: "Genuine emancipation of women is inconceivable without a general rise of economy and culture, without the destruction of the petty-bourgeois economic family unit, without the introduction of socialized food preparation and education. Meanwhile, guided by its conservative instinct, the bureaucracy has taken alarm at the 'disintegration' of the family. It began singing panegyrics to the family supper and the family laundry, that is, the household slavery of women. To cap it all, the bureaucracy has restored criminal punishments for abortions, officially returning women to the status of pack animals. In complete contradiction with the ABC of communism the ruling caste has thus restored the most reactionary and benighted nucleus of the class regime, i.e., the petty-bourgeois family" (*Writings of Leon Trotsky, 1937-38*, 2nd ed., 1976, p. 129).

3. The most important factor facilitating this retrogression was the cultural and material backwardness of Russian society, which did not have the resources necessary to construct adequate child-care centers, sufficient housing, public laundries, and housekeeping and dining facilities to eliminate the material basis for women's oppression. This backwardness also helped perpetuate the general social division of labor between men and women inherited from the tsarist period.

But beyond these objective limitations, the reactionary Stalinist bureaucracy consciously gave up the perspective of moving in a systematic way to socialize the burdens carried by women, and instead began to glorify the family system, attempting to bind families together through legal restrictions and economic compulsion.

As Trotsky pointed out in *The Revolution Betrayed,* "The retreat not only assumes forms of disgusting hypocrisy, but it also is going infinitely farther than the iron economic necessity demands."

The bureaucracy reinforced the family system for one of the same reasons it is maintained by capitalist society – as a means of inculcating attitudes of submission to authority and for perpetuating the privileges of a minority. Trotsky explained that "the most compelling motive of the present cult of the family is undoubtedly the need of the bureaucracy for a stable hierarchy of relations, and for the disciplining of youth by means of forty million points of support for authority and power."

As part of this counterrevolution, the old tsarist laws against homosexuality were dusted off and reintroduced.

Reinforcement of the family enabled the bureaucracy to perpetuate an important division inside the working class: the division between man, as "head of the family and breadwinner," and woman, as responsible for tasks inside the home and shopping – in addition to whatever else she might do. On a more general level, it meant maintaining the division between private life and public life, with the resulting isolation that affects both men and women. Bolstering of the nuclear family also reinforced the bureaucracy through encouraging the attitude of "each family for itself," and within the framework of a policy of overall planning that has little to do with satisfying the needs of the workers, it allows the bureaucracy to minimize the costs of social services.

The conditions created by the proletarian revolution and Stalinist counterrevolution in the Soviet Union have not been mechanically reproduced in all the deformed workers states of Eastern Europe and Asia. Important differences exist, reflecting historical, cultural, economic, and social variations from one country to another, even one region to another. However, despite differences of degree in the participation of women in the process of production or the extent of child-care centers and similar social services, maintenance of the economic and social inequality of women and policies aimed at reinforcing and justifying the domestic labor of women remain official policy in all the deformed workers states.

4. According to the official 1970 Soviet Union census, 90 percent of all urban women between the ages of 16 and 54 hold jobs outside the home. Yet the average Soviet woman spends four to seven hours a day on housework in addition to eight hours on an outside job.

The perpetuation of the responsibility of women for the domestic chores associated with child-raising, cooking, cleaning, laundry, and caring for the personal needs of other members of the family unit is the economic and social basis for the disadvantages and prejudices faced by women and the resulting discrimination in jobs and wages. This deeply affects the way women view themselves, their role in society, and the goals they seek to attain.

A survey made in Czechoslovakia at the end of the 1960s revealed that nearly 80 percent of women interviewed accepted the idea of staying in the home until their children reached the age of 3 years, if their husband agreed and if their income was sufficient to provide for the needs of the family. This is hardly surprising when one considers that, in the same period, out of 500 women interviewed who held supervisory positions on their jobs, half said they had to perform all of the domestic work in their homes (four or five hours per day).

While 50 percent of the wage earners in the Soviet Union are women, they are concentrated disproportionately in less-skilled, lower-paying, less responsible jobs, and in traditional female sectors of production and services. For example, 43.6 percent of all women still work in agriculture, while another quarter are employed in the textile industry. Eighty percent of all primary and secondary school teachers, and 100 percent of all preschool teachers, are women. In 1970 only 6.6 percent of all industrial enterprises were headed by women. According to 1966 statistics, average women's wages in the Soviet Union were 69.3 percent of men's- up from 64.4 percent in 1924!

In 1970, in the East European countries as a whole, the salary differential ranged between 27 and 30 percent, despite the laws on equal pay that have been in effect for decades in these countries. This reflects the fact that women do not work the same jobs as men. Not only do they continue to be pushed toward the lower-paid "women's occupations," and not only are women often overqualified for the jobs they hold, but very few of those who complete apprenticeship programs for better-paying, more highly skilled jobs (notably, in heavy industry) continue working in these sectors. Domestic responsibilities make it difficult to keep up with new developments in one's specialty. Also protective laws establishing special conditions under which women can work often have discriminatory effects that prevent them from holding the same jobs as men.

In the Soviet Union in 1976, more than 40 percent of all scientists were women, but only 3 out of 243 full members of the Soviet Academy of Science were women. In the national political arena, only 8 of the 287 full members of the Communist Party Central Committee were women. There are no women in the Politburo.

In the Soviet Union and Eastern Europe, as in the advanced capitalist countries, sufficient material wealth and technology today exist to significantly alleviate the double burden of women. Yet the distortions introduced in economic planning and the productive process because of the absence of democratic control over production by the workers and the domination of the privileged bureaucratic caste are a source of resentments. Women feel the dead weight of the bureaucracy in this respect even more than men because they are forced to compensate for the distortions in the economy through the double day's labor they perform.

In the last decade, these potentially explosive resentments have forced the various bureaucratic castes to plan expanded production in consumer goods and increased social services. But the supply of consumer goods continues to lag behind the needs and growing expectations. Social services also remain sorely inadequate. For example, while child-care facilities are more widespread than in advanced capitalist countries, according to official figures in early 1978, child-care facilities in the Soviet Union could accommodate only 13 million of the more than 35 million pre-school age children.

In Czechoslovakia and Poland at the beginning of the 1970s, only 10 percent of children under 3 could be accommodated in nurseries; of children between 3 and 6, there were places for only 37 and 45 percent, respectively. This is the case although women comprise between 40 and 45 percent of the work force in these two countries. Despite all the difficulties that such conditions create for working women, some of the Stalinist officials in these countries are reviving the theory of the "natural division of labor" between men and women. In Czechoslovakia and Hungary, the "solution" put forward to alleviate the lack of social services and at the same time attempt to reverse the declining birth rate is in essence a "salary for housework" allotted to mothers of one or two children until they reach the age of 3 years. This system is accompanied in Czechoslovakia by an increase in family allocations for the third and fourth child, as well as a substantial increase in the birth bonus for each child (which is nearly the equivalent of a month's salary). Obviously, such measures can only have the effect of pressing women to stay in the home, given the double day of work that accompanies having an outside job.

The number of public laundries is insignificant – in Czechoslovakia, Poland, and the USSR the existing laundries satisfy only 5-10 percent of the needs.

Similarly, the number of men and women workers who eat in public cafeterias has sharply decreased since the 1950s. Because of high prices and bad quality, only 20 percent of the population in Czechoslovakia, eat their main meal outside the home – as opposed to 50 percent in earlier years.

All these conditions go in the direction of burying women in the home, a tendency fostered by the propaganda of the bureaucracy in favor of part-time work for women. This is expressed in East Germany, for example, in the extra day off each month given to women so they can do their housework. Of course, only women are given this "special privilege."

In October 1977 the same reactionary tendency was, in fact, incorporated into the revised Soviet constitution as an amendment to Article 35 that is supposed to guarantee equal rights to women. The amended constitution projects "the gradual shortening of the work-day for women with small children." Soviet leaders explained that this new constitutional provision reflected the line of the party and the Soviet state to improve the position of "women as workers, mothers, childraisers, and housewives."

This reinforcement of the social division of labor between men and women is also expressed through government policies in these countries aimed at increasing the birth rate to alleviate labor shortages. (East Germany is the only current exception.) At the same time that abortion has become more available to women in capitalist countries, the attempt to foster population growth has led to the restrictive measures concerning abortion throughout Eastern Europe.

In fact, the Stalinist bureaucracies have repudiated the view of Lenin and other leaders of the Russian revolution that unrestricted access to abortion is a woman's elementary democratic right. While legal abortion is generally available in the Soviet Union and Eastern Europe, the ruling castes have repeatedly curtailed this right, frequently placing humiliating conditions as well as economic penalties on women seeking abortions (such as denial of paid sick-leave time to obtain an abortion or refusal to cover abortions as a free medical procedure).

With the exception of Poland, sexual education and widespread information on contraceptive methods were explicitly rejected in most East European countries until very recently. Family planning centers were nonexistent, and access to contraceptive methods such as the pill or sterilization was strictly limited (in Czechoslovakia at the beginning of the 1970s, only 5 percent of women used such methods). But none of these measures have succeeded in reversing the continued stagnation in the birth rate or lowering the number of abortions. Faced with this "problem", the bureaucracy exercises great imagination in devising methods to encourage women to have more children. They consider everything *but* measures to socialize domestic tasks. In Poland, they are considering a "salary for housework," or a tax on the income of housewives who refuse to have children, or raising of the age of retirement for women from 60 to 65 years in order to release money for a maternity fund, or possibly lowering the retirement age for women to 55 years to enable them to help take care of small children.

In China, on the other hand, the Stalinist bureaucracy has introduced special economic penalties for couples with more than two children, in order to try to limit population growth. But the principle is the same. The right to choose is subordinated to the economic decisions made by the bureaucracy.

In all the Eastern European countries and in China the bureaucracy promotes policies aimed at reinforcing sexual repression. The extreme housing shortage, the kind of education given to children from earliest infancy, the frequent refusal to rent hotel rooms to non-married couples, pressure to postpone marriage, all reflect the dominant social mores and the bureaucracy's opposition to any form of sexual liberation. Given their place within the family, women are of course the first to feel the weight of these repressive norms and policies.

5. Women in the deformed and degenerated workers states will not win their full liberation short of a political revolution that removes the bureaucratic caste from power and restores workers democracy. Although there are as yet few signs of any rising consciousness concerning the oppression of women, there is no impenetrable barrier between the advanced capitalist countries and the workers states. Women in the workers states will inevitably be affected by the radicalization of women elsewhere and the demands they are raising.

The struggle of women for their liberation will be a significant component of the process of challenging and overturning the privileged bureaucratic regimes and establishing socialist democracy. Demands for the socialization of domestic labor in particular are an important aspect of the transitional program for the coming political revolution.

In some respects, in comparison with the capitalist countries, the economic independence and status of women in the workers states provide a positive contrast. But Soviet history also strikingly confirms the fact that the family institution is the cornerstone of the oppression of women. As long as women's domestic servitude is sustained and nurtured by economic and political policy, as long as the functions of the family are not fully taken over by superior social institutions, the truly equal integration of women in productive life and all social affairs is impossible. The responsibility of women for domestic labor is the source of the inequalities they face in daily life, in education, in work, and in politics.

6. The Stalinist counterrevolution in respect to women and the family, the vast inequality of women in the Soviet Union especially, more than 60 years after the October Revolution, today comprises one of the obstacles to winning radicalized women elsewhere to revolutionary Marxism. As with all other questions, the policies of Stalinism are often equated with Leninism rather than recognized for what they are – the negation of Leninism. Women fighting for their liberation elsewhere often look to the USSR and the deformed workers states and say, "If this is what socialism does for women, we don't need it." Many anti-Marxists point to the situation of women in these countries as "proof" that the road to women's liberation is not through class struggle. Thus the fight to win the leadership of feminists in other parts of the world is interrelated with the development of the political revolution in the deformed and degenerated workers states, as well as with our ability to project a different image of the socialism we as authentic Marxists are fighting for.

II. The Fourth International and the Struggle for Women's Liberation

Our Perspective

1. The Fourth International welcomes and champions the emergence of a new wave of struggles by women to end their centuries-old oppression. By fighting in the front lines of these battles, we demonstrate that the world party of socialist revolution can provide a leadership capable of carrying the struggle for women's liberation through to its conclusion. Our goal is to win the confidence and leadership of the masses of women by showing that our program and our class-struggle policies will lead to the elimination of women's oppression along the path of successful proletarian revolution and the socialist reconstruction of society.

2. The perspective of the Fourth International stands in the long tradition of revolutionary Marxism. It is based on the following considerations:

a. The oppression of women emerged with the transition from preclass to class society. It is indispensable to the maintenance of class society in general and capitalism in particular. Therefore, struggle by masses of women against their oppression is a form of the struggle against capitalist rule.

b. Women are both a significant component of the working class, and a potentially powerful ally of the working class in the struggle to overthrow capitalism. Without the socialist revolution, women cannot establish the preconditions for their liberation. Without the mobilization of masses of women in struggle for their own liberation, the working class cannot accomplish its historic tasks. The destruction of the bourgeois state, the eradication of capitalist property, the transformation of the economic bases and priorities of society, the consolidation of a new state power based on the democratic organization of the working class and its allies, and the continuing struggle to eliminate all forms of oppressive social relations inherited from class society – all this can ultimately be accomplished only with the conscious participation and leadership of an independent women's liberation movement.

Thus our support for building an independent women's liberation movement is part of the strategy of the revolutionary working-class party. It stems from the very character of women's oppression, the social divisions created by capitalism itself and the way these are used to divide and weaken the working class and its allies in the struggle to abolish class society.

c. All women are oppressed as women. Struggles around specific aspects of women's oppression necessarily involve women from different classes and social layers. Even some bourgeois women, revolting against their oppression as women, can break with their class and be won to the side of the revolutionary workers movement as the road to liberation.

As Lenin pointed out in his discussions with Clara Zetkin, action around aspects of women's oppression has the potential to reach into the heart of the enemy class, to "forment and increase unrest, uncertainty and contradictions and conflicts in the camp of the bourgeoisie and its reformist friends. (...) Every weakening of the enemy is tantamount to a strengthening of our forces."

Even more important from the point of view of the revolutionary Marxist party is the fact that resentment against their oppression as women can often be the starting point in the radicalization of decisive layers of petty-bourgeois women, whose support the working class must win.

d. While all women are oppressed, the effects of that oppression are different for women of different classes. Those who suffer the greatest economic exploitation are generally those who also suffer the most from their oppression as women. Thus the women's liberation movement provides an avenue to reach and mobilize many of the most oppressed and exploited women who might not otherwise be touched so rapidly by the struggles of the working class.

e. While all women are affected by their oppression as women, the mass women's liberation movement we strive to build must be basically working-class in composition, orientation, and leadership. Only such a movement, with roots in the most exploited layers of working-class women, will be able to carry the struggle for women's liberation through to the end in an uncompromising way, allying itself with the social forces whose class interests parallel and intersect those of women. Only such a movement will be able to play a progressive role under conditions of sharpening class polarization.

f. In this long-term perspective, struggles by women in the unions and on the job have a special importance, reflecting the vital interrelationship of the women's movement and the workers movement and their impact on each other.

This is testified to by the deepening radicalization of working-class women today, the growing understanding of forces in the women's liberation movement that they must orient to the struggles of working women, and the willingness of sections of the trade-union bureaucracy in some countries to begin to take a few initiatives around women's demands. All these developments point to the future character and composition of the women's liberation movement and the kind of class forces who will come forward to provide leadership.

g. Struggles by women against their oppression as a sex are interrelated with, but not totally dependent on or identical with, struggles by workers as a class. Women cannot win their liberation except in alliance with the organized power of the working class. But this historical necessity in no way means that women should postpone any of their struggles until the current labor officialdom is replaced by a revolutionary leadership that picks up the banner of women's liberation. Nor should women wait until the socialist revolution has created the material basis for ending their oppression. On the contrary, women fighting for their liberation must wait for no one to show them the way. They should take the lead in opening the fight and carrying it forward. In doing so, they will play a leadership role within the workers movement as a whole, and can help create the kind of class struggle leadership necessary to advance on all fronts.

h. Sexism is one of the most powerful weapons utilized by the ruling class to divide and weaken the workers movement. But it does not simply divide men against women. Its conservatizing weight cuts across sex lines, affecting both men and women.

Its hold is rooted in the class character of society itself, and the manifold ways in which bourgeois ideology is inculcated in every individual from birth. The bosses pit each section of the working class against all others. They promote the belief that women's equality can be achieved only at the *expense* of men-by taking men's jobs away from them, by lowering their wages, and by depriving them of domestic comforts. The reformist bureaucracy of the labor movement, of course, also plays upon these divisions to maintain its control.

Educating the masses of workers, male and female, through propaganda, agitation, and action around the needs of women is an essential part of the struggle to break the stranglehold of reactionary bourgeois ideology within the working class. It is an indispensable part of the politicalization and revolutionary education of the workers movement.

i. The full power and united strength of the working class can only be realized as the workers movement begins to overcome its deep internal divisions. This will only be achieved as the workers come to understand that those at the top of the wage-scale do not owe their relative material advantages to the fact that others are discriminated against and specially oppressed. Rather it is the bosses who profit from such stratification and division. The class interests of *all* workers are identical with the demands and needs of the most oppressed and exploited layers of the class – the women, the oppressed nationalities, the immigrant workers, the youth, the unorganized, the unemployed. The women's movement has a particularly important role to play in helping the working class to understand this truth.

j. Winning the organized labor movement to fight for the demands of women is part of educating the working class to think socially and act politically. It is a central axis of the fight to transform the trade unions into instruments of revolutionary struggle in the interests of the entire working class.

In countering the efforts of the employers to keep the working class divided, we strive to win the ranks of the unions, and especially the young, combative rebels. The more successful we are in winning this battle, the more we will see the labor bureaucracy divide. Those who refuse to defend the interests of the great majority of the most oppressed and exploited will be progressively pushed aside.

The struggle by the revolutionary party to win hegemony and leadership in the working class is inseparable from the battle to convince the working class and its organizations to recognize and champion struggles by women as their own.

k. The struggle against the oppression of women is not a secondary or peripheral issue. It is a life-and-death matter for the workers movement, especially in a period of sharpening class polarization.

Because women's place in class society generates many deep-seated insecurities and fears, and because the ideology that buttresses women's inferior status still retains a powerful hold, especially outside the working class, women are a particular target for all clerical, reactionary, and fascist organizations. Whether it is the Christian Democrats, the Falange, or the opponents of abortion rights, reaction makes a special appeal to women for support, claiming to address women's particular needs, taking advantage of their economic dependence under capitalism, and promising to relieve the inordinate burden women bear during any period of social crisis.

From the "Kinder, Kirche, Küche" propaganda of the Nazi movement to the Christian Democrats' mobilization of middle- class women in Chile for the march of the empty pots in 1971, history has demonstrated time and again that the reactionary mystique of motherhood-and-family is one of the most powerful conservatizing weapons wielded by the ruling class.

Chile once again tragically showed that if the workers movement fails to put forward and fight for a program and revolutionary perspective answering the needs of the masses of women, many petty- bourgeois and even working-class women will either be mobilized on the side of reaction, or neutralized as potential supporters of the proletariat.

The objective changes in women's economic and social role, the new radicalization of women and the changes in consciousness and attitudes this has brought about, make it more difficult for reaction to prevail. This is a new source of revolutionary optimism for the working class. The mass explosion of feminist consciousness in Spain as one of the most significant components of the rising class struggle in the post-Franco era also demonstrates the speed with which the ideological hold of the church and state can begin to crumble in a period of revolutionary ferment, even in sectors of the population where it has been very strong.

1. While the victorious proletarian revolution can create the material foundations for the socialization of domestic labor and lay the basis for the complete economic and social equality of women, this socialist reconstruction of society, placing all human relations on a new foundation, will not be accomplished immediately or automatically. During the period of transition to socialism the fight to eradicate all forms of oppression inherited from class society will continue. For example, the social division of labor into feminine and masculine tasks must be eliminated in all spheres of activity from daily life to the factories. Decisions will have to be made concerning the allocation of scarce resources. An economic plan that reflects the social needs of women, and provides for the most rapid possible socialization of domestic tasks, will have to be developed. The continuing autonomous organization of women will be a precondition for democratically arriving at the correct economic and social decisions. Thus even after the revolution the independent women's liberation movement will play an indispensable role in assuring the ability of the working class as a whole, male and female, to carry this process through to a successful conclusion.

Our class-struggle strategy for the fight against women's oppression, our answer to the question of how to mobilize the working class on the side of women, and the masses of women on the side of the working class, has three facets: our political demands, our methods of struggle, and our class independence.

Our Demands

Through the totality of the system of demands we put forward – which deal with every issue from freedom of political association, to unemployment and inflation, to abortion and child care, to workers control and the arming of the proletariat – we seek to build a bridge from the current needs and struggles of the working masses and their level of consciousness to the culminating point of socialist revolution. As part of this transitional program we put forward demands that speak to the specific oppression of women.

Our program points to the issues around which women can begin to struggle to loosen the bonds of their oppression and challenge the prerogatives of the ruling class. It recognizes and provides answers for all aspects of women's oppression- legal, economic, social, sexual.

We direct our demands against those responsible for the economic and social conditions in which women's oppression is rooted – the ruling class, its government and agencies. We orient the women's liberation movement toward clear political goals. We present our demands and propaganda in such a way as to show how a society no longer based on private property, exploitation, and oppression would radically transform the lives of women in all spheres.

Our interlocking set of tasks and slogans includes immediate, democratic, and transitional demands. Some can and will be wrested from the ruling class in the course of the struggle leading toward the socialist revolution. Such victories bring inspiration, increasing confidence, and self- reliance. Other demands will be partially met. The most fundamental will be resisted to the end by those who control the property and wealth. They can be won only in the course of the conquest of power and the socialist reconstruction of society.

In fighting for these demands – both those providing solutions to the specific oppression of women and those answering other needs of the oppressed nationalities and working class as a whole – masses of women will come to understand the interrelationship of their oppression as victims of class rule.

Our demands directed toward eliminating the specific oppression of women are centered on the following points:

1. Full legal, political, and social equality for women

No discrimination on the bases of sex. For the right of all women to vote, engage in public activity, form or join political associations, live and travel where they want, engage in any occupations they choose. An end to all laws and regulations with special penalties for women, the extension to women of all democratic rights won by men.

2. The right of women to control their own bodies.

A woman has the sole right to choose whether or not to prevent or terminate pregnancy. This includes the rejection of population-control schemes which are tools of racism or class prejudice and which attempt to blame the evils of class society on the masses of working people and peasants.

a. An end to all government restrictions on abortion and contraception, including for minors, immigrant workers, and other noncitizens.

b. Free abortion on demand; no forced sterilization or any other government interference with the right of women to choose whether or when to bear children. The right to choose whatever method of abortion or contraception a woman prefers.

c. Free, widely disseminated birth control information and devices. State-financed birth control and sex education centers in schools, neighborhoods, hospitals, and factories.

d. Priority in medical research to development of totally safe, 100 percent effective contraceptives for men and women; an end to all medical and drug experimentation on women without their full, informed consent; nationalization of the drug industry.

3. An end to the hypocrisy, debasement, and coercion of bourgeois and feudal family laws.

a. Separation of church and state.

b. An end to all forced marriages and the buying and selling of wives. Abrogation of all laws against adultery. Abolition of laws giving men "conjugal rights" over their wives. An end to all laws, secular or religious, sanctioning penalties, physical abuse, or even murder of wives, sisters, and daughters for so-called crimes against male "honor".

c. Abolition of all laws forbidding marriage between men and women of different races, religions, or nationalities.

d. Marriage to be a voluntary process of civil registration.

e. The right to automatic divorce on request of either partner. State provision for economic welfare and job training for the divorced woman.

f. Abolition of the concept of "illegitimacy." An end to all discrimination against unwed mothers and their children. An end to the prisonlike conditions that govern special centers set up to take care of unwed mothers and other women who have nowhere else to go.

g. The rearing, social welfare, and education of children to be the responsibility of society, rather than the burden of individual parents. Abolition of all laws granting parents property rights and total control over children. Strict laws against child abuse.

h. An end to all laws victimizing prostitutes. An end to all laws reinforcing the double standard for men and women in sexual matters. An end to all laws and regulations victimizing youth for sexual activities.

i. An end to the mutilation of women through the practice of infibulation or clitorectomy.

j. Abrogation of all antihomosexual laws. An end to all discrimination against homosexuals in employment, housing, child custody. An end to the insulting stereotyping of homosexuals in textbooks and mass media, or portrayal of homosexual relations as perverted and against nature.

k. Violence against women- often sanctioned by reactionary family laws – is a daily reality that all women experience in some form. If it is not the extreme of rape or beatings, there is still the ever present threat of sexual assault implicit in the widespread circulation of pornographic literature, and the obscene comments and gestures women are constantly subjected to in the streets and on the job.

We demand the elimination of laws predicated on the assumption that female rape victims are the guilty party; establishment of centers – independent of the police and courts – designed to welcome, counsel, and help battered wives, rape victims, and other female victims of sexual violence; improvement of public transportation, street lighting, and other public services that make it safer for women to go out alone.

Violence against women is a vicious product of the general social and economic conditions of class society. It inevitably increases during periods of social crisis. But we strive to educate women and men that sexual violence cannot be eradicated without changing the foundation from which the economic, social, and sexual degradation of women flows. We expose the racist and anti-working class use of antirape laws to victimize men of oppressed nationalities. We oppose demands raised by some feminists to inflict drastic penalties on convicted rapists or to strengthen the repressive apparatus of the state, whose cops are among the most notorious brutalizers of women.

We oppose any kind of censorship of literature, even under the guise of campaigns against pornography.

4. Full economic independence for women.

a. Guaranteed jobs at union wages for all women who want to work, coupled with a sliding scale of hours and wages to combat inflation and unemployment among men and women. A shorter work -week for all.

b. Elimination of laws that discriminate against women's right to receive and dispose of their own wages and property.

c. Equal pay for equal work. For a national minimum wage based on union scale.

d. No discrimination against women in any trade, profession, job category, apprenticeship, or training program.

e. Preferential hiring, training, job upgrading, and seniority adjustments for women and other superexploited layers of the labor force in order to overcome the effects of decades of systematic discrimination against them. No preferential hiring for men in traditionally female-dominated trades and industries.

f. Paid maternity leave for father and mother with no loss of job or seniority.

g. Paid work leaves to care for sick children to be given to men and women alike.

h. The extension of beneficial protective legislation (providing special working conditions to women) to cover men, in order to improve working conditions for both men and women and prevent the use of protective legislation to discriminate against women.

i. A uniform retirement age for men and women, with each individual free to take retirement or not.

j. Part-time workers to be guaranteed the same hourly wages and benefits as full-time workers.

k. Compensation at union rates throughout periods of unemployment for all women and men, including youth who cannot find a place in the work force, regardless of marital status, or previous employment record. Unemployment compensation to be protected against inflation by automatic increases.

5. Equal educational opportunities.

a. Free, open admissions for all women to all institutions of education and all programs of study, including on-the-job training programs.

Special preferential admissions programs to encourage women to enter traditionally male-dominated fields and learn skills and trades from which they have previously been excluded.

b. An end to all forms of pressuring women to prepare themselves for "women's work," such as homemaking, secretarial work, nursing, and teaching.

c. Special education and refresher courses to aid women reentering the job market.

d. An end to portrayal in textbooks and mass media of women as sex objects and stupid, weak, emotionally dependent creatures. Courses designed to teach the true history of women's struggles against their oppression. Physical education courses to teach women to develop their strength and be proud of their athletic abilities.

e. No expulsion of pregnant students or unwed mothers, or segregation into special facilities.

6. Reorganization of society to eliminate domestic slavery of women.

The family as an economic unit cannot be "abolished" by fiat. It can only be replaced over time. The goal of the socialist revolution is to create economic and social alternatives that are superior to the present family institution and better able to provide for the needs currently met, however poorly, by the family, so that personal relationships will be a matter of free choice and not of economic compulsion. To ultraleft propaganda and agitation for the "abolition" of the family, we counterpose:

a. Free, government-financed twenty- four-hour childcare centers and schools, conveniently located and open to all children from infancy to early adolescence regardless of parents' income, employment situation, or marital status; trained male and female personnel; elimination of all sexist educational practices; child-care policies to be decided by those who use the centers.

b. Free medical care for all and special child-care facilities for children who are ill.

c. Systematic development of low-cost, high-quality social services such as cafeterias, restaurants, and take-out food centers available to all; collective laundry facilities; housecleaning services organized on an industrial basis.

d. A crash, government-financed development program to provide healthful, uncrowded housing for all; no rent to exceed 10 percent of income; no discrimination against single women or women with children.

* * *

These demands indicate the issues around which women will fight for their liberation, and show how this fight is interrelated with the demands raised by other oppressed sectors of society and the needs of the working class as a whole. It is in struggle along these lines that the working class will be educated to understand and oppose sexism in all its forms and expressions.

The women's liberation movement raises many issues. The development of the movement has already demonstrated that not all will come to the fore with equal force at any given time. Which demands to raise at any particular time in the course of a particular struggle, the best way to formulate specific demands so that they are understandable to the masses and able to mobilize them in action, when to advance new demands to move the struggle forward – the answer to those tactical problems is the function of the revolutionary party, the art of politics itself.

Our Methods of Struggle

1. We utilize the proletarian methods of mobilization and action in order to achieve these demands. Everything we do is geared to bring the masses themselves into motion, into struggle, whatever their current level of consciousness. The masses do not learn simply by being exposed to ideas or by the exemplary action of others. Only through their own direct involvement will the political consciousness of the masses develop, grow, and be transformed. Only through their own experience will millions of women be won as allies in the revolutionary struggle and come to understand the need to get rid of an economic system based on exploitation.

Our goal is to teach the masses to rely on their own united power. We utilize elections and other institutions of bourgeois democracy to clearly present our program to the broadest possible numbers of workers. But we counterpose extraparliamentary mass action – demonstrations, meetings, strikes, occupations – to reliance on elections, lobbying, parliaments, legislatures, and the bourgeois and petty- bourgeois politicians who haunt them.

Our class-struggle methods are geared to awakening the initiatives of the great majority of women; to bring them together; to destroy their domestic isolation and their lack of confidence in their own abilities, intelligence, independence, and strength. Struggling together with them, we aim to show that class exploitation is the root of women's oppression and its elimination the only road to emancipation.

Just as we strive to develop the class consciousness of the women's liberation movement, we try to win the workers movement to take up the struggle against each aspect of women's oppression.

In every struggle, we aim to educate women to understand the class inequality that sharpens the oppression of the most exploited. We try to lead the movement to address itself first and foremost to mobilizing women of the working class and oppressed nationalities. Through the system of demands we advance and the propaganda we put forward, we strive to move the struggle in an anticapitalist direction. We highlight the social implications of demands and expose the logic of profit and the conditions of class society that limit the capacity of the ruling class to implement in practice even the concessions wrung from it through struggle.

2. The oppression of women as a sex constitutes the objective basis for the mobilization of women in struggle through their own organizations. For that reason the Fourth International supports and helps build the women's liberation movement.

By the women's movement we mean all the women who organize themselves at one level or another to struggle against the oppression imposed on them by this society: women's liberation groups, consciousness-raising groups, neighborhood groups, student groups, groups organized at workplaces, trade-union commissions, organizations of women of oppressed nationalities, lesbian-feminist groups, action coalitions around specific demands. The women's movement is characterized by its heterogeneity, its penetration into all layers of society, and the fact that it is not tied to any particular political organization, even though various currents are active within it. Moreover, some groups and action coalitions, though led and sustained by women, are open to men as well, such as the National Organization for Women in the United States and the National Abortion Campaign in Britain.

While most women's groups initially developed outside the mass organizations of the working class, the deepening radicalization has led more and more working-class women to find ways to organize themselves within their class organizations. In Spain, large numbers of women joined the COs (Workers' Commissions) and brought life to their women's committees. In France, thousands of women now participate in trade-union commissions as well as Family Planning organizations and women's groups. In Bolivia, miners' wives have formed housewives' committees affiliated to the COB (Bolivian Workers Federation).

But all these are forms of the turbulent and still largely unstructured reality called the independent or autonomous women's movement.

By independent or autonomous we do not mean independent of the class struggle or the needs of the working class. On the contrary, only by fusing the objectives and demands of the women's movement with the struggle of the working class will the necessary forces be assembled to achieve women's goals.

By independent or autonomous we mean that the movement is organized and led by women; that it takes the fight for women's rights and needs as its first priority, refusing to subordinate that fight to any other interests; that it is not subordinate to the decisions or policy needs of any political tendency or any other social group; that it is willing to carry through the fight by whatever means and together with whatever forces prove necessary.

Clearly, not every group within the movement measures up to those criteria fully or equally, but such is the character of the independent women's liberation movement we seek to build.

3. The dominant organizational form of the women's movement has been all- female groups. These have emerged in virtually all arenas from the schools and churches to the factories and trade unions. This expresses the determination of women to take the leadership of their own organizations in which they can learn and develop and lead without fear of being put down or dictated to by men or having to compete with them from the start.

Before women can lead others they must throw off their feelings of inferiority and self-deprecation. They must learn to lead themselves. Feminist groups that consciously and deliberately exclude men help many women to take the first steps toward discarding their own slave mentality, gaining confidence, pride, and courage to act as political beings.

The small "consciousness raising" groups that have emerged everywhere as one of the most prevalent forms of the new radicalization help many women to realize that their problems do not arise from personal shortcomings, but are socially created and common to other women.

If they remain inward-turned and limit themselves to discussion circles as a substitute for joining with others to act, they can become an obstacle to the further political development of the women involved. But they most often lay the groundwork for women to break out of their isolation for the first time, to gain confidence, and to move into action.

The desire of women to organize themselves in all-female groups is the opposite of the practice followed by many mass Stalinist parties that organize separate male and female youth organizations for the purpose of repressing sexual activity and reinforcing sex-stereotyped behavior- i.e., the inferiority of women. The independent all-female groups that have emerged today express in part the distrust many radicalizing women feel for the mass reformist organizations of the working class, which have failed so miserably to fight for their needs.

Our support for and work to build the independent women's liberation movement distinguishes the Fourth International today from many sectarian groups that claim to stand on Marxist orthodoxy as represented by their interpretations of the resolutions of the first four congresses of the Third International. Such groups reject the construction of any women's organizations except those tied directly to and under the political control of their party.

To those "Marxists" who claim that women's liberation groups organized on the basis of women only divide the working class along sex lines, we say it is not those fighting against their oppression who are responsible for creating or maintaining divisions. Capitalism divides the working class-by race, by sex, by age, by nationality, by skill levels, and by every other means possible. Our job is to organize and support the battles of the most oppressed and exploited layers who are raising demands that represent the interests of the entire class and who will lead the struggle for socialism. Those who suffer most from the old will fight the most energetically for the new.

4. The forms through which we work can vary greatly depending on the concrete circumstances in which our organizations find themselves. Our tactics are dictated by our strategic aim, which is to educate and lead in action forces much broader than ourselves, especially the decisive forces of the working class, to help build a mass women's liberation movement, to strengthen a class-struggle wing of the women's movement, and to recruit the best cadre to the revolutionary party.

Factors that must be taken into account include the strength of our own forces; the size, character, and political level of the women's liberation forces; the strength of the liberal, Social Democratic, Stalinist, and centrist forces against whom we must contend; and the general political context in which we are working. It's a tactical question whether we should organize women's liberation groups on a broad socialist program, work through existing organizations of the women's liberation movement, build broad action coalitions around specific issues, work through trade-union commissions or caucuses in other mass organizations, combine several of these activities, or work through some altogether different forms.

No matter what organizational form we adopt, the fundamental question to be decided is the same: what specific issues and demands should be raised under the given circumstances in order to most effectively mobilize women and their allies in struggle?

5. There is no contradiction between supporting and building all-female organizations to fight for women's liberation, or for specific demands relating to women's oppression, and simultaneously building mass action coalitions involving both men and women to fight for the same demands. Campaigns around the right to abortion have provided a good example of this. Women will be the backbone of such campaigns, but since the fight is in the interests of the working masses as a whole, our perspective is to win support for the movement from all organizations of the working class and the oppressed.

6. Our perspective of trying to mobilize masses of women in action can often best be achieved in the present period through united-front-type action campaigns, which mobilize the broadest possible support around concrete demands. This is all the more true, given the relative weakness of the sections of the Fourth International and the relative strength of the liberals and our reformist, class-collaborationist opponents. For many women and men, participation in the actions organized by such campaigns has been their first step toward support for the political goals of the women's liberation movement. The united-front-type abortion campaigns in numerous countries provide an example of this type of action.

Through such united-front-type actions we can bring the greatest power to bear against the capitalist government and educate women and the working class concerning their own strength. Insofar as the liberal "friends" of women, the Stalinists, Social Democrats, and trade-union bureaucrats refuse to support such united campaigns for women's needs, they will isolate and expose themselves by their own inaction, opposition, or willingness to subordinate women's needs to their search for an alliance with the supposedly "progressive" sectors of the ruling class. And if mass pressure obliges them to support such actions, this can only broaden the mass appeal of the campaigns and increase the contradictions within the reformist and liberal forces.

As we have already seen so clearly around the abortion question, such united- front-type action campaigns are of particular importance in deepening the interaction between the independent women's movement and the labor movement, since they put the greatest pressure on the labor bureaucracy to respond.

7. Because our orientation is to build a women's movement that is basically working-class in composition and leadership, and because of the interconnection between the fight for women's liberation and the transformation of the trade unions into instruments that effectively defend the interests of the whole class, we give special importance to struggles by women in the unions and on the job. Our aim is to organize women to actively participate in their unions and in the women's liberation movement.

Here as elsewhere in capitalist society, women are subject to male domination, to discrimination as an inferior sex that is out of its "natural place." But the growing number of women in the work force and their deepening consciousness of their double oppression have already brought significant changes in the attitudes of working women, strengthening their inclination to organize, unionize, and fight for their rights.

Women workers are involved in many struggles for general demands relating to the economic needs and job conditions of all workers. They also frequently raise the special needs of women workers such as equal pay, maternity benefits, child-care facilities, and preferential hiring and training. Both are central to the struggle for women's liberation as well as to the working class in general. Such struggles and demands by women workers will assume a greater weight as the class struggle deepens under the impact of the economic crisis. They will have a greater and greater impact on the women's liberation movement.

Most women who enter into such struggles do not think of themselves as feminists. They simply think they are entitled to equal pay for doing the same job as a man, or believe they have a right to be employed in some traditionally "masculine" line of work. They often protest vigorously that they are not feminists.

Working women who become involved in struggles on the job confront the same issues and conditions that have given rise to the independent women's movement.

They often face sexist harassment and abuse which is organized and promoted by their foremen and supervisors. Even when it comes from their fellow workers, it is often the result of an atmosphere fostered by the employer. Women face the sometimes difficult job of fighting to convince the union to defend them against serious harassment and victimization by management personnel. They have to convince fellow workers that when they give women a hard time on the job, they are only doing the boss's job for him, and playing into his divide-and-rule tactics.

As women begin to play an active role, to take on leadership responsibilities, to prove their leadership capacities to themselves and others, to gain confidence and play an independent role, they develop a greater understanding of what the women's liberation movement is fighting for. The correct presentation of clear, concrete demands and objectives by the feminist movement is indispensable in reaching and involving millions of working women whose conscious political development begins as they try to confront their problems as women who must also work a job to earn a living.

8. The growing weight and role of women in the labor movement has an important impact on the consciousness of many male workers, who begin to see women more as equal partners in struggle and less as weak creatures who must be coddled and protected.

In this context, demands for preferential hiring, training, and job promotion for women in the traditionally male-dominated sectors of the economy have a special importance.

a. They challenge the division within the working class along sex lines, divisions that are fostered and maintained by the bosses in order to weaken the working class and hold down the wages and working conditions of the entire class.

b. They help educate both male and female workers to appreciate the material effects of discrimination against women, and the need for conscious measures to overcome the effects of centuries of enforced subjugation.

c. As women begin to break down the traditional division of labor along sex lines and establish their equal right to employment and their ability to perform "male" jobs as well as men, sexist attitudes and assumptions within the working class are undercut and the social division of labor in all spheres is challenged.

Struggles that open the doors for women to enter the educational, occupational, and leadership realms previously dominated by men pose in the clearest possible manner the eradication of women's inferior social status. Along with demands that raise the basic democratic rights of women, and those that go toward socializing the domestic labor women perform, such as the expansion and improvement of child-care facilities, they have a powerful educational impact within the working class.

9. Such demands also have a special importance as part of the fight to transform the unions into revolutionary instruments of class struggle and challenge the sexist bias of the labor bureaucracy. The union

bureaucracy bases itself on the most privileged layers of male workers, who usually see preferential demands as a threat to their immediate prerogatives. The most conscious elements of the bureaucracy thus adamantly oppose those demands raised by the most oppressed and exploited sectors of the working class which are aimed at eradicating the deep divisions within the class.

An important part of our strategic orientation to develop a class-struggle left wing in the trade-union movement is to utilize the growing weight of forces like the women's liberation movement to pose the key social and political issues on which the labor movement should be playing a leadership role.

As the ranks of the unions are won to support such struggles the reactionary antiwoman and therefore anti-working class policies of the labor bureaucracy will be exposed and new forces will come forward to lead.

10. There are many difficulties in organizing women workers. Precisely because of their oppression as women, they are less likely to be unionized or to have a strong class consciousness. Their participation in the labor force is frequently more sporadic. Their double burden of responsibilities and chores at home is fatiguing and time-consuming, leaving them less energy for political and trade-union activity. The gross inadequacy of child-care facilities makes participation in meetings especially difficult.

For these reasons, the fight to convince the trade unions to take up the special demands of women is inseparable from the fight for trade-union democracy. Trade-union democracy includes not only issues such as the right of the membership to vote on all question, election of all leadership bodies and personnel, and the right to form tendencies. It also implies special measures that permit women to participate with full equality-child-care facilities organized by the union during meetings, union commissions that deal specifically with women's needs, the right to meet in women's caucuses when necessary, special provisions to meet during working hours, and measures to assure adequate representation of women on all leadership bodies. Within the workers movement, challenging sexist attitudes and practices is an integral part of the fight for trade-union democracy and class solidarity.

11. If we give special importance to the struggles of women working outside the home it is not because we deprecate the oppression suffered by housewives. On the contrary, we understand and put forward a program that answers the deep problems faced by women in the home, the overwhelming majority of whom are working-class women, who will spend some part of their life in the labor market in

addition to carrying out their domestic responsibilities. We offer a perspective of escape from the mind-deadening drudgery of housework, the isolation it imposes on each individual woman, the economic dependence of housewives, and the fear and insecurity this produces. We counterpose our program of socialization of housework and the integration of women into the productive labor force on an equal basis to the alternatives offered by reaction – a glorification of housework and motherhood and proposals to compensate women for their domestic slavery through wages for housework or similar superficially alluring schemes.

As capitalism in crisis shifts more and more economic burdens onto the individual family, it is often housewives, responsible for trying to stretch the family income to cover the basic necessities, who first take to the streets in protest over food shortages and soaring inflation. Such movements can be a first step toward political consciousness and collective action for thousands of women. They offer an opening and a challenge to the labor movement to join with and help provide leadership and direction for such protests – which can develop with explosive rapidity. Demands for joint worker-consumer price surveillance committees provide common ground for the labor movement, protesting housewives, and other consumers.

Unlike housewives, however, working women are already semiorganized by the labor market. Their place within the working class, within the workers movement, and their economic status put them in a position to play a pivotal leadership role in the struggles of women and of the working class as a whole.

12. There is no contradiction between building the independent women's liberation movement, building trade unions, and building a revolutionary Marxist Party of women and men.

The struggle for socialism requires all three. They serve different functions. The mass feminist movement mobilizes women in struggle around their needs and through their own independent forms of organization. The trade unions are the basic economic defense organizations of the working-class. The mass revolutionary Marxist party, through program and action, provides leadership for the working class and its allies, including women, and uncompromisingly orients all facets of the class struggle toward a combined drive to establish a workers government and abolish capitalism.

There is no objective basis for a separate revolutionary Marxist women's organization. Unless women and men share equally in the rights and responsibilities of membership and leadership in a party that develops a political program and activities that represent the interests of all the oppressed and exploited, the party can never lead the working class to accomplish its historic tasks.

We maintain that there are no exclusively "women's issues." Every question of concern to the female half of humanity is likewise a broader social question of vital interest to the working class as a whole. While we raise demands that deal with the specific oppression of women, we have no separate program for women's liberation. Our demands are an integral part of our transitional program for the socialist revolution.

13. The program of the revolutionary party synthesizes the lessons of struggles against all forms of economic and social exploitation and oppression. The party expresses the historic interests of the proletariat through its program and action. Thus it not only learns from the participation of its members in the women's liberation movement. It also has an indispensable role to play. Through our work to build the independent women's movement, we deepen the party's understanding of women's oppression and the struggle against it. And we also strive to win ever greater forces to an effective strategy for women's liberation, that is, to a class-struggle perspective.

We do not demand agreement with our program as a precondition for building the independent women's movement. On the contrary, a broad-based movement, within which a wide range of personal experiences and political perspectives can contend in a framework of democratic debate and discussion, can only strengthen the political confidence and combativity of the movement. It enhances the possibility of developing a correct perspective.

However, we do not strive for the organic unity of all components of the women's movement at all costs. We fight for the broadest possible unity *in action* on the basis of demands and activities that genuinely reflect the objective needs of women, which is also the program in the interests of the working class.

We try to build the strongest possible wing within the women's liberation movement of those who share our class-struggle perspectives. A consistent struggle against all aspects of women's oppression means resolutely combatting all attempts to divert women's struggles into the reformist deadend of managing the rulers' austerity programs, or towards a search for individual solutions. We strive to recruit the most conscious and combative to the revolutionary party.

Our goal is to win the leadership of the women's liberation movement by showing women in practice that we have the program and perspectives that can lead to liberation. This is not a sectarian stance. Nor does it indicate a manipulative attempt to dominate or control the mass movement. On the contrary, it reflects our conviction that the struggle against women's oppression can be won only if the feminist movement develops in an anticapitalist direction. Such an evolution is not automatic. It depends on the demands put forward, the class forces toward which the feminist movement orients, and the forms of action in which it engages. Only the conscious intervention of the revolutionary party and its ability to win the confidence and leadership of women fighting for their liberation offers any guarantee that the women's struggle will ultimately be victorious.

14. We are concerned with all aspects of women's oppression. However, as a political party based on a program that represents the historic interests of the working class and all the oppressed, our prime task is to help direct the women's liberation movement toward political action that can effectively lead to the eradication of private property in which that oppression is rooted. Around every facet of women's oppression we strive to develop demands and actions that challenge the social and economic policies of the bourgeoisie and point toward the solutions that would be possible were it not for the fact that all social policies are decided on the basis of maximizing private profits.

Our approach to the struggle for women's liberation as an eminently political question often brings us into conflict with petty-bourgeois radical-feminist currents, who counterpose the development of new individual "life-styles" to political action directed against the state. They blame men instead of capitalism. They counterpose reforming men as individuals, trying to make them less sexist, to organizing against the bourgeois government which defends and sustains the institutions of class society responsible for male supremacy and women's oppression. They often attempt to build utopian "counterinstitutions" in the midst of class society.

As revolutionists we recognize that the problems many women seek to resolve in this way are real and preoccupying. Our criticism is not directed against individuals who try to find a personal way out from under the intolerable pressures capitalist society places on them. But we point out that for the masses of workers there is no "individual" solution. They must fight collectively to change society before their "life-style" will be significantly altered. Ultimately there are no purely private solutions for any of us. Individual escapism is a form of utopianism that can only end in disillusionment and the dispersal of revolutionary forces.

Our Class Independence

1. Political independence is the third facet of our class-struggle strategy for the fight against women's oppression. We do not defer or subordinate any demand, action, or struggle of women to the political needs and concerns of either the bourgeois or reformist political forces with their parliamentary shadowboxing and electoral maneuvers.

2. We fight to keep women's liberation organizations and struggles independent of all bourgeois forces and parties. We oppose attempts to divert women's struggles toward the construction of women's caucuses inside of or oriented to capitalist parties or bourgeois politics, as has occurred in the United States, Canada, and Australia. We oppose the formation of a women's political party, such as arose in Belgium and has been advocated by some feminist groups in Spain and elsewhere. The election of more women to public office on a liberal-bourgeois or radical petty-bourgeois program, while a reflection of changing attitudes, can do nothing to further the interests of women.

Women's liberation is part of the historic struggle of the working class against capitalism. We strive to make that link a conscious one on the part of women and of the working class. But we do not reject support from bourgeois figures or politicians who voice their agreement with any of our demands or goals. That strengthens our side, not theirs. It is their contradiction, not ours.

3. We strive for united-front action on specific demands and campaigns with the broadest possible forces, especially the mass reformist parties of the working class. But we reject the political perspectives of the Stalinist and Social Democratic parties.

The policies and conduct of both these currents within the working-class movement are based on preserving the institutions of the capitalist system, including the family, regardless of any lip service they may pay to the struggles of women against their oppression. Both are ready to subordinate the needs of women to whatever class-collaborationist deal they are trying to negotiate at the moment, whether it be with the monarchy in Spain, the Christian Democrats in Italy, or the bourgeois opposition parties in West Germany or Britain. The Stalinists never tire of telling women that the road to happiness is through "advanced democracy" or the "antimonopoly coalition." They advise women not to demand more than "democracy" (i.e., capitalism) can give. The Social Democrats, especially when they are managing "austerity" programs for the bourgeoisie, are never slow to implement the cutbacks in social services demanded by the ruling class, measures that frequently hit women the hardest.

4. It is only through an uncompromising programmatic and organizational break from the bourgeoisie and all forms of class collaborationism that the working class and its allies, including women struggling for their liberation, can be mobilized as a powerful and self-confident force capable of carrying the socialist revolution through to the end. The task of the revolutionary Marxist party is to provide the leadership to educate the working masses, including the women's movement, through action and propaganda in this class struggle perspective.

Tasks of the Fourth International Today

1. The new rise of the women's liberation movement has proceeded unevenly on a world scale, and feminist consciousness has had varying degrees of impact. But the speed with which revolutionary ideas and lessons of struggle are transmitted from one country to another, and from one sector of the world revolution to another, ensures the continuing spread of women's liberation struggles. Increasingly widespread questioning of the traditional role of women creates an atmosphere conducive to Marxist education and propaganda, as well as concrete action in support of the liberation of women. Through our press and propaganda activities the Fourth International has growing opportunities to explain the source and nature of women's oppression, our program for eradicating that oppression along with the class society in which it is rooted, and the revolutionary dynamic of women's struggle for liberation.

2. The involvement of our sections and sympathizing organizations in the women's liberation movement in numerous countries has shown that considerable potential exists for helping to organize and lead action campaigns around issues raised in the struggle against women's oppression. Such campaigns often provide opportunities especially for our women comrades to gain valuable experience and to play a leadership role in the mass movement. They are frequently an avenue through which even relatively small numbers of comrades can play a significant political role and win influence among much broader forces. Our support for and active participation in the women's liberation movement has already won us many new members.

The orientation of the sections and sympathizing organizations of the Fourth International is to commit our forces to building the women's liberation movement and action campaigns around specific issues like abortion, child care, the right to a job, and other aspects of our program.

We also encourage International solidarity in the women's movement, and where possible, international coordination of action campaigns around common issues. The International campaign on abortion in which our sections have frequently played a decisive role, is a good example of the type of international coordination that is possible.

3. In addition to participating in all the various independent organizational forms that have emerged as part of the radicalization of women, we must integrate women's liberation propaganda and activity into all our areas of work, from the trade unions to the student milieu. It is especially among the youth – students, young workers, young housewives – that we will find the greatest receptivity to our ideas and program and readiness for action.

Women's liberation work is not the responsibility of women comrades alone, although they will have to lead it. As with every other question, the entire membership and leadership of the party must be knowledgeable about our work, collectively participate in determining our political line, and take responsibility for carrying our campaigns and propaganda into all areas of the class struggle where we are active. Male as well as female comrades will help to drive this forward.

4. To organize and carry out systematic women's liberation work, sections of the Fourth International should establish commissions or fractions composed of those involved in this work. Such fractions would include male as well as female comrades depending on the activities in which we are involved.

They should help the appropriate leadership bodies to give regular attention to all aspects of our work around issues and demands raised by the women's liberation movement, including proposals for internal education of our own membership. By establishing such commissions and fractions which – together with the leadership bodies – are responsible for discussing and implementing systematic work we can take maximum advantage of the opportunities and openings, and make our own membership fully aware of the political importance of the struggle for women's liberation.

5. Systematic education about the history of women's oppression and struggles, and the theoretical and political questions involved, should be organized within the sections of the Fourth International. This education should not be limited to special schools from time to time

but must become part of the daily life of the organization. It must be part of the basic political education of each member as they acquire and deepen their understanding of the fundamental positions of revolutionary Marxism.

We have no illusions that sections can be islands of the future socialist society floating in a capitalist morass, or that individual comrades can fully escape the education and conditioning absorbed from the everyday effort to survive in class society. Sexist attitudes can and do sometimes find expression within the ranks of the Fourth International. But it is a condition of membership in the Fourth International that the conduct of comrades and sections be in harmony with the principles on which we stand. We educate the members of the Fourth International to a full understanding of the character of women's oppression and the pernicious ways in which it is expressed. We strive to create an organization in which language, jokes, personal violence, and other acts expressing chauvinist bigotry toward women are not tolerated anymore than acts and expressions of racist bigotry would be allowed to pass unchallenged.

6. Women members of our organizations face special problems, both material and psychological, stemming from their oppression in class society. They often face the same time-consuming domestic responsibilities as other women, especially if they have children. They are marked by the same lack of self-confidence, timidity, and fear of leadership that all women are educated from birth to consider as "natural." These obstacles to the recruitment, integration, and leadership development of women comrades must be discussed and consciously dealt with within the party.

As on all other questions, the leadership has the responsibility to take the lead:

Conscious attention must be given to the education, political development, and leadership training of women comrades. This should be a constant concern of all leadership bodies at all levels of the sections and the International. Consideration should be given to assuring that women are encouraged and, more importantly, helped to take on assignments that challenge them to develop their full capacities – teaching classes, writing articles, giving political reports, being public spokespersons and candidates for the organization, leading areas of work. Only by taking such deliberate and conscious measures can we maximize the development of our women cadre and assure that when they are elected to leadership bodies at all levels, this reflects a genuine expansion of a self-confident and strong political leadership cadre, not an artificial measure that can prove destructive to both individual comrades and the organization as a whole.

Within such a general framework of conscious leadership development, we strive to maximize the number of women in the central leadership bodies of our sections and sympathizing organizations and international.

This process will be facilitated by the fact that a growing number of comrades will be in the vanguard of women fighting their way into non-traditional jobs as part of the industrial working class. The self-confidence they gain from being part of the most powerful and organized sectors of the proletariat, the respect they earn from both male and female workers, and the experience they acquire as leaders of our class, are a crucial part of transforming the consciousness of our organization and developing party leaders who are women.

For women comrades especially the difficulties created by the gross inadequacy of state-funded child-care facilities are often a barrier to their full participation in meetings and other activities. As our sections grow and become more working class in composition, we will be recruiting more comrades who have children.

In our public activities and through our intervention in the mass movement, we strive to make broader social forces conscious of the need for organized child care. We try to win the labor movement to support and put high priority on the fight for socially organized and funded child-care services. We demand that mass workers organizations such as trade unions organize meeting times to facilitate the participation of women members, and utilize their resources to provide child-care facilities.

Internally our comrades must be constantly aware of the extra burdens and obstacles that stem from social and economic inequality generated by capitalism, especially for women and comrades of oppressed nationalities. We make allowances for this. In this perspective the leadership has the obligation to work with comrades who have family responsibilities to try to find collective solutions that will enable them to minimize the obstacles to their political activity. For example, when a comrade with children is asked to take on a full-time assignment, the leadership has the responsibility to discuss and try to resolve the special needs, financial or otherwise.

At the same time, we recognize that there are limits to what the party can do. The party itself cannot assume the material obligation to eliminate the economic and social inequalities among comrades created by class society. We cannot assure the social services capitalism does not provide. The party does not have a generalized obligation to provide child care in order to equalize the personal situations of all comrades, nor can child-care duties be imposed on any comrade.

Such an approach would change the very purpose and character of the party as a political organization. What binds us together is our common determination to destroy the system that perpetuates inequality, our agreement on the program to accomplish that aim, and our loyalty to the party based on that program.

The process of educating our own members will take place along with, and be facilitated by, the growing involvement of our sections in the struggle for women's liberation. The impact of this struggle on the consciousness and attitudes of all comrades has already been profound. The transformation of the women cadre of the international, reflecting our involvement in the struggle for women's liberation, is a development of historic dimensions. The growing self-confidence, political maturity, and leadership capacities of the women comrades of the Fourth International constitute a significant expansion of the effective forces of revolutionary leadership on a world scale.

The new rise of women's struggles internationally and the emergence of a strong women's liberation movement prior to revolutionary struggles for power is a development of prime importance to the world party of socialist revolution. It increases the political power of the working class and the likelihood that the international revolution will be successful in carrying through to the end its task of socialist reconstruction. The rise of the women's liberation movement is an additional guarantee against the bureaucratic degeneration of future revolutions.

The struggle to liberate women from the bondage in which class society has placed them is a struggle to free all human relationships from the shackles of economic compulsion and to propel humanity along the road to a higher social order.

November 1979.

Resolution on Internal Women's Caucuses

11th World Congress World Congress
of the Fourth International

In recent years a number of sections of the Fourth International have adopted resolutions permitting the organization of women's caucuses – that is, internal meetings open to women comrades only.[2]

While we support and fight for the right of women to form such caucuses in non-Leninist organizations, we are opposed to such groups within the revolutionary party.

The emergence of women's caucuses in some sections has reflected very real political problems and leadership defaults.

There has been insensitivity to the depth of the special problems women comrades face, failure to understand the political importance of the women's liberation movement and its place in the class struggle, slowness in responding to the rise of the feminist movement, or reluctance to assign comrades to women's liberation work and integrate it into all arenas of our political activity. Because of these errors we have unnecessarily lost valuable cadres and political opportunities. This kind of situation has frequently led to an explosion of resentment by comrades, especially women, who recognize that sexist attitudes often underlie these errors and make them more difficult to correct.

In an effort to change this kind of situation, women comrades in a number of sections have demanded the right to meet together in caucuses, from which all male comrades are excluded, to discuss the internal situation in the party.

Our support for the right of women to caucus in organizations in the mass movement flows from the fact that other organizations are not based on a revolutionary Marxist program that represents the historical interests of women and the working class. Their leaderships are not democratically elected to defend such a program. There is a contradiction, for example, between the interests of the trade-union

---

[2] *This resolution was submitted by the United Secretariat. The vote of delegates and fraternal observers was: 63 for, 36.5 against, 3 abstentions, 10.5 not voting.*

bureaucracy and the needs of the union membership and of women. In that situation the right to organize women's caucuses becomes a question of elementary democracy and part of the struggle to put the union on a class-struggle political course.

But the revolutionary Marxist party can accomplish the historic tasks it has set itself only if it is capable of uniting in its ranks and leadership the most conscious and combative representatives of the working class and especially its most oppressed and exploited layers. To do this it must overcome the deep divisions fostered by capitalism and forge a cadre that has profound confidence in its common commitment and understanding of the tasks. This is concretized in the program of the revolutionary Marxist party, which synthesizes the experiences, demands, and interrelation between the struggles of all the exploited and oppressed and integrates them in a strategic line of march toward the proletarian revolution.

From this program we derive our organizational norms. Just as we have only one program, we have only one class of membership. Every comrade, male or female, Black or white, worker or petty bourgeois, young or old, literate or illiterate, has the same rights when it comes to determining the party's program and activity, the same responsibilities for implementing those decisions. The party's political program, line of intervention, and internal functioning must be democratically discussed and decided with all members participating. All internal fractions, commissions, tendencies, or other formations must be organized democratically – i.e., open to all members assigned to a particular area of work or all members who agree on the platform of a tendency, regardless of sex, race, age, language, class origin, or whatever.

In a revolutionary Marxist party, whatever its shortcomings and weaknesses may be, there is no inherent contradiction between program, leadership, and ranks. Thus the organization of women-only caucuses cuts across the internal democracy of the party and the construction of the kind of organization we need to realize our working-class program.

Since they are usually established for the express purpose of discussing internal problems *only,* women's caucuses are incapable of charting a course to resolve internal contradictions. That can only be done by charting a correct course of intervention in the mass movement to build the party. In the process the membership is educated and transformed.

Repeated experiences have shown – in practice as well as in theory – that the formation of women's caucuses does not help to resolve the problems that led to their formation. Rather they create centrifugal dynamics, fostering the impression that the party is a federation of conflicting interest groups each one fighting for its own program and priorities rather than an organization united on the basis of a common program and assessment of tasks. Often the caucuses reinforce the attitude that it is only the women comrades who are responsible for resolving the problems. They turn the women in on themselves in a destructive way. They deepen the frustration and political disorientation of both male and female comrades, and often hasten rather than prevent the departure of women from the organization.

Because they are not based on internal democracy caucuses also undermine our centralism in action. They stand in contradiction to our program and our democratic centralist organizational norms.

Strong pressure to organize such caucuses is a danger sign that the *leadership* has failed to meet the political challenge of educating the party on all aspects of the struggle for women's liberation and its place in the work of the party. The problems cannot be resolved by condemning the women comrades who are seeking a solution. The response must be fundamentally political, not organizational, and the leadership must take the responsibility for correcting errors, and educating and leading.

The problems that exist can be resolved only through a full political discussion leading to (a) the implementation of consistent work on women's liberation, integrated into all areas of activity; and (b) conscious measures of cadre development which can integrate women comrades and overcome sexist habits and attitudes.

November 1979

The women's movement and feminism in Latin America (1991)

Resolution on women in Latin America
13th World Congress

Introduction

Starting with a critical look at the XI World Congress resolution, "The socialist revolution and the struggle for women's liberation", this resolution aims to be a guide to action for our organizations in their central task of organizing a women's liberation movement — alongside the masses of Latin American women, other feminist sectors and other revolutionary organizations — that can take its place and play a decisive role in the revolutionary process and in building a socialist society.

1. The Latin American peoples are subjected to imperialist domination, with the corresponding poverty and distorted development of our societies. But the relationship with imperialism is changing, continually creating more social, economic and political contradictions leading to the emergence of new movements and a rise in the consciousness and strength of the masses — among them women — about their capacity to change things.

The last 30 years have seen deep and sudden changes in our countries, changes that have transformed the face of the sub-continent and the life of its peoples, in particular those of women:

• massive migration to the cities has resulted from the structural crisis in agriculture and the uneven industrial development;

• semi-proletarian masses have emerged in the big cities as another group of the dispossessed;

• the model of capitalist accumulation based on import substitution has changed to that of secondary export and modernization;

• the debt crisis;

• the erosion of the populist state;

• imperialism has implemented a strategy of low-intensity conflict — controlled transition from military dictatorships to "democratic" civilian governments combined with repression;

• later, the invasion of Grenada and Panama and the growing use of US military bases directly on Latin American territory, often with the excuse of the "war against drugs".

All of this has meant growing impoverishment, increasing violence and the exacerbation of social differences and contradictions.

At the same time, the triumph of two revolutions, in Cuba and Nicaragua, despite the problems they are experiencing, represent a possibility for change in the eyes of the masses in the sub-continent.

It is in this context, that of the 1980s, that Latin American women have entered onto the political scene of the sub-continent.

I. The crisis, the state, the church and women's oppression

2. In the context of the economic crisis the responsibility for family spending and domestic work, socially assigned to women, has increasingly become more difficult. Hyper-inflation means housewives in the cities having to go from market to market searching for the lowest prices, eating less so that their children can have a little more and facing the anguish of simply not having anything to give their family at mealtimes. In the countryside, domestic work is increased by the work involved in caring for animals and preparing products to sell.

The lack of basic public services in the Latin American countryside means that domestic labour has to be carried out in brutal conditions. It means covering huge distances to find water or wood, and chronic and endemic suffering from curable diseases, especially for children. In the poor urban neighbourhoods women carry out their domestic work very often without water or electricity, in insalubrious conditions, without enough schools for their children, without medical facilities. Women's workload is multiplied by these conditions.

3. The growing pauperization of the masses has forced women to seek an income so that the family can survive.

In the majority of Latin American countries, from 1950-1980 the percentage of women in the workforce went up. In addition, in the majority of cases where we have data, between 1975 and 1984 women's participation in the workforce increased in relation to the total active population.

4. The possibilities of peasant women finding paid employment have decreased, forcing women to become unwaged tenant farmers, day-workers or tenants at the same time as taking on the tasks in the home.

5. In some cases, for example Brazil, Mexico and Uruguay, women have gone into industry in significant numbers. But, even in these cases, women generally go into all-female departments where they suffer discrimination in work conditions, wages and promotion opportunities, while at the same time continuing to do "women's work" in the home (double work day).

With the sole exception of Brazil, women who enter the workforce swell the ranks of the active population mainly in the service and informal sectors. For most of them this means more work, but not a proletarianization in the exact sense of the word. These changes are very evident in many large cities, where in recent years the numbers of itinerant salespeople, beggars and prostitutes have increased. With a dearth of stable salaried jobs, women have gone into the streets to earn their living any way they can.

Women and the state

6. With the economic and political crisis, the Latin American bourgeoisies and their governments are continually trying to create new bases of consensus to maintain their domination over society. Insofar as women have increasingly entered public life over the last few years, although the majority still find themselves locked away in the home, the bourgeois governments try to legitimize themselves in women's eyes, negotiating with the organized women's movements and presenting themselves as champions of women's democratic and civil rights. This has meant an ideological offensive from many governments and bourgeois forces towards women in general, demonstrated by their electoral discourse and in the appointment of women to state posts.

7. In some countries, like Brazil, Mexico, Argentina and Uruguay, the ruling bourgeois parties have encouraged the creation of institutions and organisms whose objective is to develop programmes specifically directed at women as the oppressed sex. The majority are devoted to research, propaganda and proposing legal reforms, without having any executive powers as such.

8. Most countries adhere to the United Nations Convention on the elimination of all forms of discrimination against women. This has

been followed by the express recognition at a constitutional level of equal civic rights for men and women.

In addition, many governments have introduced legal changes on their own initiative concerning to formal equality and social rights, such as divorce.

The modernizing offensive of many states is reflected in the labour field, where they evoke "egalitarianism" with the aim of making it easier to exploit women even more, and thus helping to legitimize their economic policies.

9. It is at the level of their economic programmes that governmental policies are increasingly affecting women's lives.

In many countries the state has implemented programmes that tend to legitimize and institutionalize the informal labour market: training and loans so that women can earn additional income without leaving the home. This disguises unemployment, saves the bosses paying workers and makes it more difficult for workers to organize.

Some governments have introduced temporary employment programmes originally directed at men. But it has been women who have filled them, without any job security and receiving "emergency" wages.

Alongside their modernization programmes, some governments have set up plans "to combat extreme poverty" using voluntary female labour power to carry out public works.

10. In many countries, the state has carried out an aggressive population-control policy, using the indiscriminate distribution of contraception and forced sterilization. This policy is often directly tied to its dealings with international financing agencies and requests for foreign credit. The lack of left alternatives defending women's right to decide on having children makes it that much easier to apply this policy whose goal is to lower the birthrate and convince the population that its poverty is because "we are too many".

11. Some governments have established specialized police centres for dealing with battered and raped women. The aim is not only to try and put over the image that they are champions of women's well-being, but also —and especially — to broaden and legitimize their repressive apparatus.

The church

12. The weight of the Roman Catholic Church in Latin America is enormous — politically, socially and culturally. But during the last 20 years the church in Latin America has been thrown into crisis. This is shown by the existence of various currents within it, including that

aligned with the Vatican and its theological and political orientation, and the current known as liberation theology, with its many tendencies.

The hierarchy linked to the Vatican in general supports measures tending to maintain the current ruling system, and thus has a very conservative position in relation to women — for example opposing legal changes on divorce, contraception and abortion. In various ways it promotes a policy of strengthening the existing family system and the submissive role of women within it.

The current identified with liberation theology is in general linked to the process of self-organization of the poor masses. As a general rule, a very high proportion of the members of the Church base communities and bible study groups are women. Because of this some priests are more sensitive to the specific oppression they suffer and the need to take political action around it. But their political vision is limited by the contradiction between their adherence to a traditional moral view from which they do not distance themselves and women's concrete and changing needs, especially concerning sexuality, motherhood and fertility control. There have been few theological contributions from women's point of view and its relation to the overall road to liberation envisaged by this current.

In the last few years there has also been an increase in the activity of different protestant groups in Latin America. There are liberation theology currents among them which have had an important feminist theoretical production, particularly in academic spheres. However, most of them are evangelical sects characterized by an extremely conservative social and political outlook, which is particularly reactionary in relation to women.

The family

13. All these changes in society have had profound effects on family life for the whole of the Latin American masses. There are strong pressures towards the disintegration of the family, with no material possibility of adopting the bourgeois family model in practice.

In the countryside, millions of families still make up productive units, generally with a rigid distribution of roles according to sex, placing women on the lowest rungs of the power hierarchy when it comes to decision-making, both formally and in practice. But women are nevertheless part of the productive community, although this is relatively isolated from the rest of the world.

At the same time, 26 million indigenous Americans, mainly concentrated in Peru, Ecuador, Bolivia, Guatemala and Mexico, maintain their own customs, traditions and ways of communally taking responsibility for productive work to different degrees. The pressures on these nationalities to abandon their culture are enormous, but they are resisting "Latinization".

However, the structural crisis of agriculture and a relative capitalization of the countryside exercise a strong pressure towards the disintegration of the peasant family as a self-sufficient unit of production, without this meaning its transformation simply into a unit of consumption.

With the concentration of the population in the Latin American cities and the strengthening of capitalist relations of production, within the big and small bourgeoisie and sections of the industrial proletariat a bourgeois family has formed. However the big majority of the emigrados do not form part of the working class properly speaking: quite simply, underdeveloped capitalism has no other use for its labour force than as a gigantic reserve army of labour.

But even in those families where one or more members manages to get a paid job (as a manual or white-collar worker), it is rare that the wage is enough for each worker to maintain their own nuclear family, even though they are obliged to face the labour market as individuals.

In other cases the pressures are such that the family simply disperses, giving rise to the mass phenomenon of abandoned children. In addition, women are increasingly becoming heads of household.

Alongside this, the crisis generates tensions at a social level, leading not only to an increase in the number of assaults and rapes but also to more and more violence within the family.

II. The dynamic of the Latin American women's movement today

14. At the end of the 19th and beginning of the 20th century, the first organizations of women as such appeared on the basis of an initial identification between women in the same immediate community who shared immediate problems and common concerns. This led to traditions of:

• women organizing in support of workers' struggles since the last century.

• women's struggles for the right to work, particularly in "women's" industries which have produced thousands of experienced cadres for the workers' movement in general.

• local mothers' clubs to deal with specific community problems.

There is also a certain tradition of women organizing around their demands as a sex. Bourgeois women organized from the end of the last century around the right to education, access to the professions and, in some cases, around the right to vote. But in the framework of the general peaks of the class struggle there were mass women's organizations based in the working class which fought for demands like the vote, land, work and education for women in the popular layers.

15. In the 1970s and 1980s many feminist groups emerged of the type also emerging in Europe, the USA and Canada, and influenced by them. Although in Brazil there was the emergence of a mass feminist movement for a short period at the end of the 1970s and beginning of the 1980s, in Latin America this process was not at all general and did not generate the building of an organically constituted movement with a mass character

The majority of these groups were characterized by ideological and theoretical discussion, and concentrated their activity principally in consciousness-raising and propaganda, introducing for the first time for many years the "woman question" into intellectual and left circles and society as a whole.

However, even though in some cases the work of the feminist and consciousness-raising groups was able to stimulate a mass response, it did not result in building general structures with a more permanent character among different layers of women active at the time, which could have maintained the continuity of a specific movement. The activities of feminist groups were also concentrated in the big cities or even, in some countries, limited to the capital cities alone.

The dedication to discussing and propagandizing around "themes" related to women's oppression — housework, violence, sexuality, abortion — did touch on vital issues for all women. But because they had a fundamentally propagandist vision and of building the movement by the multiplication of small groups this made it difficult to establish a platform that could unite the groups, or that was attractive and accessible to the majority of women.

The vast majority of women were, and are, permanently organized around the question of the survival of themselves and their families and around the question of democracy, their situation determined by the semi-colonial character of our countries and the resulting poverty. In addition, the middle layers have not suffered from contradictions in a sufficiently massive way to provoke a louder response in this sector, which is relatively big.

This situation led to a crisis of political perspective for the "autonomous groups", and in many cases to their disappearance or absorption in governmental projects.

16. But some groups and many individual women began to create other types of instruments to express their feminist concerns:

a) Aid and/or educational institutions, mainly financed by international agencies. Their central activities vary a lot. They do not always explicitly define themselves as feminist, but they have an important weight in feminist currents through their work, made easier by the funding they receive.

b) Non-funded projects of support/relations to women (centres providing various services, social activities, meetings, film clubs, local groups, or work with peasant or indigenous women, for example).

c) Groups publishing various journals.

d) Christian women's groups.

e) Trade-union commissions or groupings.

f) Women organized inside left political parties.

All these expressions of feminism have prospered in the 1980s insofar as their work has been guided by an attempt to relate to Latin American reality today and women's day-to-day lives.

17. The daily life and world outlook of millions of Latin American women have been transformed. They have been forced to emerge from the shadow of the home and throw themselves into public life, trying to sustain their families via activities they would never previously have contemplated.

A whole generation of young women has been raised in conditions of crisis, in general by mothers who have lived through these changes. For this reason, their frame of reference in practice is not the model of a woman whose life is confined to the four walls of the home.

At the same time, the extension of public education and the penetration of the means of mass communication into the countryside and the city in recent years have meant that millions of women's horizons have been broadened— although sometimes in a distorted way.

18. With their growing participation in the labour market, millions of women have been forced to try to find a collective solution to deteriorating living standards and democratic rights — given the impossibility of finding individual solutions. Consequently, they are increasingly involved in political and social movements in general,

which can involve millions of women, often giving them their first experience of struggle.

At present, the majority of women are organized in relation to their social situation, around their living and working conditions (family survival, conditions of domestic and paid work), and around the most brutal political problem, the struggle against repression, for human rights and democracy.

In the last 15 years, new movements have emerged whose base of support and activists are almost exclusively women: the urban struggle and the fight for freedom for political prisoners and the disappeared.

The popular and civic urban movements fight for solutions to the problems of housing, services and high prices suffered by millions of people who live in extremely precarious conditions. Women, being responsible for all aspects of family care and mostly not having paid jobs — with its corresponding absence from the home — are both the most motivated and the most available to participate in this type of movement, which is centred in the neighbourhoods.

On the other hand, women are the rank-and-file driving force for the committees of relatives of political prisoners' and the disappeared, mainly from identification with their role as mother and wife and their responsibility for freeing their children, husbands and brothers from the clutches of repression.

The development of trade union and peasant struggles has also involved many women. In sectors where there is an almost exclusive concentration of working women, thousands have taken to the streets for the first time.

Peasant and indigenous women, on the other hand, often organize as women to take up problems linked to the need for better conditions for carrying out domestic work and for the well-being of their families, such as fighting for their own rights to land and loans, and the need to have their own income to increase family revenue.

19. This entry into public life in distinct forms and at different levels creates a contradictory dynamic at the level of women's consciousness: the majority go into public life as wives and mothers; a minority, but a politically significant minority, enter as young women workers.

Leaving their homes and neighbourhoods, they come up against the government, the employers, the trade-union bureaucracy, the para-military groups and the local bosses in the countryside and the city. In sum, they do exactly what prevailing values say a woman should not do.

The central contradiction which millions of Latin American women confront is the need to fulfil the traditional role of women in the family, in the home, and in domestic work in its fullest sense, and the impossibility of so doing given general living conditions without breaking with this tradition. The existence of this contradiction is the objective basis for the perspective of building a mass women's liberation movement in Latin America and the Caribbean.

Conditions are being created at a mass level which open up the possibilities for an increase in women's consciousness of their oppression as women. When they take to the streets, motivated by both necessity and solidarity, this brings them up against obstacles for realizing their objectives. If they realize them, if they succeed, they have to change their behaviour, their conception of themselves, their conditions of struggle. To establish new conditions of solidarity, and thus improve the conditions of struggle, they have to confront their own oppression as a sex. There will be no positive solution to this contradiction without breaking with the social, political and personal conditions that create and maintain the traditional model of women — as mother, wife and housewife — on the basis of the political struggle of the masses, of which women are in the front ranks and the leadership.

This contradiction is sharpened by:

• Today the mass of women have access to the means of mass communication and, despite its deficiencies, millions of women also have access to formal education. By both these means, they are aware of the enormous possibilities offered by today's world for individual development at the same time as the models which are presented for women — both traditional and "modern". This new knowledge, and the models themselves, are in open conflict with the reality of their lives.

• For the first time; millions of women have access to contraception, which makes it possible to envisage controlling their own bodies, and to make choices concerning maternity and sexuality no longer determined by procreation, despite all the risks implicit given that they have this access because of a policy of controlling births that is dangerous in its motivation, and undemocratic in its application.

• The establishment of governmental programmes on sexist violence, at the same time as being a way of broadening and even legitimizing the repressive apparatus of the state, also legitimize the social character of sexist violence, the testimonies exposing the brutality and high number of cases which exist.

• Bourgeois propaganda around women's equality — albeit to back up a birth-control policy, to win votes, to legitimize a regime in the eyes of the international community — introduce at a mass level as never before, and in some cases for the first time, the idea that women and men have equal rights before the law and in society. At the same time, within the independent mass organizations which struggle against state policy and the bourgeoisie, and particularly those raising the banner of the struggle for real democracy, women encounter discrimination and marginalization in most cases both from the rank-and-file and from the leaderships.

20. But recognizing these contradictions and overcoming them through a conscious struggle for liberation is not automatic. It depends on many factors in the social struggle, on the degree of organization among women and of the class struggle in general: the general relationship of forces between the bourgeoisie and the workers; the capacity of the bourgeoisie and its state to propose demobilizing and self-legitimizing policies to women; the development, strength and relations of the revolutionary and reformist organizations with the women's movements that emerge and their positions on the question of women. All these factors influence the development of a sector of the women's movement capable of linking up in practice the project of building a mass movement with a feminist character and the more general starting points of radicalization and mobilization of women. However the existence of this contradiction is the objective basis for the advances of the last few years towards building a political women's liberation movement in our continent.

21. In general, the central dynamic of the situation today in Latin America points to this contradiction being resolved favourably. Women are participating as never before in political and social struggles; they are organizing increasingly as women by social sector; there exists a growing and renewing feminist fringe or pole of the women's movement; and non-bourgeois political organizations are increasingly under pressure to confront their traditional anti-women's liberation positions. Taking into account the advances and setbacks in each country in terms of its specific situation, the general dynamic is towards the formation of mass women's movements with the emergence of a large number of groups of different types which , as part of their platform of struggle and basis of unity, increasingly tend to raise gender demands in combination with demands relating to survival and democracy.

22. In the course of the struggle for their immediate demands, the mass of women continually confront obstacles flowing from their specific oppression: they are restricted by "not having permission" to go out of their houses to activities, having nowhere to leave their children, feeling guilty for "abandoning" them, being insulted by men in meetings of the movement; their organizations are weakened by the competition among women and the lack of self-confidence and training of their members. All these obstacles are worse inside mixed organizations of women and men. Also they are even more despised and humiliated by the authorities than men, and they raped by the police and military. These obstacles have to be overcome in order to go forward. Sometimes they constitute such an insuperable obstacle that there is a regression in the struggle. But at other times they lead to attempts to propose practical solutions in the form of collective demands.

In these cases the natural leaders of many women's movements, and often the organized women's groups themselves, search for elements which explain the existence and the dynamic of the obstacles in order to be able to overcome them. Moving closer to more feminist sectors in general gives them the possibility of understanding and building the necessary instruments of struggle and organization to confront their contradictions as women. At the same time, many feminist groups have been participating in the popular organizations. On the other hand, in the last ten years a significant number of feminist activists have emerged within the political parties who have succeeded in maintaining a much more organic presence in the women's movement, over and above their struggle to change the mentalities of these parties on gender oppression.

All this has begun to generate a social and political decomposition of the feminist pole in the women's movement. Undoubtedly many active women still mistrust feminism. But many others are beginning to identify with it as such, identifying with feminist ideas and recognizing their usefulness for understanding and changing their reality. On the other hand, the traditional feminist sectors can no longer deny the "feminist legitimacy" of women who combine their activity in the women's movement with party activity, as they tended to do in the past.

Empirical proof of this decomposition can be seen in the increasing attendance by women from the popular sectors in the Encuentros Feministas Latinoamericanas y de Caribe (Latin American and Caribbean Feminist Meetings) from 1981 to 1990. It has been this combined dynamic of contradictions in women's struggles in the popular sectors for class demands and the interaction with feminist layers of the women's movement — including more and more who are primarily mobilized around class demands or as party militants — which has made it possible in many sectors to put forward gender demands in the programmes of struggle and as the basis for the mass mobilizations of women in the last few years.

23. The forms of coordination between the different sectors of the women's movement vary a lot in their objectives, scope and duration.

Sometimes permanent coordinations exist, fundamentally to provide a space for political discussion, contact and mutual support rather than around actions or campaigns, although these can result from the same coordinations.

Other forms of coordination, which at times combine clearly feminist forces with both political parties and the broader women's movement, have emerged in the context of particular national political situations.

A series of working networks have also been formed both at national and sub-continental level around the campaigns or ongoing activities of their members. In many countries, contacts between feminist groups have been limited to local, regional or national conferences, sometimes resulting in information networks between groups being established without the existence of any common political platform.

The majority of women who are involved in permanent coordinations tend to be so on the basis of their social situation.

Although at the beginning of the 1980s the initiative for events around March 8 or November 25 or other general activities was taken by layers linked to the small feminist groups, the social composition of these activities and the initiatives for them are much more frequently start from women linked to the popular and trade-union sectors of the movement.

On the level of the sub-continent, there have been various contacts and opportunities for discussion, basically in the Encuentros of Latin American and Caribbean feminists and the three conferences of the Continental Women's Front Against Intervention. There has also been a multiplication of international meetings and events which play the same role. It is in this type of event that the Cubans and Nicaraguans have had growing contact with the Latin American feminist pole.

24. The general dynamic of women's lives today is: a) that more women than ever before are entering social and political struggle; and b), that they find themselves objectively in contradiction with their oppression. But in making the big jump from transforming these

conditions into a political movement of women for their liberation, there are a series of political problems that have to be analysed and overcome:

a) The diverse demands of women in struggle

Women's initial demands usually have a specific local focus, which makes it difficult to unify their struggles. This lack of unity and, for the same reason, contact with many more women, not only creates difficulties for winning the immediate struggle but impedes their thinking about their oppression as a social question.

However, although there are immediate demands that unite the women of a whole sector, this does not mean that a general political movement takes shape which sees itself as a women's movement. Obviously, the unity of women organized as such, even by sector, has a big multiplying effect in other sectors. But, insofar as the movement is not politically extended to unify women from different sectors, there is a big danger that even stronger sectors can see their gains pushed back.

Finally, where the different popular organizations advance gender demands these are also very different and difficult to unite in struggle. And it is in struggle and through progress around their concrete rights that women will appreciate the usefulness of organizing for their demands as a gender.

b) Clientelism and self-helpism: two dangers in building the movement

Women, particularly in the neighbourhoods and peasant communities of Latin America, have two ways of surviving: by making demands on external agencies or trying to find a solution through their own resources.

Placing demands on the state in relation to social and political problems has the enormous advantage of putting the responsibility where it should be, on society as a whole and its institutions, and more easily gives mass action a political character. Successful struggles and mobilizations advances both their overall consciousness and their strength and confidence in themselves.

Practice has taught us, however, that reliance on the state is not without its dangers. On the one hand there could be a clientelist dynamic and, on the other, in partially winning certain demands women can become absorbed into administrative tasks of providing services.

The other form of self-organization for assuring survival, that of self-solution/self-administration, has the advantage that it is a process of cooperative self-organization which presents immediate solutions to urgent problems and gives greater value to domestic labour, creating the seeds for its socialization.

But it also has two real dangers: the legitimization of the established role of women as those responsible for domestic tasks and family well-being, and apolitical self-helpism.

c) The difficulties for the political participation of women workers

It is clear that there is no automatic correlation between the mass entry of women into the labour market and their involvement in political and/or trade-union struggle as workers:

• They basically work in "feminine" industries and sectors, such as services and in the informal sector in general. As in the rest of the world, their jobs are often similar to the work they do in the home, or require great meticulousness.

• The informal sector usually means working in isolation or in small workshops, where there is very often a paternalist relationship with the employer or boss.

• Even in those cases where women have entered big industry, the majority have to put up with a double workday as well as having other restrictions in the time they can allocate for trade-union or political participation.

• The working woman continues to see herself primarily as a mother and/or wife and not a worker, even when she is the family's only breadwinner.

• Fellow workers often apply pressure to prevent her participating actively in trade-union life; and the trade-union leaderships are not only unconcerned by women's specific conditions, but frequently openly block women's participation.

• Most women who become trade-union activists are unmarried or childless. Because of this, they usually identify less with the majority of women workers.

Aside from these difficulties, in many places little attention is given by revolutionary organizations to women's trade-union work.

For all these reasons, the organization of working women has not increased at the same tempo as their incorporation into the labour market.

d) The state's attempts to co-opt

In the case of countries where the state has a relatively aggressive policy towards women, the need to respond with alternative political proposals that strengthen the mass movement is obvious. Without presenting a political alternative to state initiatives it will be increasingly difficult to maintain class independence, because the state will appear to be more useful than the movement in the eyes of the masses.

e) The predominance of sexism in the leaderships of the mass movement

Insofar as the initial rise in consciousness of most women comes through the struggles of the more general movements, usually led by male leaderships, the machismo of these latter is a big obstacle to their advance. This is particularly important in the absence of a specifically women's political movement which raises at a national, unified level the gender demands that women in various sectors are beginning to put forward today. In its turn, the leaderships' sexism is an obstacle to building this movement.

25. Over the last few years, the non-bourgeois mass leaderships have changed their approach to women's situation and their role in society and in struggles.

In many countries the crisis of the Communist parties includes questioning the old Stalinist conception of the women's movement as an "auxiliary" to the mass movement in general.

At the same time, revolutionary organizations are discussing revolutionary strategy, a discussion in which the role of women and the struggle against gender oppression is also raised, at least potentially. However, in almost all cases these leaderships reject this point as part of the strategic discussion and strongly resist any serious consideration of the subject.

However, within all types of left political parties there are feminist nuclei and currents emerging which are putting forward different alternatives around the need for women to fight for gender demands. They influence the orientation of their parties, not only in line with their political capacity, but also in function of the more or less democratic traditions of discussion, the social insertion of the party and its overall political capacity to recognize and confront the real problems of women in struggle.

26. The discussions within the women's movement and its feminist pole have evolved positively, passing from the initial examination and

affirmation of basic points on oppression to defining the routes for building mass women's movements around their specific demands.

Elements of broader debates on politics and society in general influence this discussion. Thus, existing political tendencies exert a certain pressure on the discussion on feminism:

• Modernizing bourgeois ideology, which legitimizes competence as a social norm and reduces democracy to the relationship between the citizen and the state, divorcing it from social classes and problems.

• Social-democratic positions, today accompanied by a poltiical offensive throughout the sub-continent, which support gradualist and institutionalist tactics.

• Imperialist propaganda which identifies market mechanisms with democracy on the one hand, and socialism with dictatorship on the other.

• Perestroika and the crisis in Eastern European countries, which as well as reaffirming the false distinction market/democracy vs. socialism/dictatorship, has brought pressure to bear on revolutionaries, thus weakening the influence of a perspective of revolutionary rupture as a solution to the problems of the Latin American masses.

Given these pressures, some feminists have been incorporated into bourgeois projects, particularly with the controlled transitions to democracy that have taken place in several countries. Given the weakness of feminism and the anti-feminist positions of the majority of the socialist and left oppositions, they have placed their confidence and/or decided to work in bourgeois women's projects in order to "really change women's situation" in relation to the regime. Among many of them positions predominate based on the necessity and possibility of "democratizing the state", and creating "space for women" within it. Others identify with ideas around the "feminine essence" as something morally superior to the "masculine essence", which is one way of denying the need to build an autonomous mass women's movement.

However, the great majority of feminists are independent of the bourgeoisie and the state, and consider themselves as being in some way on the left, with a broad range of positions that identify with the elimination of capitalism and a socialist perspective. In this sector, which in general takes the broad women's movement as its point of reference for the struggle against gender oppression, the debate is particularly diffuse, thus making it difficult to characterize the currents within it.

Under discussion, among other things, are:

• The relation between gender oppression and class exploitation/oppression.

• The struggle for democracy and feminist demands.

• What sort of power do women want?

• Women as political and social subjects.

• The validity or not of the concept of the vanguard in a strategy for change.

III. Our orientation

27. Confronted with any form of oppression, the only solution is the self-organization of the oppressed to fight it. The case of women is no different. It is the independent self-organization of women themselves that can impose reforms to the law and to current government economic policy, and changes in the social and political organizations of the masses, to improve their immediate situation and encourage and create better conditions for their continued struggle. On the basis of self-organization, as the fundamental foundation of their liberation movement, they can reach the numerical strength and political development necessary for having a favourable influence on future events, both today and after the revolution.

It is only through a process of self-organization that women can succeed in transforming themselves, collectively and individually, in public and private, in such a way that the traditional role filled by women can be replaced with a new concept and a new reality of what is woman, creating this through the struggle itself.

28. A thoroughgoing, consistent feminist struggle is not simply to achieve formal equality between women and men, but to completely revolutionize relations between them, eliminating the historico-social construction of gender. This change cannot be fully realized in the framework of class society, particularly in the present Latin American context of exploitation and oppression in countries that are dominated by imperialism. In this sense, it is in all women's interest to struggle for the overthrow of the oppressive patriarchal capitalist system and for building a socialist, democratic and pluralist society. Only such a revolution and a new society can lay the bases for completely eliminating the oppression currently experienced by women.

However, women's oppression is not automatically eliminated either with the anti-capitalist revolution or in post-capitalist society. For women to be able to transform their own lives, to be revolutionary subjects in the taking of power and the overthrow of the present bourgeois regimes, and to have the strength to favourably influence the events in a post-revolutionary society, it is necessary now that they build a political movement based on their demands as a gender.

The formation of this movement will transform them into a political subject, which fights for its own interests; women's objective historical interest in eliminating patriarchal class society laying the basis for their transformation into a revolutionary subject. This transformation could in practice go along with the political development of the movement itself and its vanguard.

29. To build this movement today, we have to start from the conditions, the forms of organization and the demands that women feel to be theirs, whether they are gender demands or not. Self-organization of women by social sector around their most pressing demands is an essential element in strengthening women socially, collectively and thus individually, creating greater possibilities for the development of consciousness of gender oppression, even though this is not automatic.

Undoubtedly, women's struggle for their own demands will be closely linked to the struggles of all working people, even with the rise of their own political movement. In building this movement general class demands will combine with gender demands as the basis of unity. Nevertheless, this dynamic will certainly include ups and downs in the promotion of specifically feminist demands.

A better level of organization of the popular movement will encourage greater recognition of women's struggle for their own demands. This is because a better level of coordination and unity not only means more chance of winning but also a higher level of politicization, the establishment of a more global basis for unity and an understanding of the need to organize in an ongoing way, not just for tackling one problem but a whole series of problems.

In practical terms, it also creates the possibility for a better division of labour within organizations of struggle and for giving more attention to seriously analysing their reality.

The coming together of forces whose objective is extending women's consciousness of their specific oppression is more effective in reaching larger numbers of women.

But there is no mechanical relationship between the general popular movement and women's advance. Women have to have their own political expression. And they will only succeed if there is a conscious effort in every movement to promote the growing discovery and politicization of gender oppression, which we can call the feminization of the demands, organization and political dynamic of the women's movement.

30. In the very process of building the movement, different problems are raised:

a) Given the diversity of demands, which reflect not only different needs but also different levels of consciousness, we must take every opportunity to bring together struggles and establish a system of demands that can move towards the formation of an increasingly clearly defined political movement.

b) Given the dangers of clientelism and self-helpism, we have to reinforce the internal democracy of both the mass organizations in general and the political space and organizations for women, as well as ensuring democratic functioning in the women's movement as a whole. On the other hand, the political nature of women's demands should be emphasized — they cannot be met by charity — along with the absolute necessity of keeping the movement independent from the bourgeoisie and the state.

c) Despite the difficulties faced by women workers in terms of their political and trade-union participation, this should not lead to the conclusion that their involvement in the women's movement is not central. The numbers of women who have gone into the labour market has meant that, despite all the obstacles to their participation, more women are active in trade unions than ever before. And when they enter into a collective process of consciousness raising and struggle around their oppression as women as well as workers, they advance politically more rapidly and consistently than other sectors because of their living and working conditions and their numerical concentration — in sum, their social situation.

d) Given the attempts of the state to coopt the women's movement, particularly its feminist pole, in addition to strongly maintaining its autonomy for historical reasons there must also be political perspectives for the type of changes considered necessary from now on at governmental level. We should promote the following criteria for these within the movement. Distinguishing between two things: services that the state is obliged to provide with the greatest control on the part of the users; and a position of accepting or promoting the state organizing women (the example of the Women Today programme in Argentina). In the case of legislative proposals, it is more feasible to maintain the independence of the women's movement in proposing or supporting this or that draft law. But at the level of the executive (ministries for health, justice, social or family welfare), the form of the relationship between the movement and particular state programmes is more complicated. If we demand a programme of maternity healthcare, for example, and win it, we cannot simply leave the state to determine its form, content and application. But neither can the movement take full responsibility for it. The criterion that we can adopt is proposals for and vigilance over such programmes, but without accepting direct responsibility for their functioning.

In the case where the left controls municipalities, the objective of its programmes should be to increase the possibilities for self-organization of the movement, as was done with the Glass of Milk programmes in many municipalities in Peru. The simple implementation of the programme, without women's self-organization, will neither guarantee its future nor strengthen the women's movement or the long-term objectives of the left itself.

e) Because of the prevailing sexism in the mass movements and their leaderships, mechanisms have to be established within them to increase women's space and promote discussion — not only around concrete action proposals and demands, but also around the origins, manifestations and solutions to women's oppression: that is, a theoretical discussion.

31. To enable this process to move forward, the feminist pole in the women's organizations and movement has to be strengthened:

a) Strengthening the recomposition of this pole to include more women leaders of the mass movement so that they — along with the women of the autonomous groups, the non-governmental organizations, the political parties and the youth who today would like to get involved in this struggle — can forge a real vanguard of the whole women's movement.

b) Establishing more opportunities for political and theoretical discussion in the vanguard through conferences, coordinations around concrete campaigns, publications, seminars, and so on.

c) Orienting this pole so that its priority becomes the relationship with the general women's movement, so that it can:

• take advantage of each opportunity to put forward unifying gender demands;

• take advantage of each opportunity to unify the women's movement;

• ensure the continuity of the movement;

• encourage reflection and theoretical production — a collective memory for the movement;

• develop independent alternatives to the proposals of the bourgeoisie and the state.

To do this there has to be the development of a political alternative within the feminist pole in alliance with other sectors which have a similar vision. If other revolutionary currents and parties which are today absent from this political elaboration become convinced of feminism this will also help the development of this alternative.

If the clearly feminist expressions of the women's movement are weakened, in time the organization of the mass of women will also tend to be undermined. The mass sectoral organizations will tend to disperse or be manipulated for other ends, which implies a political weakening which will in time lead to an organic erosion.

32. The reason for the existence of our organizations is to be a useful political instrument for our peoples organizing themselves, proposing and implementing their own projects as a nation in line with their interests, against the interests of the bourgeoisie and imperialism. The revolution and the new socialist society that we seek to create can only be the work of the toiling people as a whole, and for this reason our revolutionary Marxist current has a conception of feminism that encompasses a profound transformation, the subversion of the existing order.

For this reason we must be the foremost promoters of the women's liberation movement and of the discussion within the mass movement and the left — particularly the revolutionary left — around the necessity of building this movement and the ways of doing so.

33. In nearly all our sections women's work is being reorganized and we are reformulating our political perspectives for building the women's movement.

This fits into the general framework of the need to tackle the question of building our organizations with greater effectiveness, and is part of this task. In particular, in relation to women's work the reorganization must confront the following problems:

• To a greater or lesser degree, our sections did not understand the central dynamic of the radicalization of the majority of women and have had to make a turn towards the mass sectors, working on the basis of immediate demands.

• The fact that feminism did not develop on a mass scale, the non-centralization of the general women's movement as a political movement and the sexist pressures of society as a whole are strong countervailing pressures to our maintaining consistent feminist positions.

• Today there are many comrades, men and women, who have not been formed in our programmatic feminist vision and this makes the elaboration of a concrete political orientation for the movement difficult.

• All this means that the objective difficulties which all women comrades face have been inadequately considered by the leaderships, leaving comrades to confront them individually.

• Consequently, little effort is made to include in political leadership tasks.

Obviously, the possibilities for each section resolving this situation vary with its social insertion and accumulation of cadres and the degree of progress in forming a leadership team.

34. Our general objective must be to elaborate concrete political strategies and implement them in the struggle itself. But to do this we need to:

a) educate comrades in our feminist programmatic vision;

b) clarify our theoretical positions in line with the central discussion in each country, in order to intervene with the greatest clarity;

c) develop adequate organizational forms in each case to:

• ensure efficiency and not overload comrades doing women's work with tasks;

• ensure that the whole of the party, and in the first place all women comrades, participate in elaborating the political orientation for women's work.

d) Counterbalance, within the limits of our possibilities, the obstacles which confront women comrades:

• making it easier for comrades who are mothers to participate;

• special education measures for women comrades;

• consciously promoting women to take on tasks, in particular seeking to establish a proportional relationship between the number of women on the leadership bodies and the membership, which will mean using a system of targets or quotas in elections.

Changing forms of the struggle for women's liberation (1991)

Resolution on Women in West Europe/North America
13th World Congress

Introduction

Since the 1979 11th World Congress resolution "The Socialist Revolution and the Struggle for Women's Liberation" important changes have taken place in the forms of women's radicalization in western imperialist countries.

That resolution noted the mass resurgence of feminist ideas and organizations. It came at the end of a period marked by large-scale mobilizations on the abortion question, by self-organization of sizeable sections of the female population and by workers' struggles in which women had played an important role.

Breaking with a tradition of indifference or distrust towards feminism by our movement, the text advocated building independent women's movements in every country according to the rhythms and particularities of local situations. It affirmed the strategic character of building such movements as an indispensable condition for challenging women's oppression and achieving real socialism.

Since then we have to note a decline of "organized feminism", but this does not mean a generalized decline in women's radicalization. The centre of gravity of radicalization has changed, as have the channels by which it is expressed. The essential question facing feminists is to find ways of linking up with the new generations of radicalizing women in order to build feminist movements that preserve the gains of past years and that can once again have an influence on the political scene.

The decline can probably be explained by two interlinked factors. The economic crisis has altered the overall balance of forces in favour of the bourgeoisie; reformist organizations have accepted the logic of austerity. In some countries, the media have been pushing the idea that we are now in a "post-feminist" era, where equality between the sexes has already been achieved. In this context, which is also marked by a relative lack of workers' activity in many countries, the weakness of the women's movements meant that they could not swim against the stream and impose anti-capitalist demands; winning genuine women's liberation seemed to be a utopian idea.

During the 1970s it was possible for the various currents of the women's movement to unite and engage in mass action in alliance with trade-union and democratic organizations nationally and internationally to win and defend women's rights, such as abortion. The granting of legal reforms slowed down this type of mobilization.

Our analysis of the nature of women's oppression has not changed. The absolute need to build an autonomous movement — the only guarantee that there is a radical and effective struggle against oppression — has in no way disappeared. What remains is to make tactical adjustments to a new conjuncture.

I. The changes in women's situation and different bourgeois policies

The general trends in the social situation of women described in the 1979 resolution remain fundamentally valid today, but new elements should be incorporated:

❖ Continuation of the massive participation of women of all ages and from all family situations in the labour market, although their integration into waged work takes place fundamentally through part-time work. Wage discrimination and sharp segregation between "masculine" and "feminine" jobs — running through training, promotion, working conditions, etc. — is continuing and even deepening.

❖ Better technical possibilities exist for women to control reproduction, but in the majority of cases these are limited by laws limiting women's right to decide.

❖ Continuing massive presence of women in public education to the level of high-school graduation and university entry. Mixed schools have not meant real co-education. Women's presence is limited to humanities faculties, and in any case diminishes sharply in higher levels.

❖ The development of legislation which postulates formal "equal rights", outlawing discrimination, penalizing sexual violence etc., without taking positive steps to enable women to overcome their historically disadvantaged position.

❖ An increasing choice by women to live alone, with or without children, as seen in the number of divorces requested by women, single-parent families, women living alone, etc. Obviously this situation does not always represent a free choice — insofar as it is does, it is made possible by women's increased economic and legal independence.

❖ Black and immigrant women continue to suffer from racism, which combines with and reinforces their oppression as women.

❖ Greater social recognition and rejection of maltreatment within the family and the sexual violence which men use against women.

❖ Increasing participation of women in public spaces until now reserved for men; exclusion has been replaced by integration in unequal conditions in all spheres of public and social life.

❖ Liberalization of sexual habits and customs, recognition of women as sexual beings, although this is still not expressed in greater sexual equality between men and women.

All this reflects the political activity of feminist organizations and has meant an important development of women's consciousness, their personal autonomy and self-esteem; and a change of the socially established stereotypes for men and women. All these elements have created a situation which is different and more complex — because contradictory — than that of 1979.

This reality has been noted by those who defend the social and economic order, forcing them to re-elaborate their discourse so that it seems more in tune with the new situation. It has also led to a differentiation in the policies developed, although there is obviously a basic and firm agreement to preserve the family institution, the fundamental pillar of oppression, and to keep women in the workforce in a particular form. But the bourgeoisie is far from having a single, clearly-defined plan to achieve its goals.

A. Changes in the traditional family and different bourgeois policies

The changes indicated above have introduced important fissures in the traditional model of the family, determined by the seclusion of women in the home, dedicated to domestic tasks and care of the children, and by the relations of domination which existed within it.

Some of these changes are:

❖ the increase in the number of non-married, cohabiting couples;

❖ the large increase in the number of single-parent families;

❖ the soaring divorce rate;

❖ the increase in the number of lesbians and gay men living open and proud lives;

❖ the decline in the birth rate, reflecting women's change of attitude to bringing up children as their only preoccupation;

The increase in legal complaints for domestic violence is an important indicator of the change in women's self-esteem, and the cracks made in women's relationship of emotional and sexual dependence on their husbands.

This change in women's consciousness and the social rejection of this most brutal expression of women's oppression has also demanded greater attention to the problems which exist in the family: media attention and campaigns around battered women in the 1970s; exposures of physical and sexual abuse of children; the problems of children of separated parents. However, there are not sufficient of the social services necessary (battered women's centres, etc.) to meet the demand.

There are a number of different bourgeois responses to this situation which also reflect national particularities:

a) Constant promotion of the ideal of the happily-married couple in a permanent union, with a mother responsible for the home and two children, despite the fact that most women work. This is particularly the case for the white working-class family. Capitalism is less concerned with defending or promoting the unity of black and immigrant families, which it will happily break up through immigration laws, deportation orders or police harassment.

Another aspect is the European bourgeoisies' insistence on the "dramatic consequences" of the falling birth rate. The need to "reverse this trend" is used to reinforce the idea that women's fundamental role is within the family, producing children (directed at white women). At the same time this prepares the ground for cuts in social spending and throwing the burden — especially of the care of old people — back into the family, under the pretext that there will not be enough workers to contribute to social security funds.

b) Certain sections of the bourgeoisie have become more flexible on questions such as the status of children born outside marriage or legal recognition of cohabiting couples. This flexibility aims at incorporating the structural changes in the way people live their lives into the system, because capitalism requires the continued existence of the nuclear family as the general model even if different variations can be accepted.

No alternative to this style of living exists on a mass scale. The indices given for the "crisis of the family" can be countered in different countries by various elements including the rise in the number of marriages, the possibility to register "illegitimate" children in the names of both parents, the incorporation of certain types of "acceptable" homosexuals (white, male and middle class) into the norm through offering a possibility of "marriage", and so on.

c) Some openly reactionary sectors of the bourgeoisie use the "crisis of the family" to press for measures of moral order — in Europe this often includes the idea of a maternal wage, eroding the incomes of single parents and attacks on lesbian and gay men. These currents are still markedly on the extreme right of the political scene, even if some churches have put themselves in the vanguard of this struggle but they have had some success in the British state and in Germany, and they do influence more mainstream bourgeois thinking on the family. In the United States, they have a larger mass base and have been openly encouraged by successive governments.

Those who do not adapt to the nuclear family or the dominant sexual model are often considered marginal, while women who accept the more or less established rules of social behaviour are considered more favourably.

B. Women's massive presence in the workforce on terms determined by their specific oppression

Contrary to the most pessimistic predictions, the economic crisis has not led to women being pushed back into the home. In all the European countries, women's economic activity continues to rise. Even if the rate of women's unemployment is higher than men's everywhere, nowhere has there been a systematic attempt — as there was during the 1930s — to replace female workers by male ones.

The reasons for this are evident. Outside of women's own increased reluctance to return to the home, it is the change in economic organization over the past 40 years that is responsible for this new attitude of the bourgeoisies. The development of the tertiary sector has led to the creation of a large female workforce, not highly skilled but sufficiently so that they cannot be replaced from one day to the next by an unskilled metalworker or a redundant miner.

In addition, women's low wages encourage the bosses to keep these workers. This continuous entry of women into waged work has taken place on varying scales according to the country. But the forms that it takes are determined everywhere according to the situation of domination over women. Modern capitalism faces a contradiction for it is dependent on female labour outside the home, but it is also dependent on "free" female labour inside the home.

The precarious conditions in which women are integrated into waged work form a whole which goes from discrimination in professional training, in hiring conditions and wages, and which finishes in the feminization of poverty.

The expressions of this specific insertion of women into the world of work are as follows:

a) Increase in part-time work

In countries with the highest levels of female employment part-time work has reached its highest levels. Part-time work is most likely to be exclusively female: 80% of all part-time workers are female, and in West Germany and Denmark the figure rises to 95%. The majority of women workers in Britain — the first European country to promote part-time work on a large scale — are part-timers. This carries with it low pay, low status, high productivity levels and lack of union organization and maternity rights.

Lack of adequate child-care facilities for children below school age is the key factor that forces women into part-time work. Although it seems the only possibility for them others — particularly young women — want to work full-time but cannot get jobs.

Trade unions in Europe have generally not responded to the special needs of part-time workers.

b) Job segregation

The expansion in female employment has not been spread across the occupational jobs and groupings. Job segregation has even increased with the rise in women's rate of activity and is the key factor in their lower average pay. Women are predominantly employed in the service rather than industrial sector. Among semi-skilled women workers, many of them work separately from men in jobs like wiring and routine assembly work. Nor, despite anti-discrimination legislation and changes in education, have we seen women breaking into male-dominated jobs or a marked increase of women working in the top professions.

c) New technology

A quiet revolution is taking place using new technology to structure and restructure the hierarchical sexual division of labour at work, at a time when the workers' movement is on the defensive. These changes are geared to the interests of a capitalist, imperialist and patriarchal society.

Introduction of new technology not only brings job losses but also deterioration in women's working conditions. According to recent surveys in the tertiary sector, women just do not have the "promotional characteristics" — post-entry qualifications, an unbroken service record, geographical mobility — to take advantage of the new managerial and administrative opportunities. Men are more often encouraged to retrain, while women are left to occupy the lesser-skilled jobs (such as computer operators rather than programmers).

d) Flexibility and the reorganization of work

To get the most out of the new machines capitalists are demanding that workers work around the clock — introducing shift work, weekend work and attempting to lift the ban on nightwork for women. An increasing number of firms (banks, insurance) are also proposing to exploit women's dual role by installing terminals in their homes.

The arguments used to try and convince women workers to accept flexible hours are not the same as for male workers. The argument directed at women emphasizes the possibility to combine "their" family responsibilities with waged work. For men, the arguments emphasize increased leisure time.

All the attacks outlined above go in the direction of introducing flexible jobs, hours, wages and employment patterns. The ruling class tries to creates a divide between a small minority of skilled workers — usually male, of the dominant nationality — and an increasingly large marginal layer of unskilled, precariously employed workers made up of women, a section of young workers, immigrants, and unskilled males, who only have temporary jobs and are not covered by social security. It needs to cement the sexual division of labour at work as it reorganizes production to achieve these aims.

e) Unemployment and social security

Since 1974 there has been lower economic growth and higher levels of unemployment than at any time since World War II. In nearly all countries the proportion of women registered as unemployed is higher than for men — in Austria, Greece and Portugal the unemployment rate among women is double that for men. (Of course, official statistics mask the full scale of female unemployment as many women fail to register as unemployed.)

No capitalist state ever recognizes women as workers on equal terms with men. One example is the series of measures taken recently in various European countries that tend to exclude even more women from social security coverage, while married women without jobs have never qualified for benefits. The new restrictions on unemployment benefits give priority to heads of household (usually men). Such measures reinforce the fiction that a woman's place is in the home and that women's work only provides a "supplement" to family income. They deny women's right to economic independence.

C. Attacks on abortion rights and women's right to control their own bodies

a) The USA has been at the forefront of the attacks on the right to abortion with the recent attempt to reverse the 1973 Roe v Wade ruling, which gave women a constitutional right to abortion. This frontal legal attack is combined with grass-roots fanatical mobilization by extreme sectors of the "Moral Majority" and evangelical churches, taking the forms of burning down clinics and physically preventing women from entering them. However, it now seems that the Republican Party will downplay its hardline opposition to abortion which unexpectedly turned out to be a vote-loser.

This offensive has also developed in a less frontal way through attempts to limit existing laws: reducing time-limits or limiting women's right to decide, giving greater power to parents and husbands or lovers, demanding parental permission for minors, etc. Attempts to restrict the laws meet massive rejection expressed in mobilization. In some countries, (Belgium, Spanish State) there have been big mobilizations to broaden the scope of the existing laws.

Another line of attack is the severe restrictions on health service resources making access to abortion difficult.

The badly-named pro-life organizations, whom we should better call "pro-foetus", are developing an international campaign with extensive means and economic resources, as well as counting on the support of sectors of the political, judicial and medical establishment. They are attempting to erode the social climate favourable to abortion created by the activity of the feminist movement. These forces use a discourse that tends to criminalize and culpabilize women, using the communication media, schools etc, with particularly aggressive rhetoric and propaganda.

However, abortion as a right is never secure under capitalism as it conflicts so strongly with the subordinate role ascribed to women in our society. In fact, all legal changes on this front have failed to give abortion to women as a right — instead it is framed in legislation as a "necessary evil" of the modern world. We have certainly not seen the end of such attacks. But, at the same time, the bourgeoisie knows that it has to reckon on women's ability to fight back against any challenge to this right, limited as it may be. The great majority of women now consider that this is a fundamental element in their battle for independence.

There have also been a series of attacks on other aspects of women's rights to control their own bodies, around issues of surrogacy, new reproductive technologies and donor insemination.

b) The response of bourgeois governments to the AIDS epidemic consisted of a wave of hostility particularly directed against the male gay community, with demands for the registration and segregation of victims and potential victims. While US figures show that while only 8% of AIDS victims are women, in New York it is already the primary cause of death for women of child-bearing age. The extension of AIDS beyond the gay community has forced most Western governments to take it more seriously. This has led to some sex education campaigns about "safe sex" in the mass media or in the schools. However, the right wing uses this issue to attack sexual freedom in general. It has also been used to reinforce racist ideology.

D. Public spending cuts

A symptom of the economic crisis is the tendency of the capitalist class to cutback on the costs of reproducing the labour force. Social services are more expensive than women's unpaid labour in the home.

The state aims to transfer the burden of these services back onto the individual family. Attacks on maternity rights, creche and nursery provision, health and community services not only increase the level of female unemployment because these are female intensive areas, but they also step up the unpaid work and the oppression of women in the home.

E. Women in the bourgeois political arena

a) Legal rights

Throughout the 1970s most governments (right or left) — under the pressure of women's mobilizations — introduced a series of major legal reforms on women's rights, although American feminists' attempt to enshrine equal rights in the constitution was defeated after a hard battle. However, these laws have generally had little practical impact. The deepening economic crisis has made governments even less willing to bear the costs themselves or to impose the extra costs involved upon employers. But these laws have had an important effect in raising women's expectations and willingness to struggle.

b) Women as voters

The changing social position of women has been accompanied by a change in their pattern of support for the existing political parties. Before World War II the general pattern was for more women than men to vote for right-wing parties. A gender reversal is now underway.

A number of parties of both right and left have engaged in wide-ranging tactics to win over women voters. This has taken a number of forms, including pseudo-radical feminist arguments ("re-evaluating motherhood", reconciling work and family life), establishing ministries for women's rights, feminizing their image, etc.

c) Women in bourgeois political institutions

The absence of women from representation in the legislative assemblies and government has led to increasing demands for reform. A number of bourgeois parties have responded with proposals to increase the representation of women, but it is remarkable how little impact this has so far had. There has been a small increase, reaching 20%-28% in the Scandinavian countries and the Netherlands, but not exceeding 10% or 12% in the other imperialist countries of Europe.

II. Reformist strategies in relationship to women

The reformist leaderships are caught in the contradiction between maintaining their traditional relationship to the base of the mass workers' organizations, and thus to women at the base beginning to express specific aspirations, and their general logic of "managing the capitalist crisis".

The reformist discourse varies from country to country. The general framework tends to be a pro-equal rights position, but without being prepared to take the positive action necessary to make them a reality. In some countries the argument is that "the basics have been won". In others, where a more specifically feminist gloss is given to reformist ideas, we see arguments developing for women's low pay to be alleviated through an incomes policy. Increasingly, the reformist leaders, both in and out of power, are being pushed rightwards — accepting the logic of the capitalist crisis and refusing to fight against the basic inequalities women face at work and in society. To the degree that the labour movement confines itself to the narrow, economist concerns of the traditional industrial sectors of the working class, the parties of the ruling class will have some success in recruiting layers of women behind their own fake "feminist" banners.

a) The trade-union leaderships

The paper policies adopted by many unions over the last twenty years in themselves were quite progressive and could represent a real step forward for women. But the specific structures in the trade unions nationally, locally or in the workplaces (women's commissions, officers or secretariats) usually receive no real support from the leadership and the real battle is often for thorough implementation of these policies. Hence their effects and achievements have been limited, though not negligible, in areas such as equal pay, sexual harassment and childcare.

On many occasions, the trade-union leaderships have turned their backs on women's demands, ignoring or even opposing them, thus deepening elements of conflict between working class men and women. This helps to justify the relations of domination which exist between men and women in the working class, and makes convergence with the feminist movement more difficult. The French unions have not mobilized an active opposition to the imposition of flexibility and part-time work, and the disappearance of the CGT women's monthly journal *Antoinette* is final evidence of this union federation's policy to stop all specific work aimed at women. In Belgium we saw women workers left to fight alone at Galerie Anspacht in Brussels and at the Bakaert-Cockerill steelworks near Liege over the introduction of part-time work and the loss of jobs. In Italy, the FIAT union did not oppose the introduction of nightwork for women.

b) The leaderships of the reformist parties

In 1979 we noted that social democracy and Stalinism (particularly the latter) were slow to respond to the rise of the modern feminist movement, and that their response was influenced by two factors: i) commitment to the family; and ii) the need to maintain and strengthen their influence with the workers' movement.

Since 1979 the inter-dependence of the struggles of women and the workers' movement has necessitated a more developed response. Women as voters, as trade unionists and as political activists comprise an important political entity that these parties have to consider. Most parties have adopted and developed policies formally supporting women's equality, in some cases including immigrant and black women and lesbians, although the policy that has flowed from this has been patchy and partial. The reformist leaderships in some countries have shown a willingness to incorporate leading spokespersons of the feminist movement as researchers, journalists, counsellors, MPs and top civil servants in women's ministries or committees of local councils. This is made possible because the socialist and feminist revolution which many women were expecting — along with the rest of the left — did not come about and women still wanted to see changes here and now.

i) The Socialist parties

Most Socialist Parties have adopted specific "positive action" measures, albeit superficial, aimed at winning women's votes, and particularly increasing their representation as parliamentary candidates. The left currents within these parties have sometimes been able to use this opportunity to pass progressive measures.

Social-democratic governments particularly have attempted to integrate feminists into institutional work, encouraging moderate feminism oriented simply to obtaining small reforms, producing changes which appear the natural result of the evolution of a democratic society, blurring the role and combativity of women in winning these changes. However the gains are real, however small, and they may be used as a lever on social democracy.

The creation of women's ministries or institutions emerges from the need to give an institutional response to the social pressure of women. The French and Spanish experiences show that women's ministries, although long on speeches about equality, in practice accept the traditional sexual division of labour and are no guarantee that women's interests will really be defended, particularly in the context of austerity policies. Their lack of executive capacity and respect for official policy put clear limits on their activity, but their existence can be positive in reaching broader layers of women. The contradiction between their formal and practical positions can provoke debate and differentiation between the women in these parties, some of whom are prepared to engage in united action.

ii) The Communist parties

The current upheavals in Eastern Europe and the discrediting of Stalinist rule have thrown most CPs into crisis. However, we should not expect any significant about-turns in the CPs' policy and practice on women.

They will continue either to deny the need for women's autonomous organization and struggles or push a (sometimes very sophisticated) rightwing version of gender politics, for example arguing for a "feminist incomes policy" which increases women's wages at the expense of men's. However, as their crisis provokes significant ruptures and departures we can hope for a questioning of traditional policies and a greater readiness from some layers to get involved in united feminist struggles.

In conclusion we can say that the impact of the women's liberation movement, its lasting effect on political consciousness and the political agenda, have made it impossible for the mass organizations not to respond in some way, however inadequately, opening up increased possibilities for united action with women from these organizations.

III. Women's radicalization and self-organization and the autonomous women's liberation movement

The birth of the women's liberation movement reflected the profound structural change in the lives of the mass of women. The feminist movement succeeded in revealing the social character of women's situation and giving an expression to the revolt of women as a gender. Despite the changes that have occurred, women's lives are characterized by discrimination, subordination and oppression. All these factors mean that the basis for women's activity and radicalization of women continues.

Many of the ideas expressed by the movement have been accepted by a big majority of society. At the beginning of the 1980s, there was a decline and a disintegration of the movement, sometimes as the product of integration into institutional and/or social service work, or dilution into different types of sectoralized organizations. In many cases women's organizations continue, although isolated and focused on concrete and/or one-off activities. Today, except in the Spanish state, there are no national coordinating structures of women's groups, which implies an element of weakness of the movement, a sectoralization of the struggles and demands. But women's active resistance to concrete attacks on their rights has continued and new organizations have emerged on specific themes or initiatives of temporary coordination, allowing optimism for the future.

Women's greater participation in various types of struggles — in the unions, political parties and other movements — is a feature of the situation. Although this has not always been translated by an organizational strengthening of the movement the potential exists for this and for a political expression of gender consciousness.

In many countries there has been a greater convergence between the struggles waged by women on their problems as a gender and those of the whole of the workers' movement; the workers' organizations are a point of reference for many women to solve their problems. As a relatively new active force in the workers' movement, many women can be more combative than the workers' movement as a whole and challenge the class-collaborationist policies of the bureaucracy. The investment of feminists in the labour movement is aimed at transforming the labour and mass movement to make them reflect women's needs and to make it possible for women to become a permanent part of these organizations.

A. Women wage-workers

In several countries in Northern Europe large numbers of women have joined the trade unions as they entered the labour market over the last period. In some countries this has even helped prevent a dramatic decline in trade-union membership of the kind experienced in the 1930s. In Scandinavia, the level of women's unionization reaches 50%, and in Britain, Italy and Belgium it is around 30%-33%. In France, given the overall weak rates of unionization (5% in the private sector, 10%-12% in the public), the number of unionized women is very low, almost nil in some sectors.

a) Women trade unionists

The active participation of women workers has played a key role in a series of workers' struggles. In West Germany women workers in the steel industry have been in the forefront of the campaign for a 35-hour week. They adopted as their own the demand for a 7-hour day, first articulated by social-democratic women in Sweden in 1972.

The strike that took place in the National Health Service in 1982 in Britain involved large numbers of women workers and won significant solidarity from other workers, such as miners, firefighters and teachers.

The women in Denmark's unskilled all-women union (KAD) played an exemplary role in the near general strike that took place in Easter 1985 following the break-up of negotiations between employers and the main trade-union federation. The women's union took the initiative to form an inter-union strike committee on one of the industrial estates, and it was here that the strike held out longest. The women successfully forced the trade-union bureaucracy to release funds for the strike.

Working-class women also fight for their specific demands. In 1984 for example a group of women workers in Asturias (Spanish state) demanded to be employed in the mines, where the men from their communities have always worked. With the support of the women's secretariat of the CCOO, and against the media and the

UGT, they won and a group of them were finally employed in surface work, winning the support of their fellow workers.

At a more generalized level, we saw at the end of the 1980s a wave of struggles in majoritarily feminine professions — particularly nurses — which affected most West European and North American countries. They brought a whole generation of women to the front of the social scene. Among other things, they demanded recognition of their professional qualifications — highlighting the inequality between their situation and that of male technicians, and refusing the status of handmaidens to doctors — thus going beyond simply demanding women's right to work. In addition — particularly in France — they developed structures of self-organization to control their struggles from top to bottom.

b) Solidarity struggles

Two examples of women's involvement in solidarity struggles with strikers are:

❖ The Spanish steelworkers' wives who organized a women's coordination to build support for the struggle at a national level against the Gonzalez government's decision to close the Sagunto steelworks, which were the mainstay of the local economy. They often adopted vanguard positions which were more radical and action-oriented than the steelworkers who were threatened with the loss of their jobs.

❖ Born out of the NUM dispute with the Tory government in 1984-85, the Women Against Pit Closures movement was a nationally-organized autonomous network of women's groups based in the mining communities. These groups had to fight for the right to have their own bank accounts, representation in NUM branch meetings and the right to picket alongside the men. Many of the women were miners' wives and new to active politics, yet their resolution helped to ensure that the dispute lasted so long, won so much support against Thatcher, and made links with other movements such as CND, Greenham, black and immigrant groups, lesbian and gay groups and international campaigns.

This movement arose, of course, in the rather particular context of the vanguard role of the miners' union, the length and intensity of the struggle and the relatively homogeneous nature of the mining communities. But beyond this specificity it should be emphasized that it was a dramatic example of the political power of working-class women in action, and an example for other women in Britain and elsewhere.

B. Feminist work in the trade unions and their feminization

a) Under the pressure of women's organization, and in order to keep or win women members, many trade unions have been forced to make small concessions in representation or broaden their debates to include such questions as a guaranteed minimum wage, abortion rights, sexual harassment at work, the portrayal of women in the media, specific demands of black or lesbian women, etc.

But the greater presence and participation of women in trade-union struggle and activity has not always led to a strengthening of their organization within the unions. Often these attempts clashed with the negative attitude of the trade-union bureaucracy and sometimes had to confront the distrust of the majority of the membership. Or, as in the Spanish state, they succeeded in maintaining special structures, but faced problems in terms of concrete activity. Equal opportunities committees and programmes exist in many major unions, but these are not the same as positive action.

Women's mistrust of trade-union organizations is such in certain countries that they have developed structures of self-organization outside the unions. The most striking example was the French nurses' coordination during the winter 1988 strike.

b) Women realize that for their struggles to be supported and their needs as women to be acted on, the representation of women has to increase at all levels of the unions.

There are a number of reasons for the under-representation of women in the labour movement:

❖ the sexual division of labour means that most women are in the least organized sectors;

❖ the history of the workers' movement, and the chauvinism of the traditional leaderships;

❖ the large proportion of women in the "informal" sector in certain countries.

In Britain, NUPE, a municipal and health workers' manual union, ran a successful campaign in the late 1970s to encourage women — the majority of their members — to become shop stewards. In West Germany, women in the printing and textile unions raised the demand for quotas in union structures in proportion to their numbers in the union. In Italy, the male leaders of the CGIL themselves criticize the limited presence of women in the leadership, because they are alarmed by the low level of activity or, indeed, the disaffection among women.

C. The mobilization of women in social movements

One of the striking aspects of women's radicalization in the last decade is their mass participation in the social movements — in ecology, peace movements, in solidarity committees with liberation movements or aid to the third world.

A particularly important example was the women's peace movement that developed in many European countries out of the anti-missiles struggle. Women were attracted to this movement both on the basis of a general appeal around disarmament, and because of the links — highlighted by feminist coalitions in the Spanish state and Britain for example — between militarism and patriarchy. The forms of organization this movement adopted were networks of women's peace groups, mass action initiatives, and coordination at an international level — forms learnt from the women's liberation movement. Many women, particularly young women, gained their first experience of feminist ideas in such formations. In many cases women were at the forefront of the most dynamic mass actions, as at Greenham Common.

a) Black and immigrant women

Struggles against racism have often involved black and immigrant women in a prominent way, and they have taken up their specific oppression: pinpointing sexual harassment; discrimination in housing, jobs, health and education; immigration laws; specifically racist violent images of women's bodies and violence towards black and immigrant women; and racist assumptions about black and immigrant men involved with rape and violence.

They have taken up the specific oppression they suffer due to the family forms and culture of their own communities, and launched campaigns against excision and infibulation of women and girls. Black and immigrant women have been at the forefront of placing anti-imperialist questions before the whole women's movement.

Where black women's organization is more developed, for example in Britain and North America, they have challenged many assumptions of white feminists — for example, taking up the issues of fertility control as they affect black and immigrant women such as forced abortion and sterilization. This has been in the context of xenophobic speeches from forces like Le Pen in France, and Margaret Thatcher in Britain, on the fear of being "swamped" by the "alarming" fertility of black and immigrant women. They have challenged the idea of a consensus among women, stressing that they cannot put gender before race and class.

b) Young women

The feeling that men and women are equal and that women are not oppressed because of their sex is much more deeply rooted among young women today, and talk of the women's liberation movement seems "old-fashioned". However, they can be attracted to a movement capable of developing the "traditional" themes of feminism: contraception, sexuality, violence, which enable women to radicalize quickly and build specific organizations to carry out their own feminist activity in the neighbourhoods and educational establishments.

In the recent student mobilizations young women played a more active role, as they do in the peace, anti-racist or Green movements. In France, young women of North African origin have unquestionably play a vanguard role in anti-racist mobilizations. Through this political activity they can become aware of their oppressed situation in society, in the family and in the labour market. The contradiction between their assumption that they are equal and the reality when they find that their movement is dominated by men can provoke a sharp reaction and a turn to organizing among themselves as women.

In a country like the Spanish state the youth mobilizations have given birth to groups of young women whose struggle focuses on questions such as sexuality, violence, education, etc.

It is important to explain that the solution to this oppression is a collective fight, and not an individual one or an individual search for a career. A collective fight must include those young women who are outside the education system, who are unemployed and for whom the only future seems to be to find a male breadwinner.

c) Lesbians

The fragmentation of the women's movement has been largely reflected in the lesbian movements. There are a few exceptions and there are also some countries where the lesbian community is only now beginning to grow and organize.

The fragmentation of the women's movement often involved major disagreements over issues of lesbianism and sexuality. The failure of socialist feminist currents to adequately respond to the issues and demands raised by lesbians has contributed to the relative hegemony of radical feminist ideas in the lesbian movements.

The weakness of the feminist movement is also a major factor of the de-politicization of the lesbian communities. Although lesbians remain generally much more political and radical than their gay male counterparts, the late 1980s saw the emergence of a growing preoccupation with style rather than with women's liberation on both sides of the Atlantic.

On the other hand, the campaign against the British Section 28 involved the largest lesbian and gay rights demonstration ever in Europe and was one of the most dynamic campaigns against the Thatcher government in recent years. It was notable not only for the fact that it was led by lesbians, but also the support generated in the labour movement and internationally.

D. The left parties

Women's presence in the non-revolutionary left parties has become stronger by a combination of radicalization of women in the traditional base of these parties — that is the growth of their aspirations as women under the influence of the women's movement — and the entry into these parties of certain layers of feminists previously organized in the women's movement. These women were in search of a seemingly more "effective" alternative to the women's movement, once the period of big united-front struggles was over. New political formations (such as the Greens) can also have a certain attraction for women who are seeking an overall political alternative but who reject the traditional parties which often have a very "masculine" image.

a) The traditional workers' parties

Women have organized at rank-and-file level, for example in the British Labour Party, the German SPD and Norwegian social-democracy, to fight for policies corresponding to their needs as women and for greater representation. We have already underlined the possibilities opened up for joint action by the contradiction between this battle and the attitude of the leaderships. The women's structures in these parties sometimes take more radical positions on general political questions than the parties themselves.

b) The German Greens

In this party autonomous women's caucuses exist and leadership bodies are elected on the basis of gender parity. Speakers in meetings are taken on the basis of equal time for men and women. The all-woman leadership of the parliamentary fraction caused an enormous stir when they publicly challenged the sexual harassment of men in their own party. Taking on the politics of gender does not however avoid the debate about political strategy, and women will often be

139

found to have different political views about the priorities in the struggle and what alliances the Greens should make.

E. The feminist movement

Traditional feminist themes re-emerge from time to time as new subjects of mobilization, sometimes in response to attacks on rights already won, sometimes as concrete demands to broaden these rights.

For example, in 1982, under the left government, the French feminist movement mobilized to impose the reimbursement of abortion by the social security. In 1985, women from the entire Spanish state decided to collectively defy the government's restrictive abortion law. This campaign has inspired a resurgence of activity among women on a whole host of other issues surrounding their oppression, and strengthened the national coordination led by the far left. Two thousand women in Germany met to discuss new reproductive technology, and in November 1989 120 women from all over Europe came to the Socialist Feminist Forum in Sweden. International Women's Day can provide a focus for involving all currents of the movement in united initiatives.

Different examples demonstrate the strength of the autonomous women's movement when it is able to take initiatives on questions which rally broad layers of women and bring behind it sections of the traditional organizations of the workers' movement. The self-organization of women within the labour movement is a key mechanism for effecting the necessary political interaction between the movements of women for their liberation and the organizations of the working class.

The changes in women's situation have provoked a political differentiation in the movement. This greater differentiation has been shown on the theoretical terrain. Among the new theoretical themes some — related to questions of race, class, imperialism and sexuality — show up the different situations that exist among women. Feminists' differing attitudes and relationship to the state and its institutions have also provoked discussion. Other discussions arise with new problems (for example the new reproductive technology), or on themes such as sexual violence.

The development of the struggle against men's sexual violence against women, touches one of the most vulnerable aspects of masculine domination. We situate the origin of this violence in women's oppression and raise the necessity for it to be considered as a social crime, placing the accent particularly on women's self-organization and self-esteem. Another line has been developed which situates sexual violence as the origin of women's oppression and elaborates a series of demands which include an anti-pornography movement, censorship, strengthening the police and demands for stiffer prison sentences.

The development of fundamentalist ("back to nature") alternative currents (who consider industrialization of any form as totally negative) has had a strong impact on feminist thought. The possible implications of new reproductive technologies have stimulated these discussions. These "naturalist" tendencies, profoundly anti-science, demand a serious response on our part.

At the core of these ideas is the view that women's oppression is a product of biological differences, reflected in the cultural sphere, and not a result of the social and economic organization of society. Such an analysis involves a retreat from the early perspective of modern feminism that argued that femininity and masculinity were socially constructed and could therefore be changed. Instead they advocate creating "women's space" within the framework of existing capitalist society.

The process of differentiation has produced a variety of currents among which we can identify:

❖ Radical feminists who, on the basis of their analysis of the existence of sexual classes, consider the struggle between the sexes as the only element in the struggle for women's liberation.

❖ Various strands of bourgeois feminism, chiefly characterized by their strategy of making gains for small and privileged layers of women through an alliance with the ruling class and its parties.

❖ Reformist feminists, who either do not take into consideration the factors which determine women's condition as a gender or consider them as a product of the dominant ideology or reduce them to the economic aspects. They have the perspective of reforming the state and thus place the struggle for women's liberation simply in the context of reforms and a "democratization" of society.

❖ Socialist feminists who see the struggles of women as more closely linked with the struggles of the labour movement.

❖ Revolutionary Marxist feminists — including ourselves —: we try to integrate into our theory, analysis and political practice the different contradictions which shape women's reality (gender, class, race), situating women's struggle in a revolutionary perspective and recognizing the importance of an alliance with the labour movement as a whole.

We should emphasize that the frontiers between these different currents are relatively fluid and the categories can often not be rigidly applied. Moreover, our relationship to these currents can vary: on some questions we have united-front work with radical feminists. At the same time the ideas of radical feminism, for example, have a stronger impact on women when the workers' movement turns out to be incapable of responding to women's aspirations.

IV. The orientation of revolutionary Marxists

Confronted with those who deny the specific oppression of women, who situate it in the cultural terrain, who consider it a product of biology or think that it is possible to do away with domination, subordination and oppression in the framework of this society, we affirm the existence of a material and social basis for gender oppression and the need for women to constitute themselves as a social subject, with their own political expression. The feminist movement makes possible the reaffirmation of women's identity, both individually and collectively, and is the only movement able to give a political expression to women as a gender.

The process of feminist consciousness-raising is complex and takes very different forms: on the basis of the contradictions generated by participation in social production or in the public sphere; on the basis of a political practice in other movements which makes possible a greater reflection and understanding of their particular reality and conditions for participating in the struggle; on the basis of a process of individual affirmation in the search for their individuality. All these roads can lead women to fight for their economic, emotional and sexual independence. But this often individual rise in consciousness will not become a collective strength if it is not transformed into collective consciousness, into a desire to change her own reality and that of other women.

Women's liberation work is not simply a sector of work in itself but something that must influence every other area of our work and our entire organization. Every section has to identify the layers of women that they are going to work among on a consistent basis. This is necessary in order to be in a position to take political initiatives to defend and extend women's rights.

Starting from their aspirations and the radicalizing movements in which they participate, we do everything possible to ensure that women become conscious of their specific problems, encourage their self organization to defend their specific interests and thus strengthen the autonomous women's movement.

We also take initiatives each time we can in the workplaces and unions to defend and extend women's rights. We systematically highlight the link between women's domestic responsibilities and their position in the workforce. We support women's right to self-organization and representation within the labour movement.

A. Central axes of our work

We intervene in defence of women's rights, particularly those of the most exploited women — black and immigrant women, women workers, young women and women of the oppressed nationalities.

We particularly emphasize:

❖ The fight for women's right to control her own body, participating in campaigns against any legislative backsliding on abortion and contraception; and for liberalization of laws in countries where abortion is still not a right.

❖ Intervening around the themes of violence against women (rape, battered women, against any kind of sexual harassment in the workplaces or trade unions...) through campaigns explaining the issues or by participating in women's or social movement structures concerned with these questions. Our objective is that laws should be introduced which defend women's rights and define violence against women as a crime.

❖ The fight for shorter working hours, with no loss of pay. This brings women into the fight against unemployment and flexibility and responds to women's need for leisure and time for their own personal needs.

❖ Wage equality between men and women, and the recognition of women's qualifications. We link wage demands to the themes of the right to work and economic independence for women, including through a national guaranteed minimum wage.

❖ Refusing all forms of temporary employment. We understand that some women choose to work part-time, but we emphasize the dangers (low wages, marginalization, de-skilling) and we are resolutely against imposed part-time work. We encourage collective struggle against super-exploitation in the form of temporary work, home-working and insecure "fill-in" jobs and for full rights to time off, job security and trade-union activity for part-time workers.

❖ For education, training and retraining programmes that make it easier for women to gain the necessary skills to challenge their traditional employment patterns. For positive action, including where appropriate quotas in employment and training.

❖ Demanding the abolition of all discriminatory measures limiting women's rights to social security.

❖ Participating in campaigns for the maximum extension of social services (crèches, nurseries etc.), we continue to propagandize for the sharing of domestic tasks.

❖ Opposing all discrimination against lesbians and defending women's right to freely define and exercise their own sexuality.

B. Our participation in building an autonomous women's liberation movement

What we have said before shows the decisiveness of the existence of an independent feminist movement, able to carry forward struggles on all aspects of women's daily lives, that is against their specific oppression, particularly inside the family.

This is the condition for consistently defending the specific interests of women and for transforming the trade unions into revolutionary instruments. This can only be achieved if there is a radical questioning of the traditional divisions of the working class, beginning with the sexual division of labour.

The form or shape of such an independent women's movement will vary from country to country, depending on history and present struggles. But the need for continuity — that is, passing on theoretical gains, strategic debates, the experience of previous struggles — makes this a permanent and central question. Without that — and one can see this in our own ranks and in particular in our youth organizations — we will be faced with a very alarming steps backward from the programmatic gains of the 11th World Congress.

The way forward is not simply given by the overall political situation. We do not give up actively contributing to building trade unions and forming class-struggle currents within their ranks on the pretext that political perspectives are difficult. Nor do we abandon our full involvement in building an independent women's movement where we defend our line and where we struggle to be a part of the leadership.

Positive Action and Party Building Among Women (1991)

Resolution of the 13th World Congress

"What is at the bottom of the incorrect attitude of our national sections? In the final analysis, it is an underestimation of women and of their accomplishments. That's just what it is! Unfortunately we may still say of many of our comrades, "scratch the Communist and a philistine appears." To be sure you have to scratch the sensitive spots, such as their mentality regarding women."
Clara Zetkin, Recollections of Lenin, 1919

Introduction

There are three possible approaches in considering the importance of the real integration of women and of the struggle against sex discrimination in political organizations and in particular in our organizations.

First, from the point of view of the class struggle, that is the general political struggle. The integration of women is essential if we really want to achieve the unity of workers, of the proletariat. We cannot ignore the situation of women. But in building real unity of all the oppressed, we have to work with the various contradictions that still exist among the oppressed under patriarchal capitalist domination, resulting from women's oppression and subordination. Today there is another element — the increase in the number of women in the organized labour force, a change in the social composition of the proletariat with a more acute differentiation in the exploitation based on sex differences — but this is an additional reason, not the fundamental one, for adopting an aggressive policy to integrate women into revolutionary organizations.

Second, from women's point of view, our presence and effective participation in political organizations is a fundamental aspect of developing our identification as revolutionaries. If we start from the need to incorporate individual members, in practice, over the long term, this identity is extremely weak if there are not a large number of women as it can then only be created by male discourse. This is why we are not talking about creating appendices to the revolutionary political project that give women a space, but about a construction which also involves women, in which the struggle against gender oppression is more than a programmatic discourse, but the transformation of daily practice in the field of gender with the development of the political elements necessary to transform society.

In such a perspective the very presence of women, in both numerical strength and real political weight, is essential because, together with the development of the women's movement, this is the only guarantee that the demands and needs of women will be present with the radical dimension necessary to a revolutionary process. The experience of revolutions in various countries demonstrates this clearly. However liberated from patriarchy the male comrades are, any political organization or project of social organization in which women are not represented on an equal basis reproduces the forms of domination of women and their exclusion from public life.

Finally, from the point of view of the total socialist project that we want to develop, we cannot talk about socialism only in male terms, in which women will remain in the same sort of social division and roles, where they maintain a split personality and are potential and daily victims of the power and violence of men.

We also have to respond to the present situation in the workers' movement and in society. There is an organized pressure, a pressure from women, not only for the integration of feminism and women's demands, but also for a numerical increase of women in political and trade union organizations. This stems from the pressure of the organized women's movement and from the objective changes which have taken place over the last decades in the social situation of women: at the level of education, the integration in the labour market, the extension of contraceptive means, some alterations in the structure of the family.

The bourgeoisie in various regions, in Latin America, in Europe and probably in other parts of the world, has been rather flexible and rapid in responding to the pressures created by this new situation. It has tried to broaden the base of its rule by adopting some aspects of feminist discourse and even by allocating some token spaces to women. Despite the limits of such policies, they have been made more successful by the weakness of our response. This is particularly so when, as in the majority of the cases, we have limited ourselves to the adoption of a discourse defending the rights of women without changing our political practice or increasing the effective presence of women in the spheres of power in our own organizations.

The social democratic parties have made progress in the sense of establishing quotas of women in their electoral lists or in the party leadership bodies. It is true in general that these measures have not been accompanied by radical demands for the social transformations necessary to end women's oppression. But it is also true to say that they have been more daring in their proposals to increase the number of women than most revolutionary parties and than our own sections.

We will attempt to briefly explain the difficulties in women's political participation and the obstacles deriving from these.

In political organizations, there is a general dynamic of exclusion of women. The "natural" dynamic is not the presence or participation of women but rather the reproduction of the social dynamic of discrimination and exclusion of women from public spaces.

First we can say that the division between private and public continues within our political organizations and our political vision itself. The social role attributed to women — primarily within the family and in private reproduction — prevents women from developing social and political participation on an equal footing. This is also a central element in the construction of our personality: the way in which we perceive the possibilities or absence of possibilities of entering into public life. Women's participation in political life demands a break from their education and socialization in order to enable them to move into a space which is not normally assigned to them. This division, taken at the level of a party, implies that the male comrades have enormous difficulties in relating to women as political beings and reproduce the way they divide between public and private in their relations inside the party. For this reason we accept a schizophrenic behaviour in which there is no coherence between public and private life. This is a source of permanent tensions between men and women in their relations inside a political organization.

The second question is related to the sexual division of labour. It is obvious that the clearest part of this division is the permanent allocation to women of domestic work, of responsibility for the family and home. Although there have been some progress in some countries, the bulk of domestic work and responsibility still falls on women. For most activists this bourgeois ideology which forms the family structures remains practically intact, essentially because of the privileges and facilities it offers men in their political relations. This aspect of the sexual division of labour deprives women not only of time for political activity but also absorbs most of our personal, political and intellectual energy.

Within parties this type of division is reproduced in many ways. The women do the menial work, and the men do the political work. Within political organizations we reproduce the same mechanisms of depreciation of women's work as in the labour market. It is like the reverse of the tale of King Midas: whatever we touch is devalued. The best example could be the different value given to organizational work when done by men or by women.

The third point relates to the continuation of patriarchal power established inside parties. This patriarchal power, power of men over women, manifests itself by the maintenance of an immense authoritarianism of men: women's discourse is devalued, and must be backed up by a man; in some cases, leaders use their position to obtain emotional and sexual privileges from women.

These are some of the elements that create this dynamic of exclusion of women from the political organizations.

Why this discussion is necessary in the Fourth International today

Most women comrades agree that they joined revolutionary parties to make a revolution that was both socialist and feminist. This is why we want to build parties that are socialist and feminist, and why we have put this discussion on the agenda as part of the discussion on building the Fourth International. A combination of internal and external, positive and negative, factors make it necessary to return to this discussion:

• The International as a whole failed to consolidate politically and organizationally the gains made in the debate on women's liberation at the 1979 World Congress. There has been a general decline in the political level of debate and education in the sections, and a process of depoliticization particularly on the questions of women's liberation. The debate on special measures was left unfinished and arrived at some mistaken conclusions.

• The sections were slow to analyse the changing character in the workforce and what effect this had on the political recomposition of the workers' movement. While we were able to state that in the current economic crisis women would not be driven from the workforce, we tended to underestimate the significance of the ideological offensive of the ruling class on questions of the family, reproduction, sexuality and racism. Consequently, we were unprepared for their effect on the workers' movement.

• In several countries in Western Europe and the United States a downturn in the mass activity of the independent women's movement has taken place, in other cases the women's movement, under the impact of the economic crisis, has moved to the right. All too often the sections have reacted to these events by deprioritizing women's liberation work. But when trade unions are on the defensive revolutionary organizations do not conclude that it is impossible to recruit working people. And even when there is a downturn in the women's movement or the feminist current is weak, this is not an excuse to put our feminist goals on the shelf.

• In some countries in the Third World there has been a massive process of women's organization around demands of the general struggle. When women from popular sectors began to mobilize, at the same time several of our sections started to do broader work both in unions and in other mass sectors that were on the move, amongst them women. However, this implied an enormous pressure on the women comrades who worked in specifically feminist groups to leave them because they were not "mass" organizations. Faced with this pressure, many comrades abandoned work in specifically feminist sectors, or left the sections. In this way, we lost trained women cadre and later found ourselves without participation or very often legitimacy in the feminist sectors of the women's movement when they began to move nearer to the mass movements and with a big backwardness in our level of discussion on feminism both inside and outside our organizations.

In those cases where — on making the turn to these mass women's movements — feminism became secondary, positive action measures were also weakened and women militants' situation inside the party suffered accordingly. There is also an organic discontinuity in our organizations: sections have appeared and disappeared since 1979.

• In general, the sections did not foresee these sorts of problems or think about how to help comrades to confront them. We were not conscious of how much women developed out of their direct experience as participants and leaders of the women's movement and therefore we did not take conscious measures to pass on those lessons and skills to younger women members, especially as they were unable to obtain this experience directly.

- In Western Europe we have seen the development of young women as political leaders in youth organizations. This indicates that positive action can have an impact on changing the revolutionary party as well. Two factors explain the capacity of revolutionary youth organizations to incorporate young women into leadership structures. Most importantly, youth groups are constantly preoccupied with leadership renewal. The search for new leaders places emphasis on conscious leadership development. This sets the stage for allowing young women to think of themselves as potential leaders and to receive the necessary training.

Second, young people's consciousness has been influenced by feminism and they have less need to cling to past habits. Young women are more insistent on change, young men are at least a bit more open to change.

In Third World countries, young people constitute a considerably larger proportion of the population than in industrialized countries. While the great majority of young women have not been directly influenced by feminism, they have been brought up in a period of economic and political crisis which has objectively presented them with a situation where women are more present in public life than were previous generations. Nevertheless, women continue to be subjected to the most brutal forms of oppression. At the same time, a large number of children and adolescents continue to have children themselves, which means their social and political integration takes place in ways more similar to that of adults than is the case for young women in developed countries. This is one of the reasons why neither youth movements nor youth organizations in solidarity with the Fourth International have developed. The development of young women as revolutionary leaders generally occurs in the framework of the adult organizations, which implies specific contradictions in their participation and the need to pay particular attention to their development.

In addition, most young people are freer of responsibilities than they will ever be again. This is particularly true for women. Therefore the skills and attitudes gained during this period of rapid change will be important for years to come. If women gain political confidence as leaders in the youth organization, this can provide an essential framework for advance in the revolutionary party.

- Many sections have decided to adopt some form of positive action plan following debates over the lack of full integration and/or loss of women members. These plans vary according to each national situation. Examples include inviting women's commissions to Central Committee meetings, establishing women's fractions on a national basis, holding special educationals on women's oppression, setting various targets to increase women's participation in leading bodies, holding special meetings where women can discuss and monitor a positive action plan.

The efforts that have been made in the last few years by some sections to change the situation using goals or quotas of women in the leaderships (particularly at national level) have shown that:

o It is possible in the majority of sections to considerably raise the number of women in leadership bodies; there are women capable of taking on these tasks and if they were not assigned to them previously it was because of the obstacles which existed.

o In the bodies in which more women are incorporated than previously as a result of this mechanism — insofar as this is accompanied by a discussion among them of the problems they face as militants, and the party continues to build the movement — this can improve the conditions for their political work. If more account is taken of the need for women's training, internal discussions on sexist violence take on another tone and relationship of forces, their needs are legitimized as needs for the leadership body (and not personal ones) in relation to meeting hours and forms of discussion; our external policy on women can be discussed with greater insistence and precision, etc. In summary, the conditions are created for establishing a relationship of forces between women and men which create conditions making it possible to change the unfavourable situation for women, and thus help the positive development of the organization as a whole.

However, even in those cases where women have been in a majority in leadership bodies, they have not had the same power as the men. For example, they have lacked the informal networks and political authority of the longer-serving men. The men still set the tone of the meetings and determined the political agenda. Even when women were quite numerous in the leadership, they frequently suffered from overwork and felt less effective. They saw that they had less back-up within the organization than the male comrades. Thus, positive action has not solved all the problems — in fact it has often helped to identify new ones.

• In most Third World countries where we have sections, women militants face additional types of problems in their political work: parties prefer men to establish relations with other parties because of misogynist traditions and sometimes justify excluding women from leadership on this basis; the lack of acceptance of women in public spheres; difficulties women face in fulfilling political assignments because it is often dangerous or illegal to be out at night or to travel. In cases of clandestine groups or where cultures isolate women's lives to an extraordinary extent or when the feminist movement is weak or not present at all, as in many Third World countries, the difficulties of women militants become greater. Also, recruiting women becomes more difficult.

• The general problems of leadership functioning often find their sharpest reflection among specifically oppressed layers within the party: women, youth, immigrant workers, members of oppressed nations and races, etc. This reveals both an unhealthy process of leadership selection and a weakness in finding ways to help members who face specific social obstacles to their political development. Informal discussion and collaboration between comrades to prepare meetings and decisions are important aspects of collective working, but a process from which women are usually excluded. Informal discussions with women comrades usually deal with questions other than the political discussions and decisions to take. Even when proposals are to be put forward that concern a woman comrade's political responsibilities or tasks it is not an automatic reflex on the part of male comrades to consult with her.

• Given limited resources and time pressures, sections often merely reproduce society's sexual division of labour. The criteria for selecting leadership are frequently biased against the selection of women because it has an inbuilt set of assumptions based on a "masculine" model that have not been consciously analysed. For example, when women comrades are proposed for tasks, sometimes the limits on their activity because they are mothers comes into the discussion. In the same discussion, on proposing a male comrade for this task, the discussion does not take into account that he has children, which may or may not limit his ability to take on this task. Underlying this is the tacit acceptance that childcare falls on the woman comrade, not on the male comrade. It is also common for there to be stricter criteria for evaluating women, not only in terms of their political capacities but also, in some cases, their personal behaviour.

These obstacles mean that leadership selection tends to eliminate women from these responsibilities, depending on the level of the leadership body: there are fewer women in local leaderships than in the base; fewer in the regional than local leaderships; fewer in the national than in the regional; and fewer still in the international than the national.

Given the competitive atmosphere in leadership bodies and a lack of self-confidence among women, women in leadership positions who manage to survive are sometimes forced into traditional "helping" roles, relegating themselves into seeking advice from a male mentor with more knowledge and experience or ending up by taking refuge in the technical aspect of their task.

• Political debates aimed at discussing women's problems and issues have often been hijacked for other purposes or, alternatively, women have been forced to discuss their concerns within the straightjacket of a factional framework, given that they did not have the power or experience to transform the overall climate of the organization.

We have perpetuated styles of debate that do not create forums in which genuine discussion can take place. Instead of being able to move forward on the basis of these discussions, debates become battlegrounds in which "winning" involves using forms of psychological terrorism to "smash" your opponent. Faction fights often had the effect of either demoralising women, causing them to withdraw from the leadership, or encouraging women to adopt these norms of behaviour to "prove" themselves equal to men.

This intimidating atmosphere is also difficult for many male members to deal with but unlike most women they try to overcome these problems by adjusting to the competitive mechanisms and conforming to male leadership models.

Thus it is clear that a central problem is the lack of collective functioning, which reinforces the existing sexual division of labour. (Weakness in collective functioning is also revealed by other divisions such as between youth and adults, workers and intellectuals.) It is not always possible for women to challenge such forms of functioning head on — in fact, it takes a great deal of leadership experience to figure out how to organize a successful challenge.

• Women face specific problems because of their day-to-day responsibilities and their social conditioning. Of course women come into revolutionary parties from different social and educational backgrounds, with different sexual orientations, and at different ages and periods of struggle. Therefore they have differing levels of experience, knowledge and self-confidence. Women do not always manifest their lack of confidence by timidity — the opposite can occur. Placed in positions of responsibility women can also react by becoming defensively aggressive.

But however individual women have dealt with the sections' leadership structures, the present structures of the organizations indirectly discriminate against women. If we do not adopt and monitor positive action plans, this process will only continue.

• An uneven consciousness on the problems facing women has been a historical problem for the Marxist movement. It has led to a different appreciation of feminism and what constitutes "proletarian morality." Issues such as sexual violence and intimidation have not been fully discussed and resolved in our movement. But the positive and negative experiences of several sections provide the basis for our drawing some definite conclusions regarding unacceptable behaviour towards women comrades and women in general.

***

Much that is said here has general implications for party building and is not the exclusive experience of women members. We would argue that a positive action plan represents a break with spontaneist conceptions of party building. There cannot be a policy of feminization without a worked-out project of building the revolutionary organization as a whole. The debate around positive action can be used to strengthen the whole organization, its apparatus, education and collective functioning.

Some conclusions flow from this debate:

a. The national sections need to be alert to new forms of women's radicalization and the political evolution of debates in the women's movement.

b. Sections need to stress their socialist feminist goals more boldly.

c. Women in the sections need to wage a collective battle, with the support of the whole organization, to transform the way in which the sexual division of labour manifests itself within the party.

d. Key to building a collective leadership in revolutionary parties is an awareness of how the sexual division of labour manifests itself. The only way that can be overcome inside the revolutionary organization is through a monitored program of positive action. The development of a collective leadership will not come about spontaneously, but only through a series of thought-out proposals.

Past experiences — women and the revolutionary Marxist movement

This section will outline some specific features of women's past involvement in revolutionary parties:

Under capitalism the rise of the class struggle led to a rise in women's self-activity and involvement in radical and socialist movements. The founders of Marxism contributed certain bases to a materialist understanding of women's oppression. However, the Marxist points of view in relation to women's self-organization have evolved with time according to the degree of pressure exercised by the mass of women, both within the party and in society as a whole.

At the beginning of the century, revolutionaries usually opposed the autonomous organization of women, arguing that women need to be organized as communists. But as a way to get around Bismarck's repressive laws, socialist women in Germany organized separately from men and a vibrant political movement developed. Certain specific forms of women's activity were maintained even when the law was changed (for example, celebrating International Working Women's Day, publication of a women's magazine).

Lenin, Clara Zetkin and other leaders of the Third International discussed a broader approach, particularly during the debates on the united front and work within colonized countries. Specific measures to organize women workers included women's departments of the party and women's journals. The backing of the international bodies of the Second and Third Internationals was vital to combat backwardness in different national situations. Special measures were adopted to organise women's work in the colonial world.[3]

Today we are committed to organizing women around their own needs (economic, social, ideological). This means building an autonomous women's movement on a revolutionary basis. We emphasise campaigns that involve masses of women in action and project the need to build alliances with other social movements, especially working to deepen the ties between the women's movement and trade unions. In countries where the majority of women first become active in their social sector, as in the Third World, we emphasize mass action and the need to unite women as such around their gender demands. We also seek to attract women to the revolutionary party.

---

[3] See Resolutions of the Third Congress of the Comintern, 1921 for the Theses on Methods and Forms of Work among Communist Party Women.

In the past individual women were prominent within a variety of revolutionary parties. These were primarily intellectuals who led unconventional lives, the most well known being Alexandra Kollontai and Rosa Luxemburg. Their biographies illustrate that the lives of women revolutionaries were full of personal dilemmas. But they were forced to make a stronger break with conventional morality and family life than male revolutionaries of that time and place. Clearly one vital ingredient to their survival as political people was the network of female friendship and support they built.

Modern feminism has begun to unearth information about the role of working class women in earlier socialist and working class movements (for example, utopian socialism, the suffragette movement, the German Social Democracy) but their participation was still much more limited than the possibilities open to women today.

The changing pattern of women's lives, the continued entry of women into the paid workforce, the influence of feminism, the greater cultural and political level of the mass of women and increased access to fertility control make it far more possible today to win broad layers of women to revolutionary parties, and to see them develop as leaders, than ever before. Nonetheless, the stages of women's lives and the fact that women are still the primary child-rearers means that women are still more often expected to make choices between being a mother and being a revolutionary militant, not to mention taking a leadership role in the organization. We need to do what we can to lessen the impact of the special problems women face and convince individual party members through our practice that we are serious.

Women and the Fourth International

Our information on the early history of the FI from this point of view is very limited but our initial impression is that the downturn in the 1950s included a low awareness of feminism. However a number of articles in the FI press indicate that a certain level of understanding on the nature of women's oppression existed, but there was little discussion on the issue. Traditionally women in the FI were "helpmates" who did the small organizational tasks that kept the sections going during the hard times. Often they held fulltime jobs, assuming the role of breadwinner, thereby providing the section with the possibility of paying their husbands a meagre movement salary.

The rise of the second wave of feminism had a big impact on the FI. Comrades in Canada and the United States led the turn to the women's movement, partly because the feminist movement and the campaign for abortion rights developed there earlier than in most other countries. As the result of women comrades' involvement in a feminist movement and as women were recruited to the revolutionary organizations from that movement, sections developed a relatively high proportion of women members. While the revolutionary parties of the pre-World War I socialist movement never exceeded a female membership of 10%, in the 1970s a few sections had more than 40% women members.

By the mid-1970s the sections of the FI were plunged into feminist campaigns. Our international press reflected strategic debates from the feminist movement and reported on new research on women's history. The International proved its usefulness in promoting an international campaign on abortion rights. Women's Commissions in Europe, the United States and Mexico all contributed to the 1979 debate on the political and ideological analysis that formed the resolution on women's liberation. The debate on positive action was concentrated in Europe, Canada, the U.S.A., and Australia precisely because they already agreed on many basic issues about women's oppression, because there was a mass feminist movement in these countries. Although in its analysis of the modern movement it reflected basically the experience of the advanced capitalist countries, this text was fundamental for educating comrades in the basic principles of feminism, although the discussion remained uncompleted and the assimilation of the principles laid out was partial and unequal.

Today, we have to revise some of the conclusions of the discussion. It was dominated by an inadequate and idealistic vision on the assimilation of our programme. We were not able to consolidate in terms of organization what we understood politically, because the document had an idealistic conception of the way in which men's sexist and heterosexist attitudes could be challenged and failed to analyse how they were reproduced in different generations, including among revolutionaries. This applies to all questions related to the family and sexuality — not only women's position but everything which challenges the heterosexual model, and to religious prejudices — not the individual right to religion and faith, but conservative traditions in relation to women.

The other weakness of the document was to put forward the goal of full political, social and legal equality of women as if it could be achieved by a spontaneous and gradual extension of the rights of men. This idea did not take into account the dynamic of exclusion of women from public spaces and of men's privileges.

The degree of organization of women in the FI at this stage was halted by the effects of the turn in some sections, or by the ill thought-out and schematic idea of being "a useful party" with mass influence in others, although women participated in both processes. Additionally, one aspect of the turn to industry was to emphasize sectors of the industrial working class that are overwhelmingly male. Combined with the declining impact of the women's movement, this led to a loss of women cadre, particularly the layers of women recruited in the early 1970s. Recruitment of women declined and the organization saw the work of women comrades active in the women's liberation movement as less central — leading to the marginalization of feminism within many sections.

For the women who made the turn into male-dominated industries, many faced problems of sexual harassment and isolation from other women workers. Women who stayed in public sector unions, or in "female" occupations, found their experiences ignored. There was also a loss of prestige in many sections for those women who had led a mass women's movement but who no longer had such a strong base from which to operate. Unless they could learn to operate in another milieu they were seen as less valuable to their sections and marginalized.

A crucial error was ending the International Women's Commission in the International, especially given the small number of women in the International leadership. Between 1979 and 1985, at the same time as new sections were joining the International, there was no collective reflection on the political questions posed by the women's movement in advanced capitalist countries or the rise in new opportunities, given women's self-organization in the semi-colonial world.

In several countries when our comrades pointed to how women were discriminated against in political and public life, they found themselves in a compromising position. Women faced the same situation within their own party. If we are to build egalitarian and revolutionary parties, we must overcome this contradiction and reflect the full participation of women in our own internal life and public activities.

Pressure for formal reports at the Latin American and European Political Bureaus led to reports on the situation of women in Europe and Latin America and a self-critical resolution on the Place of Women in the FI at the 1986 IEC. A document on Europe was passed at the 1987 IEC and a report was given on Latin American feminism.

A report on Women in the Third World was also on the agenda of the 1988 IEC.

The principle of positive action was revived in the 1986 debate. Both International and European structures were established for the coordination of women's work. Mechanisms for advancing political analysis and coordination for the Latin American sections were also agreed upon. But there is a discontinuity between the work and theorization we did a decade ago and what we are attempting to launch now. The women's movement has changed dramatically. Today it is vibrant in places it did not exist ten years ago, and vice versa. One question we must ask ourselves is what kind of positive action is appropriate now?

What we mean by "positive action" for women and why it is necessary

A revolutionary organization exists to organise the mass of the working class in alliance with the oppressed masses to take state power and transform all social relations of exploitation and oppression. It is this strategic goal which provides the basis for the united action of members of revolutionary parties. The active involvement of the working class in the revolutionary party is a pre-condition for even beginning to attain these goals, as it is the decisive force for revolutionary change. The hegemony of the working class must be promoted within the revolutionary organization.

Alongside this understanding must go an appreciation of the changing nature of the modern proletariat. New layers are becoming part of the proletariat both in the semi-colonial world and in Western Europe. Most often these are specifically oppressed groups, including blacks, women, oppressed national minorities — groups which the organised labour movement often ignores. If revolutionary parties are blind to colour, sex, nationality, caste and social or class position they will end up reinforcing inequality. This would be like fighting to end inequality by failing to liberate the motor force necessary to carry out the task.

Positive action for women is not counterposed to developing proposals for any other specially oppressed layer. In fact, women are often members of those other oppressed groups. Therefore many of the reforms that women want to implement will enable these other oppressed groups to play a stronger role in the party.

Positive action means taking concrete steps to break down barriers to women's participation in the political life of the party. It means recognising the discrimination that women face in society today. It takes into account the social differences between women as well as recognises the oppression that is common to them as a sex. Positive action fits best in an overall plan that takes account of the existing needs and strengths of the organization. It needs to consider the party's next steps. It requires a conscious and self-critical approach to the history and development of revolutionary organizations. It rejects the notion that these problems can "work themselves out naturally." Positive action measures are "artificial" because we want to combat the "natural" tendency.

In the life of our parties very often the forms of functioning and debating derive from the sexual division of labour. The mode of functioning, the nature of leadership and the style of work all operate on what is essentially "masculine" terrain. The privilege of individual development is counterposed to collective work. What prevails is a markedly greater value given to individual development, to personal initiatives and competition to the detriment of collective work.

If we are to build a collective leadership team that can incorporate the skills, insights and experiences of the women cadre, we must find ways to cut across this unhealthy division. Not only are skills are fragmented along gender lines, but those that have been ghettoized into women's sphere are overlooked and devalued, in the sections as well as in the labour market.

Essential to the process of developing leadership criteria is the necessity of identifying the variety of leadership skills necessary for the organization's growth, and not just those skills that are seen as typically "male." The truth of the matter is that the stress on individual initiative and competition has too often produced a battleground of contending forces rather than a coherent organization in which debates and differences are resolved in an atmosphere of genuine respect. Both the skills of abstract theorising and the skills of working collectively must be integrated into criteria for leadership. These need to be woven into the political fabric of the revolutionary party and learned by all, and renewed as the leadership is renewed.

A further problem is the different criteria for political evaluation, not only for the allocation of work but for the individuals as well. This is striking in the case of positions considered important when the situation of women is taken into account concerning their having children or not, the way they live their sexuality or other considerations which have a different weight when they apply to men or to women. It is worth mentioning here that these prejudices also apply to homosexuality whether male or female.

Thus it becomes vital that the whole organization develop a commitment to challenging that reproduction of the sexual division of labour, it is not possible to leave the task to individuals or to the women only — but women will be a major factor in assuring that we will reach our goal. It must be the whole weight of the organization that pushes against the routinism and inertia of the sexual division of labour.

In addition, the symbols used by political organizations are symbols of male power. Not only in terms of language but of aggressivity, and of everything which is developed in the representation of politics. It is very frequent to find an extremely intimidating atmosphere in debates and discussions not only in the way they take place but also because of the frighteningly large number of men which always puts women in an extremely unfavourable relation of strength. This is even more true when we have no means of fighting against social mechanisms of discrimination against women be it in terms of crèches, issues linked to maternity, times of the meetings, and all the other issues which make women's political participation difficult depending on their social situation. We know very well that there are limits: political organizations cannot get rid of the social differences that exist in society and this is all the more difficult the smaller the organizations are. But this cannot be an excuse for not attempting to find alternative ways of enabling women's political participation.

We can say that the political milieu is still marred by an atmosphere, behaviour and forms of relations which exert daily violence on women. Whether in the use of language, in offensive patronising, in manipulations, in psychological violence, fear is imposed by certain forms of functioning or debate, including the physical and sexual violence which is not absent in revolutionary organizations. And here, in general we find the development of a type of patriarchal and sexist solidarity among men which makes even more difficult to fight against this violence.

Another problem is the undervaluing of feminist work. The weakness of our intervention in the movement imposes great limitations on the feminization of our organizations. The pressure of the movement is fundamental to alter the relations of strength in favour of women. But the weaknesses or setbacks of the movement cannot be an excuse for us not to participate in it, and even less for not developing policies of effective struggle against discrimination in political organizations. Our organizations cannot be so vulnerable that they change their attitude to feminist work according to what happens in the movement. This type of change has however a negative consequence on the militancy of women and their decision to do or not to do feminist work, because this area of political work has little status. It is evident that our militant activities are valued on the basis of other elements and not by feminist work.

In addition, our male-dominated parties produce political analyses that constantly miss out a gender analysis. We can produce conjunctural analyses as if women did not exist; we discuss revolutionary processes without women; we make general political analyses of a given society as if women did not exist. On top of that, women's work remains treated as if it was only the work of women and not of the party as a whole, including its leading bodies. Here again we can see a very negative dynamic of neutralization and division of women which undermines the building of our strength as militants.

The consequence of this dynamic of exclusion means that women in general stay on the margins of the general political project. And we feel on the margins because in fact we are. Not because of any psychological problem specific to women, but fundamentally because we pay a very high personal price to try to reaffirm our revolutionary political identity every day when it does not exist inside our organizations. This leads to a great loss of women cadres, who take much longer to be replaced. And it weakens our intervention.

Recruiting women to revolutionary parties

Part of this discussion includes looking at the image our sections project. We want to make sure our sections are attractive to women and provide suitable environments for the training and development of women cadre. We can do this by considering our public image:

• We need to have a profile which clearly reflects our commitment to winning women to our perspectives. This means utilizing symbols and heroes that incorporate women's revolutionary experiences, as well as covering issues from women's perspectives — whether this means discussing problems of everyday life, sexual politics and sexual orientations, community or trade union issues, or international concerns — developing women as educators, propagandists, writers, candidates and spokespeople for the sections. It means developing collaborative relations with women who are leaders of a variety of social movements, and making sure interviews and statements by them appear in the party press whenever appropriate. That is, in every way, the presence of women in the revolutionary process is affirmed.

• The party needs to experiment with structures that can help to draw women sympathizers closer to the organization. Women's book clubs, educationals specifically designed for women (sometimes involving men, other times only for women) or more externally-oriented women's clubs are all methods to be considered. In the semi-colonial countries it has been useful to have workshops where the relationship between women's oppression and problems of daily life is demonstrated.

• The party's organizational structures and methods of operating need to be reconsidered in the light of providing a supportive and collaborative atmosphere for women. Above all, it means developing a political atmosphere in which members are not made to feel "stupid" or intimidated, either by unwanted sexual advances, sexual harassment or elitist attitudes. Central is the development of non-factional styles of debate and a comradely spirit of working together. Such an environment will reinforce women's self-confidence and allow for growth.

• We also understand that the size of the organization implies problems of a particular nature in line with its growth. The smaller the organization the more difficult it will be to identify the problems women confront as objective problems of a social character. The growth of the party with a greater number of women means giving greater attention to women's special problems. This means changing our educational methods, functioning and language, and also discussing the importance of organizing childcare for meetings and external events of the party. Independently of which collective solutions appear appropriate, it is important to note that mothers and fathers need to be sure that their children are being looked after properly. Ill-prepared childcare is just as disruptive to our functioning as ill-prepared meetings.

What other measures should a positive action plan include?

The development of a policy of positive action means the development of a general policy and not of isolated measures. A general policy to fight against the "natural" dynamic of exclusion. In that sense, it is obviously artificial since the "natural" means the exclusion of women. Here we can say that the first condition lies with the alteration of the relation of strength. To this aim we need not only to develop a general programmatic and political integration but also to develop a conscious policy to change our functioning, to ensure a fundamental policy of integration of women in the leadership and leadership tasks. We, women and men in political parties, have known for a long time that real changes do not occur if there are no changes in the leaderships.

Added to this it is fundamental for the building of the strength of women to be able to organise internally in all the ways necessary to the various objectives of building our strength: in numerical terms, in terms of the organizational conditions, of the development of solidarity amongst women. Implementation of only one measure, whichever it is, as the solution to the problem, has a limited effect.

However, it is important to give some ideas on possible measures to be included in such a policy:

Organizing our feminist work

i. Creating and/or strengthening women's commissions in the sections.

ii. Strengthening bodies that exist to organise the women's liberation work in the International and encouraging regional organizing among women in the FI.

iii. Regularly discussing women's liberation work on leading bodies and taking collective responsibility for any problems that arise. Disagreements and differences among women will emerge and should not be viewed as unhealthy. They do not have to be hidden from the organization as a whole.

iv. Inviting members of women's commissions to discussions of the leadership if they are not members of the relevant body.

Education

i. Placing a high priority on education, debate and analysis of women's liberation issues for all members and ensuring that some understanding of these issues is central to the criteria for recruitment.

ii. Organising educational events in which women play an equal or majority role. Ensuring that styles of delivery are not so traditional that they discourage women and less experienced comrades from participating.

iii. The European schools/extended fraction meetings have been relatively successful given the small resources put into building them and because they bring together comrades who have experience in organising over a long period with younger comrades who are today leading the youth organizations. The educational aspect of the Latin American fraction meetings has been important in developing a common understanding between the comrades of a certain number of theoretical and political questions. This type of initiative should continue in these two regions and be extended to others when possible.

v. The first international FI women's seminar was successful. We must ensure that the second is equally so.

Party image and profile

i. Ensuring the press has articles by and about women — and covers issues of particular concern to women. Pamphlets and other publications need to have a feminist profile.

ii. Ensuring that we have recruitment campaigns aimed at women.

Leadership

i. Ensuring that women are visible as leaders of the organization.

ii. Encouraging the development of young women as political leaders in the youth organizations and sections.

iii. Taking time to train women in branches and national leadership responsibilities so that they feel competent in the tasks they perform.

iv. Not overburdening a small number of women with so many tasks that they become "burnt out" and are forced to withdraw from activity.

v. Making knowledge of, and interest in, questions of women's liberation a criteria for participation in the leadership.

General behaviour and functioning

i. Having a code of practice that specifically outlaws forms of sexual intimidation and violence.

ii. Avoiding sexist language and jokes.

iii. Organising meetings that allow for maximum participation through adequate preparation of chairing and speaking procedures that ensure equal rights to all participants.

iv. Taking account of the problems of parents with children in planning national and local events.

v. There is a need to place a higher value on developing a convivial atmosphere in our political activity, e.g. having socials at political events.

Self-organization and democratic centralism

In relaunching the debate on this question we have to be clear about the parameters of a revolutionary organization. It is impossible to liberate women without overthrowing the private property relations which reproduce women's subordination in society. Membership in a revolutionary organization is conditioned by this understanding. No one particular form of organization can end the oppression of women.

Many comrades use this objective limitation to argue that "not much can be done, women cannot be liberated without changing the social structures and making the revolution." We must reject categorically this type of reasoning as being conservative and reactionary. Revolutionary Marxist organizations, understanding material limitations, must adopt an attitude of creating all the counter-tendencies possible today to existing oppression. We do this in relation to the limits of the workers' movement and racial oppression. It also has to be done as regards women's oppression.

But revolutionary organizations can take steps to reach out to women on their terms, look at their political experiences and adjust their own functioning to make them as women-friendly as possible. Women's fractions, commissions and organizers can help push this process forward.

In general the most positive experiences and the most political discussions take place where the leadership through the CC or the Women's Commission has structured these discussions. The idea of special women's meetings to discuss political questions relevant to women, and to which all women in the organization are invited to attend, can be a good model to promote the self-organization of women.

Criteria for leadership

The leadership question is one important aspect of the positive action debate. If approached without an overall plan it will not address the problems of women throughout the organization. We have to have objective criteria for leadership that guarantee a real change in the composition and functioning of leaderships. Just as political continuity is a factor in leadership selection, so is working in a collective team, taking the lead in developing key areas of work, having earned the political confidence of rank-and-file activists and comrades. When a leadership constantly under-represents the number of women in the whole organization it is a sign that the body itself is somewhat disfunctional. We should aim for parity where possible but this should not be a rigid, inflexible schema because women do not wish to reverse roles but to transform the workings of the party. Where parity is not possible we should adopt targets to increase women's representation in relevant leadership bodies.

One suggestion for helping to integrate new women onto leadership bodies is that they should be given time to learn their new tasks and an opportunity to identify practices in the organization they think need changing. This is best facilitated by women's commissions, fractions or a specific caucus meeting that can help to identify such areas and organize report-backs to the relevant leadership bodies. Leadership bodies need to be held accountable for the organization as a whole.

Conclusion

The aim of this document is to restart the debate on positive action. In a sense, it comes ten years after it should have been written. But it is not too late to crystallise organizational as well as political gains out of an important period of women's radicalization, backed up by the self-organization of women and promoted by the leadership.

The women's movement does not have the institutional expression of the trade unions. We have tried to create structures and an understanding inside our sections and the International so that revolutionary continuity on the problems of women are not lost or abandoned. In some countries the women's movement has faced a downturn. But the lessons are not lost for that country or internationally if the gains of modern feminism are fully reflected in both our programme and our practice. It is only by working through the proposals in all the sections that we will be able to make an international balance sheet on this question.

It is worth restating the positive nature of the policy which has been developed in the recent years by the FI. A series of important measures have been applied, which are not however sufficient. The central challenge which remains is that of obtaining this type of policy in a more complete way inside the sections. By taking such special measures, within the framework of unifying the party as a whole, we will not only counter any philistinism among communists, but win and keep more women in our ranks. This is central to ensuring that the political projects of our organizations are collective projects of women and men.

Extract from the world congress resolution on "Building the Fourth International" (1995)

Proposed by the Women's Commission of the International Executive Committee

15. The emergence of a credible socialist current will also rely on its ability to be seen as representing the aspirations of all sectors of the exploited and oppressed populations. This is not a simple banality which we just need to repeat.

To a certain extent, the Fourth International has developed its understanding of women's struggles and the mass women's and feminist movements. For the first time at the last World Congress, there was a specific resolution concerning the dynamic of women's exclusion from the political process and political parties and its effects within the Fourth International. The Congress adopted this resolution, thus specifying the positive action needed for women to take their place within the Fourth International.

This resolution represented an important advance in our understanding of how to build our organizations, and relate them to mass movements etc.

However, we have not adequately explored the implications of how the struggles of women express the changes taking place in society, and how the priority given to feminization is directly linked with the new tasks and renewed forms and themes of struggles that we have and will encounter.

In analysing the potential outcome of any given social and political situation, we must integrate a number of elements that arise from women's specific situation *as women,* combined with their class, ethnic or age status.

A starting point should be the continuing mass integration of women into the workforce — whether formal, informal or unemployed workers — although in sharply gender-defined forms.

This in turn increasingly involves women in social struggles, whether as workers, urban dwellers, peasants, consumers, etc.

However, the recent arrival of women in the workforce, and indeed in social movements in general, combined with the general trend of women's exclusion from public and collective life, tends to place women in a marginal situation within the traditional organisations of social and political life. They can thus, at times, be pushed in a more radical direction and act in defiance of the traditional leaderships.

The continuing penetration of general ideas of women's equality and rights, as a result of battles fought by the women's movement, throughout the population, influences the way in which women raise and defend "traditional" demands (for example linking the fight for pay rises with a fight to increase the status accorded to what is seen as a specifically "female" job). However this wide-spread acceptance of women's right to equality is not unchallenged. The right-wing, and in particular the growing religious fundamentalist movements, target questions of women and the family particularly. Without a determined response from women such attacks will not be defeated.

This determined response is however not guaranteed, given the decline of a radical, organised feminist movement. The growing institutionalisation of the movement through recuperation by sections of bourgeois political formations or integration into NGOs, as well as the ideological attacks of the "post-feminists", has weakened the revolutionary subversive aspect of feminism that played such an important role in winning women to revolutionary perspectives in an earlier period. The failure to renew feminist discourse, demands and ideals makes this situation worse.

This is not however simply the result of developments specific to the feminist movement, but a reflection of the general decline of revolutionary radicalism and the lack of a liberatory perspective. In certain cases it could be the reaction by women to attacks on them that stimulates a general political radicalisation. The contradiction, especially for the younger generations, between the prevailing ideas of women's rights and specific attacks, for example on abortion rights, could be such a spark.

For the organisations of the workers' movement, including revolutionary organizations, to be able to attract these potential new radicalising layers, they must overcome the specific dissatisfaction expressed by radical women with traditional forms of political and social organisation and rebuild themselves on a different basis, including the idea of parity, i.e. that women should have their full place in decision-making. Such a programmatic and organisational renewal is vital for these organisations in the present period. Without such an effort including the integration of women's contributions it will be impossible to develop a fully-rounded socialist alternative.

Our commitment to integrating these parameters into our analysis is not simply an abstract one. It should determine how we understand the priorities for revolutionary intervention. This should be one of the major elements of the profile of all the sections and sympathising organisations of the Fourth International; but this will be impossible unless we act on the proposals contained in the resolution of the last World Congress, both at an international level and within all our national organisations.

Women and Economic Integration (1995)

Discussion Text for the 14th World Congress

These theses result from a discussion in the IEC Women's Commission. The members of the Commission would like to see the general ideas presented here integrated into the document on the World Situation, obviously in abbreviated form. This is an initial attempt to develop this analysis; suggestions, reactions, and further contributions are welcome.

Restructuring and integration of the global capitalist economy — including the recent imposition of so-called structural adjustment policies involving austerity measures, privatization of the economy and deregulation of the market — and the current moves toward establishing formal trade blocks through NAFTA, the EEC and MERCOSUR, have particular impacts on women in both dependent and advanced capitalist countries. Equally important, these economic transformations and their role in undermining the political strength of the international working class depend precisely on the continuing oppression and exploitation of women. This latter point must be grasped to adequately understand the fundamental dynamics involved.

Broadly speaking, the formal trade blocks, with their goals of downward "harmonization" of economic and social policies to remove barriers to the free movement of capital, the search for cheap labour and the maximization of profits, simply codify and deepen trends already well underway.

While there are regional variations, we can point to some general implications for women and some gendered aspects of integration. We have grouped them in the areas of work, health and welfare, social gains, sexuality, and ideology:

Women's Work

The overall implications of economic integration for women's work has been to promote contradictory proletarianization of women on a world scale, forcing them into the work-force and at the same time using their role in the family and society to justify job insecurity and casualization and the return of many private services to the "private" sphere of the family, to be shouldered by women.

Today's international capitalist restructuring involves the development of export-processing industrialization by multinational corporations whereby parts of the production process (usually those that are low-skilled and labour-intensive) are located in free-trade zones throughout the Third World. These zones represent localized models of what the new trading blocks will create on a broader regional basis. Industries in these free-trade zones depend on the particular exploitation of women's labour to provide the increase in surplus-value and in profits that is the goal of global restructuring. As a result, a significant layer of Third World women are brought into industrial production and in fact into some of the most modern sectors of the economy, though under very exploitative conditions. However, this development has also been accompanied by a huge expansion of the informal sector into which most women workers, including those who have been laid off from multinational industries because of age or pregnancy, are channelled. In fact, women's work in the informal sector is used to underwrite the "cheapness" and "flexibility" of both male and female labour in the industrial sector and to provide a safety valve for periodic retrenchments in that sector. This trend toward informal-sector work is accelerated by the increasing commercialization and export-orientation of local agriculture, a shift which frequently undermines women's role in the more traditional farming economy.

In the advanced capitalist centers, there has been a shift of the job market away from industrial work toward service-sector employment, drawing large numbers of women into the low-paid "pink-collar ghetto". This shift has been accomplished without massive disruption by building off of the gendered division of labour in the family. Thus it was women who played the key role in holding families together through periods of unemployment and economic stress, and also women who more readily took up the new low-wage jobs in response to their feelings of responsibility for family survival. This expansion of the service sector has been combined with a new phase of industrial development in the U.S., Canada and Western Europe, depending largely on the labour of immigrant women. These women, vulnerable because of the combined factors of gender, race and immigrant status, often work in small workshops or at home, signalling the revival of turn-of-the-century sweatshops and the putting-out system. Such fragmentation and casualization of women's industrial work, which is paralleled by the trend toward temporary and part-time employment in the service sector, is a *central component* of capital's strategy of creating a "contingent" or "flexible" work-force.

Structural adjustment policies, and the resulting rise in unemployment, have served to drive women disproportionately out of the formal economy while also increasing their need to find some kind of income-producing work. They thus turn to the informal sector where women are increasingly forced to take jobs as day labourers, street vendors or prostitutes. In some Third World countries, unemployment has reached such proportions that men and women are now competing over informal-sector jobs, thus removing even this safety net for women.

The establishment of formal trade agreements will most certainly accelerate these developments, leading to a further "maquiladorization" of women's work in both advanced capitalist and Third World societies. One of their basic aims — aside from ensuring certain rules for capital flow and investment, while highly regulating other things like patents — will be to generalize the elimination of certain regulations of working conditions and labour relations which have not already been eliminated, using the argument that their maintenance would constitute "unfair trade practices". Undoubtedly, then, we would see challenges to rights such as:

• the right to safe, decent working conditions. Hazardous conditions in both industry and services where women are concentrated already exist — for example, danger from the use of toxic chemicals in electronics factories, fires in garment sweatshops, and the rise in stress-related injury for clerical workers using computers.

• retirement age requirements may be "harmonized" as is already being foreseen in Uruguay, where MERCOSUR could raise women's retirement age by seven to nine years to jibe with Brazil's higher age.

• maternity leave with pay, as well as child care, both legal rights in Mexico, could be eliminated formally by NAFTA.

• affirmative-action programmes, a hard-won right for both people of colour and women in the U.S. and Canada, could be challenged as an undue burden on capitalists in both countries, "prejudicing" their competitiveness.

In the agricultural sector, NAFTA and the EEC will promote the domination of agribusiness, leading to peasant women's further loss of this economic base.

Health and Welfare

These changes in conditions and security of work directly affect women's health and general well-being as well as the welfare of those family members (especially children and the elderly) for whom women are primarily responsible. Rising prices and unemployment put stress on women's own ability to provide for basic needs, while cut-backs in public spending and the dismantling of social welfare programmes decrease state support for services such as education, health care and child care. This development is particularly deleterious to women because of their perceived role in both social and biological reproduction. At the same time, the state depends on women to "take up the slack" and provide on a private basis services that were previously provided by the government, thus furthering the process of structural adjustment.

NAFTA in particular threatens to unleash new health hazards for women as it opens the way to challenging existing environmental laws as "unfair trade practices". For example, in certain communities on the U.S.-Mexican border, the problem of toxic wastes is already linked to cancers of the female reproductive system and to severe birth defects such as anacephalic children. With the general weakening of environmental regulations, such problems could become more widespread throughout North America. At the same time, NAFTA will pose a challenge to the national health care programmes of Canada and Mexico while making it more difficult to establish a comparable programme in the U.S. While this affects the whole of the working class, women, as primary consumers of health care services and as those mainly responsible for family health, will be particularly hard hit. In the case of the EEC as well, health care and other components of the state welfare system could be gradually chipped away.

Social Gains and Basic Rights

Closely related to the question of health and welfare is the effect of economic restructuring and the new trade policies on the social gains women have fought for over the past quarter-century, and in relation to which they have won at least partial victories. These include the right to reproductive freedom (including the right to abortion), the right to equal pay, and the right to freedom from sexual harassment and violence.

While the general economic crisis has already generated serious attacks on women's rights, formal trade agreements have the potential to undermine these rights in a more formal and thoroughgoing way. This is largely a result of the supranational and corporate-dominated decision-making structures proposed in these agreements, which will supersede regular legislative and executive actions. This, combined with the focus on "unfair trade practices", sets up a situation rife for the challenging of measures that help equalize women's role in the economy. While the reason for attacking these rights may have a primarily economic basis, we should note that the rights themselves help ensure women's position in many areas of society. Their significant weakening would, in fact, bring into question women's basis status as citizens. The possibility for such a development is particularly clear in North America, where NAFTA provides no guarantees for such rights. In Europe the situation is more uneven, in that the Social Charter that accompanies the EEC proposal provides common European principles on these matters, thus promoting stronger measures in certain cases (e.g. Ireland and Portugal) while watering down existing laws in others (e.g. Sweden).

Sexuality

The manipulation of women's sexuality is one of the primary ways in which capitalist restructuring uses and builds on women's oppression. This happens in several ways. First, there are the attacks on sexual and reproductive rights discussed above. In this sense, such attacks can be seen as not only an effect of economic change but also as preparing the way for further restructuring by making women more vulnerable in both economic and social terms. Second, we can find numerous instances where the entry and dismissal of women from the wage-labour force, as well as the conditions of super-exploitation under which most women work, are justified by images of female sexuality. This, for example, is very common in factories where women are alternately represented as "sexually loose" and thus "free" to be exploited, or as requiring stringent controls — including the physical organization of the workplace using the threat of sexual violence — to maintain their sexual purity, thus limiting their autonomy and mobility. Finally, there are particular instances — such as the expansion of the international sex trade in Europe, Asia and Latin America, the increase in dowry deaths in India, and the imposition of class-based population policies, for example in Singapore — in which women's sexuality is both commodified and controlled in ways that directly further the economic strategies of individual men or of capital as a whole.

Ideology

The ideological transformations that accompany global integration also have an impact on women. This too has several aspects. There is, for example, the manipulation of sexual images and norms we have just discussed. Also of importance is the ideological emphasis on individualism and privatization that parallels recent changes in economic relations. Because of women's traditional role in the family, such an ideological development affects them differentially — and also depends on their often unconscious collaboration to carry out such broad cultural change. Finally, there is the possibility that NAFTA and the EEC will play a role in undermining both memories of and aspirations for progressive national struggles. This in turn could have special implications for women, since it is through such struggles that women's demands are frequently raised and secured. For example, to prepare the way for implementation of NAFTA there are already pressures to revise the official histories of the Mexican Revolution. Such revisions would serve to weaken the collective memory of the gains of the Revolution, including those of particular importance to women such as rights to maternity leave, child care and health care. The Irish struggle provides another example, in that the dampening of its vigour because of the renewed ideology of a common Europe could also dampen aspirations for women's emancipation connected with the goal of national liberation.

Women and the crisis of civilization (2009)

The convergence of the different aspects of the crisis of global capitalism today confirms that we are faced with systemic economic, ecological and social crises, which combine to produce a crisis of civilisation.[4]

In this paper we indicate some of the ways in which this crisis particularly affects women.

Women were already at the bottom of the pile before the crises started, so it is no surprise that we feel the effects of these disasters most acutely. Women's subordinate place within the labour market, notwithstanding the limited gains made as a result of women's self organisation, remain a reflection of the sexual division of labour and inferior status of women within the patriarchal capitalist family. The family, together with the education system, continues to reproduce notions that women are inherently inferior to men —or at best have different destinies as primary care givers to children and the elderly— a particularly important notion for the state to fall back on as it slashes public services. The family continues to be the main site of violence (and repression) against women.

And make no mistake: what is tested out on women today in terms of the capitalists' attempts to make sure they do not pay for the crisis will be imposed on the whole of the working class tomorrow, as we have already seen in many other instances, for example with part-time work.

In response to all these issues, we need to make sure that the demands we raise as parties and campaigns take into account the specific oppression of women. Sometimes this will mean raising specific demands that affect women (e.g., abortion or equal pension rights), but it always means looking at what we say from women's point of view.

---

[4] This collective contribution to the discussion of the World Congress on the international situation was developed by a seminar of Fourth International women held in July 2009.

So, for example, the demand for a shorter working day/week is in the interests of the whole working class, but has particular importance for women while we also carry out the double burden of domestic labour. Another example: nationalisation of the banks has come to the forefront of our propaganda as a result of the credit crunch, though of course we understand that the economic crisis did not start and will not end with the banking crisis. But women, as one of the poorest sections of the working class, are particularly affected by rises in interest rates and limitations in the availability of credit.

Of course, the context in which these demands are formulated will be different in each national situation and need to be adapted to meet the concrete realities in which we are working. The programme developed by the Belgian comrades for the 2009 European elections, "An ecosocialist Europe will be feminist or it will not exist," is a good example of how this can be done.

Women are also an integral part of the resistance to the onslaught and the fight we see taking place to create the other ecosocialist and feminist world that is daily ever more necessary. Women's self-organisation is essential to achieving this. The steps forward that women have made in terms of the constituent assembly and the campaign against public debt in Ecuador, for example, are not because Correa decided to grant women favours but because women's self-organisation helped create the balance of forces that won these gains.

Women and Climate Change

Poverty and inequality is the lot of the majority of women in the south, and they are the first to be hit by the climate crisis, caused by emissions produced mainly in the countries of the north. Eighty percent of the 1.3 billion people in the world living under the poverty line are women.

Women produce 80% of food in the south, so desertification, the loss of water resources, etc., have a huge impact on their daily lives. When people are forced to move because the place they live can no longer provide any food because of climate change, women and children are and will be the majority of those displaced.

A report published by Oxfam in June 2009, *The Winds of Change: Climate change, poverty and the environment in Malawi*, argues that women are affected most by climate change because they have multiple roles as farmers, providers of food, water and firewood, and child carers. It also points out that women in Malawian society have no say in decision making and that climate change exacerbates existing inequalities. It further argues that there is a danger that deepening poverty will pressure women to sell sex for food and that this will further exacerbate the spread of HIV/AIDS. The spread of HIV/AIDs will further weaken the ability of the population to resist climate chaos.

In 2008 the level of global malnutrition grew by 800,000 to reach more than 1 billion people and, at the same time, diseases such as cholera that we have long known how to eliminate are now re-occurring as part of this crisis of civilisation.

The fight for women's access to decent free public education and health care, including access to abortion, contraception, and sex education, is an essential element of combating the climate crisis especially in the south. Women are often at the forefront of campaigns to defend and extend these essentials.

The neo-Malthusian answer to the climate crisis arguing that there are too many people on the planet seeks to further limit women's right to control our own bodies and is racist in that the rate of population growth is greater in the countries of the south. Our first response is to fight for the extension of women's fertility control, as well as for the eradication of poverty which means that there is less pressure on communities to provide more people. We also fight against capitalist consumerism which means that so much of what is produced has no use value and is deeply environmentally wasteful.

The growing impact of agribusiness, production of biofuels and the continuing sell-off of land to multinationals for the continued extraction of oil and other resources has resulted and will continue to result in the loss of land and of autonomy for small producers, the majority of whom are women, many from indigenous communities. Pesticides destroy organic crops of small producers.

Indigenous women and women landless farmers play a central role in defending forest ecosystems from governments who want to sell them to the highest bidder and mutinationals who want use them for the production of biofuels and to extract other resources including water, tropical hardwoods (which take hundreds of years to grow a few inches) as well as oil and other minerals. The action by Via Campesina women in Brazil, who destroyed the Aracruz Celulosa substitution for eucalyptus, was a victorious example of women playing a leading role in defending the biosphere. Women of many indigenous communities are also central to the defence of ancestral lands.

- Diminishing energy consumption by ending wasteful production including the arms industry, nuclear industry, advertising and the explosion of air transport

- For localisation of production, including agriculture
- End the use of harmful energy sources and expand sustainable energy
- Free and adequate public transport

Women and the Economic Crisis

Neoliberal globalisation has resulted in a vast expansion of insecure jobs with short-term contracts and the massive extension of part-time work. At the same time, the informal economy has spread from the countries of the south to parts of the north and to sectors that were previously part of the formal economy.

The majority of those who work in the informal economy are women and children. For example, 1-2% of the urban populations of the world make some sort of living from collecting and reselling waste on landfill sites. The majority of these are women and children. The demand from industry for recycled paper, especially from China, has already begun to fall as a result of the recession, which means the price for these products is falling significantly, and therefore so is the ability of those sectors of the population who live by collecting and reselling them to survive.

In a recession, informal sector jobs are lost at the same time that some previously in the formal sector move into the informal sector. In the south some export-oriented industries like textiles where large numbers of women have been employed have grown rapidly: in Africa for example 100,000 new jobs were created over the last 7 years. But demand has reduced as a result of the economic crisis. In the Philippines, 42,000 jobs in textiles, semiconductor and conductor industries, where a majority of workers are women, were lost in one day (Oxfam report, *Paying the Price for the Economic Crisis*, March 2009).

Export manufacturing is, of course, an area where workers have virtually no rights, so most of the women who have lost their jobs in this sector have received no redundancy pay or social security benefits. Even where there is supposedly a legal right to them, where there is no worker's organisation to ensure that this happens, the bosses ignore their legal obligations.

The growth of microcredit has been important in allowing some economic independence for growing numbers of women in the south. But the recession means that its availability is severely reduced, which will have a negative impact on women's economic and therefore social and political independence.

In terms of job losses in the formal sector, the crisis has so far impacted differently on women in different countries. The motor industry —where it exists, one of the hardest hit sectors— is generally male-dominated. In some places, generally those countries of the advanced capitalist world where the recession has already hit deeply, we have already seen big job losses in the service sector where a majority of workers are women. In countries where this has not yet happened, the service sector will be next.

Though statistics on global rates of unemployment for women and men are difficult to find, it seems that so far the differential rate of unemployment has not increased; it will, however, as the crisis has more impact on the service sector. Oxfam says the majority of jobs lost in the south are women's, while in the US, female unemployment rose faster than male in May 2009 (5.6% for women, 4.1% for men – Womenstake.org)

Despite legal protection in most advanced capitalist countries, women workers have continued to suffer particular discrimination when they become pregnant. Indeed the assumed possibility that they will get pregnant lies behind much discrimination against women of child-bearing age. But there is evidence in Britain at least that this is getting worse in the recession. The Alliance against Pregnancy Discrimination in Britain, a coalition of different groups who have come together to campaign on this issue, says:

"There has been an alarming increase in the number of pregnant women and new mothers who are being made redundant. It appears that some employers are using the recession as an excuse to break the law on discrimination. With the economic downturn has come a rise in the number of calls to our organisations from women facing maternity or pregnancy discrimination. We have examples of pregnant women being singled out for redundancy and of women returning from maternity leave to find their jobs have gone.

"Even before the recession, the Equal Opportunities Commission had already estimated that 30,000 women lose their jobs each year as a result of being pregnant, and this figure looks set to rise. This shocking impact of the recession is not only morally wrong and deeply damaging to workplace gender equality – it is illegal"[5].

The sub-prime crisis in the US, the first visible sign of today's crisis, has taken a higher toll on women – especially women of colour. Thirty-two percent of women mortgage holders have sub-prime mortgages vs. 24% of men; and African American and Latino

---

[5] http://bit.ly/aapdpdf

homeowners were 30% more likely to have received sub-prime loans (Ms Foundation for Women).

And of course poverty rates increase during economic downturns; with the increasing costs of even basic necessities like food, transportation, and energy, the number of poor families is growing. And once a family has fallen into it, poverty is difficult to escape. An estimated 60% of families in the bottom fifth of income levels remain there a decade later (Ms Foundation for Women).

And, as is historically the case, when women are faced with no current or future prospects for job opportunities, even in the informal sector, already strained by its swelling ranks, they often turn to considering marriage and child-rearing as their only "acceptable" alternative. Still others try to keep a roof over their and their children's heads by selling their bodies for sex.

- Nationalise the banks under popular control, extend provision of microcredits, and increase government aid especially to women
- For shorter working week/day with no loss of pay
- For the ending of temporary contracts. Full rights for all workers
- Against discrimination including at work on the basis of gender, marital status, age or sexual orientation
- For the creation of new jobs open to women and men
- No discrimination in pensions or state benefits

Women and Public Services

The defence of basis services —most fundamentally water, but also electricity, housing and transport— as publicly controlled and affordable —preferably free— is essential. Women have very often played a leading role in the campaigns to defend and extend these basic services, from the successful battle against the privatisation of water wars in Cochabamba, Bolivia in 2000, to the struggle against privatisation of railways and cotton and rice cultivation in Mali.

The economic crisis we face now will not see any let-up in the neo-liberal policies that privatise and starve public services of resources, affecting women both as the majority of workers in this sector and as those most dependent on the services provided. In many European countries, cuts in health services are a constant example. In France the drive to privatise pre-school care in private kindergartens rather than in nursery schools in the public school system will reduce public sector jobs and make childcare more expensive. In Mexico, state outsourcing of an increasing number of childcare centres to private manager-owners has led to a severe decline in the quality of service; the cruellest result of this so far has been the death of 48 children in a June 2009 flash fire at a childcare centre in Hermosillo, Sonora, owned by relatives of high-level government officials, operating under the same roof as a warehouse. Public horror at the corruption and impunity for those responsible distilled into a movement that cost the ruling party the governorship, but the guilty parties have yet to be brought to trial.

In countries where abortion is legal (within limited conditions), cuts in public health services are already impacting on women's access to abortion and contraception. Rape crisis centres and other services for women who have been on the receiving end of violence have also lost funding. These services will be seen by many providers as optional extras, while others will be happy to cut projects that they never supported in the first place under the guise of economic necessity.

Personal social services are increasingly being privatised in different European countries: France, Sweden, Belgium, and Britain at least. Primarily women workers are employed to do house work (cleaning of house and clothes, cooking, childcare and in some cases care of elderly or disabled people) in the homes of professional families (sometimes by the state, sometimes by private companies). They work maybe 5 or more jobs a week with a small number of hours spent at each and almost as much time travelling between jobs as working. The status of these jobs is very low and unprotected, and the extension of these services is used as an argument for reducing public services, in the retirement home sector for example.

Together with very low hourly wage rates. this means poverty for the women working there. And given that "reform" of social security systems mean that in many countries people are forced to take any job or lose benefits, it is harder for workers to refuse to take these jobs, while the bosses are provided with a pool of cheap labour. These types of developments also result in deepening divisions between women where those with more social and economic power become the employers of those —mainly black and migrant women— who do not.

- For the defence and expansion of public services under workers' and users' control
- For the extension of high quality childcare services

Migration

Over the past four decades, total numbers of international migrants have more than doubled, but the percentage of the world population migrating has remained fairly constant. There are now 175 million international migrants worldwide or approximately 3.5 per cent of the global population. About half this number is women, despite the common misconception that migrants are men. Most migration takes place to adjacent countries, and some takes place within countries as well as across continental borders.

In many countries of the south, remittances sent back by migrant workers play a crucial role in the economy. For the Philippines in 2008, annual remittances amounted to US$16.4 billion and in March 2009 alone, total remittances were US$1.47 billion. In seven Latin American and Caribbean countries, remittances even account for more than 10% of GDP and exceed the dollar flows for the largest export product.

As the crisis deepens, women's migration will increase further for a number of reasons: women moving to work abroad because they cannot sell their labour power at home, or if they can, they cannot sustain their families on the income offered. For example, 4.5 million families in the Philippines cannot meet the minimum requirement for food.

In some situations, in fact, the majority of migrants are women: for example, from the Philippines 70% are women, employed mainly as undocumented domestic workers. The RMPP (Philippines section of the Fourth International) works in Europe to organise Filipina migrants and to try to win rights for undocumented workers.

Filipina women, like other women from Asia, Africa, Latin America and Eastern Europe, working as domestic workers are part of the global domestic care chain, where women in first world countries who want to be liberated from their domestic functions and pursue fulfilment in the public space by working have to find someone to replace them in their domestic functions. So, migration of domestic workers is a form of demand-based migration founded on the gender division of labour in receiving countries. This demand is met by Filipina women, many of whom have children of their own in the Philippines. Given the gendered division of labour in Philippine households, they cannot expect their husbands to take on their domestic workload in their absence. Furthermore, the husbands might themselves be migrant workers elsewhere (mainly in construction).

For migrant women, the solution to this problem is to in turn employ live-in domestic workers to care for their family while they are gone. In the non-migrant family, the absence of the mother creates a demand for care for her own children. Since they cannot afford to pay a domestic worker, this work is taken on by an elder daughter while the mother is at work.

At the end of the global care chain, this daughter assumes the role of mothering for her younger siblings, giving her less time to play, study, or work outside the home. Alternatively, the migrant's mother cares for her children. Such grandparent fostering is a common constellation in societies of emigration. It takes pressure off the eldest children, but means that grandmothers can experience forty or fifty years of continuous child-rearing responsibility. While every woman in the chain feels she is doing the right thing for her family, hidden costs are passed along and eventually end up with the older daughter in the non-migrant household. As childcare work is passed down the chain, it diminishes in value and becomes unpaid at the end.

Migrant families are deprived of their mothers' personal affection and care since they are already commoditized in the global market and traded internationally. This "new commodity" in the global market is well promoted and supported by the state. For example, the two women presidents of the Philippines (Aquino and Arroyo) made these migrant women "heroines" because they sacrifice their families in order for the Philippine nation to progress through remittances. President Arroyo promised the Middle East countries to send efficient and reliable domestic workers. They both called the migrant women workers the "new heroes" to pacify them in the face of the emotional distress of separation and exploitation.

The migrant women and their families are the sacrificial lambs of this neoliberal globalization. During global financial crisis, women migrants working in the domestic households are directly affected and cannot even claim severance pay when they lose their jobs because they are mostly undocumented.

Governments like that of the Philippines ignore their own legal obligations to protect migrant workers from their country (Republic Act 8042 (Migrant Workers and Overseas Filipino Act of 1995). For example, since 2002, six Filipino migrant workers have been executed in Saudi Arabia including one woman, and a number of others have been held on death row for crimes they clearly did not commit. The violence (beatings, rapes, forced detention) meted out to women migrant domestic workers from Asia, Africa, and Latin America in the receiving countries has been well-documented.

Of course not all those who migrate become migrant workers. Men, women, and children are displaced in huge numbers as a result of wars —including civil wars— and by climate change, which makes the places they were living uninhabitable. People try to escape political persecution by leaving their country of origin. Women may run from violence within the family or from forced marriages. Many of these flee as refugees, hoping for a place of safety in the country to which they run. Unfortunately the lot of the majority is to be treated as outcasts and scroungers.

Trafficking in women has also increased. The most publicised form has been trafficking for sexual exploitation of women, particularly from Eastern Europe, Latin America, and Asia to Western Europe, creating a huge network of forced sex workers. But there is also an increase in women being sold within their own countries as domestic slaves: recently, Peruvian feminists' research showed that the largest number of women in their country subjected to trafficking were actually indigenous women kidnapped and sent to work as servants in other towns inside Peru. This is a sign of deepening inequality within countries.

Women who are refugees and/or subject to trafficking have even fewer rights than migrant women workers. The majority of refugees remain within other countries of the south. The conditions of refugees in the advanced capitalist countries has become worse over recent years with the "development" of more repressive measures in North America, Europe, and Australasia to keep out refugees as much as possible. This has taken a number of different forms, from making it harder for people to cross borders in the first place, imprisoning many of those —including pregnant women and children of all ages— who do so in barbaric conditions, and making access to what welfare provision still exists in the "host" countries more and more difficult.

Not only the far right, but increasingly mainstream politicians scapegoat refugees for the economic crisis. In Italy, the passage of an emergency law on rape in February 2009 was a cynical attempt by Berlusconi to scapegoat refugees, particularly Roma, for violence against women, while at the same time giving the state more power in general.

- Against the informal economy. For the regularisation of migrant workers' status

Ideology

The crisis of civilisation is also the motor for the growth of reactionary ideas. Berlusconi's policy of blaming immigrants for all the effects of the crisis and using this as an excuse to introduce strong "security" —that is, anti-immigrant— laws is just an extreme example.

Religion has an increasing hold on greater sections of the population, and fundamentalism within all major religions continues to be a threat. Women's bodies are seen as a key terrain of struggle for all fundamentalists.

A striking example is the way in which the reactionary elements of the Catholic Church in Ireland used the threat that the Lisbon Treaty of the European Union would force Ireland to legalise abortion to build support for their reactionary opposition to the Treaty, despite the fact that it contains no such provision. This forced the EU to give a formal guarantee that adoption of the treaty would not mandate Ireland to legalise abortion, as it had also been forced to do on the question of preserving Irish neutrality.

The collusion between right-wing governments and religious hierarchies continues from Italy to Iran, even if there has been a change in the US, where this is no longer the case. One important consequence of the latter is the overturning of the Bush government ban on funding for projects that gave even contraceptive advice —let alone abortion services— to women. This opening will potentially have a positive impact on women's rights, especially in Africa. However, the murder of Dr. Tiller, one of the few physicians in the US openly prepared to perform late-term abortions, reminds us that fundamentalism is still alive and well in the US itself.

Further, the Bush regime's fundamentalist doctrine had a profoundly negative impact on the fight against HIV/AIDs, especially in Africa, that has destroyed the lives of so many women. Sixty-one percent of those with the disease in sub-Saharan Africa are women. But in some countries there, infection rates among young women far surpass those of their male peers. For example, in Swaziland, four times as many females aged 15-24 are infected as males. Lack of access to accurate information about how the disease spreads, as well as pharmaceutical companies' greed, which has severely limited the availability of anti-retrovirals in the communities that most need them, have been the most important causes of this devastation.

In Nicaragua, the Sandinistas ditched their political principles on the question of abortion in 2008, apparently in order to win the election, although there was no real indication that in fact this would increase their vote. But they not only abandoned their own position, they also decided to actively attack the women's movement, bringing criminal charges against nine prominent feminists in the case of a therapeutic abortion given to a nine-year-old rape victim. It just so happened that most of these nine women had also been involved in supporting President Ortega's step-daughter in her case against him for sexual abuse.

In Mexico we have seen collusion between the right wing PAN government and the PRI to introduce "right to life" legislation in 13 states – making the extension of the right to abortion up to 12 weeks which the PRD introduced in Mexico City more difficult. Such developments were possible because the gains in Mexico City, while positive, took place at the level of the superstructure and were not achieved through mass mobilisations, with the resulting change in mass consciousness that this would have involved.

In Brazil, the Lula government has continued to compromise with the Vatican to the point of considering the possibility of putting religious education on the school curriculum. At the end of 2008, Congress chairman MP Arlindo Chinaglia created a Parliamentary Commission of Inquiry into abortion with as a mandate for no less than the institutionalisation of criminalisation of women who defend legalisation of abortion and those who are obliged to carry it out. Moreover, the Judiciary of the State of Mato Grosso do Sul, in the town of Campo Grande, which cited more than 10,000 women for practising abortion, using as proof the medical records requisitioned in a clandestine clinic. Out of these women, some 1,200 are facing trial.

In Afghanistan, one of only three countries in the world where women die earlier than men, we have had the grotesque spectacle of the passage of a law legalising rape within marriage and debate of a clause that would allow a man to legally starve his wife if she refused to have sex with him. This is the country where those who have waged war against it since 9/11 have cynically claimed to do so in defence of women's rights, but where the government they installed is just as reactionary and as in hock to Islamic fundamentalists as their predecessors (who, anyway, were a creation of US imperialism).

The new Afghan constitution allows a separate "family code" for the Shia population and it is under this provision that the current debates are taking place —in the run up to a general election. In this context, as in many others, women's lives and bodies are instrumentalised. Afghan women have organised against this —with at least moral support from feminists elsewhere— however their protests have been viciously attacked by fundamentalists.

As feminists we also face an ideological attack from a different direction: post feminism and masculinist ideas. Starting from the idea that feminism has "gone too far," these currents use differentialist theory to attack women's individual rights to abortion, divorce and protection against violence.

- For full separation of religion from state, an end to religious influence in the framing of laws and the operation of the legal, health or education services.
- For the right to free abortion, contraception and sex education

Violence

The crisis of civilisation is marked by an increase in violence at all levels of society as alienation deepens.

Whether in the private or public spheres, women are victims of violence: in France one woman dies every three days from conjugal violence. At work masculine domination leads to widespread physical/psychological/sexual violence and the increasing tension in workplaces as the crisis deepens can only deepen this phenomenon.

War is of course the most obvious and brutal (and brutalising) example of violence. War in the late 20th and 21st century has become a phenomenon in which it is routine for massive casualties to take place amongst civilian populations, therefore affecting huge numbers of women and children.

From the time of the wars in the Balkans and then again in the wars in the Great Lakes in Africa, we have seen the increasing use of rape as a weapon of war.

Evidence of the extent of rape in Bosnia between 1992 and 1995 by Serb forces in particular forced the International Criminal Tribunal for the former Yugoslavia (ICTY) to deal openly with these abuses, and in 1996, for the first time, rape was recognised as a war crime. According to the Women's Group Tresnjevka, more than 35,000 women and children were held in Serb-run "rape camps" in which Muslim and Croatian women were held captive, raped and deliberately made pregnant. This occurred in the context of a patrilineal society, in which children inherit their father's ethnicity, hence the "rape camps" aimed at the birth of a new generation of Serb children —and the continuation of ethnic cleansing by another means.

Similar horrors have also been experienced by women in the Great Lakes region of Africa. Their bodies have become battlegrounds because women are seen only as vehicles through which new generations are produced; and, in ethnic warfare, preventing the enemy from reproducing equates to the ultimate prize. Against this background, sexual violence has become a deliberate and effective war-time strategy in the region.

Violent sexual acts directed toward women to brutalise and instil fear in them and the general population do not discriminate by age, with girls as young as four months and women as old as 84 suffering the same fate. UN agencies working in eastern Democratic Republic of Congo (DRC) estimate that approximately 50,000 women were raped in the region between 1996 and 2002, and close to 55% of women have experienced sexual violence during the conflict in South Kivu. An estimated 250,000 women were raped during the Rwandan genocide.

In Haiti, an Amnesty International report (November 2008) said a trend has emerged involving groups of armed men assaulting girls, the legacy of rape as a political weapon that emerged during the armed rebellion that ousted Aristide in 2004. Rape became a political weapon by armed insurgents to spread fear and to punish women believed to have supported the democratic government. "Rape has now become a common practice among criminal gangs," said the report. Of 105 rape cases reported by November 2008, 55 percent involved girls under age 18. In 2007, 238 rapes were recorded; 140 of these involved girls between 19 months and 18 years of age. All this is taking place despite the fact that UN troops have been in Haiti since 2004.

Women in Palestine and particularly in Gaza continue to suffer brutally as a result of the Israeli occupation. Pregnant women beginning labour or needing medical attention at earlier stages of their pregnancies are routinely refused passage through the check points into the Israeli state, at the same time that hospitals in Gaza are denied medical supplies, even when they are brought by aid convoys. Countless women have miscarried or died themselves as a result of this barbarity. 192 women died in the Israeli bombardment of Gaza at the beginning of 2009. And the siege of the area continues to impact extremely negatively on the whole society including on the physical and mental health of women and children.

In other places we have seen the impact of increasing militarisation of societies usually resulting in the criminalisation of civil society and violent repression by the state apparatus. Sexual violence including rape has been increasingly used as a tool. In Atenco, Mexico in 2006 the police launched a brutal attack on the social movements resulting in two dead and 26 women being sexually assaulted. The war on drugs, especially in Latin America, and the war on terror are two sides of the same coin here.

We have also seen the use of horrendous forms of sexual torture by US forces —including women—in Abu Graib and in Guantanamo. These abuses, used mainly against male detainees who are presumed to be religious, are clearly intended as much to humiliate the victims as to physically assault them.

We further see that prejudices —racism, anti-semitism, homophobia and sexism where these had been rolled back by the gains of the movement— are again on the increase, together with the spread of Islamaphobia. At the same time these prejudices are expressed more violently so we see a marked increased in murders as a result of these brutal beliefs.

In the case of women, we have the grotesque phenomena of feminicide, which first came to light around the case of Juárez City in the state of Chihuahua in Mexico from the early 1990s and continues to this day. What became clear as women organised and fought back around this issue however, is that the murder of hundreds of women just because they are women is not unique to this one Mexican city. Rather the phenomenon is pervasive throughout the national territory of Mexico and in other Latin American countries including Guatemala, Salvador, Honduras, Costa Rica, Chile, Argentina and also in Spain. Feminicide has to be understood as the (il)logical extension and normalization of other forms of violence against women, and like other such crimes is carried out by men in a number of different relationships to the women involved.

- For full and free support systems for women victims or potential victims of violence, such as women's centres, the independent right to benefits and housing, adequate training of social work, police and justice departments.

The Feminist Challenge to Traditional Political Organizing (1997)

Penelope Duggan

The purpose of this report is to look at the challenges to and criticisms of traditional political organizational forms, primarily those made by the women's movement but also by other social movements, and consider whether they are well-founded or not. [6]

1. Dissatisfaction with "politics"

The first thing to note is that there is a general dissatisfaction with what is considered as politics, that is bourgeois parliamentary representational politics. One of the main indicators of this is the growing abstentionism in parliamentary elections in Western Europe at least. The reasons are easy to see: the scandals over corruption, the confusion between politics and the media—"soundbite politics"—and the loss of control over elected representatives.

In the 1930s and 1940s there was a certain coherence to politics: parties represented different interests, they negotiated and made

---

[6] This *Working Paper* originated as a report by Penny Duggan to the first IIRE Women's School in 1991. It has evolved and matured since, having been given in whole or in part at all sessions without exception since then. It has become far broader in scope than at the beginning and thus, perhaps, schematic in parts. The report given to the first IIRE New Questions School in November 1995 was transcribed by Peter Drucker and used as the basis for the *Working Paper*.

The fact that the text began as an oral report helps to explain its informal and anecdotal character, which has deliberately been preserved. The fact that Duggan speaks out of her own activist experience makes her perspective all the more valuable, both as a feminist critique from within the Marxist tradition and as an intransigent response to challenges to Marxism from outside the tradition. In this sense she makes an important contribution to the IIRE's project of a thoroughgoing, critical renewal of Marxism in dialogue with other paradigms.

Penny Duggan, historian and director of the IIRE Women's Studies Programme, has worked for many years to increase the feminist content of our educational and research activities. Together with Heather Dashner, she co-edited our *Notebook for Study and Research* no. 22, *Women's Lives in the New Global Economy*. She lectures on the historical development of the women's movement and women in broader political movements.

compromises in the interests of their "natural constituencies", in a division of labour with the trade unions. The great result of this type of politics was the establishment of the welfare state. Now in Western Europe at least this coherence is disappearing and there are rising levels of abstentionism in national elections. There can be exceptions, as in the presidential elections in Algeria in 1994. Islamic fundamentalism called for a boycott because it was obvious that all the elections would do would be to approve the president who had been put in place by the army generals two or three years ago. Nevertheless there was a very high level of turnout in the vote: something between 60 and 70 percent of the Algerian population went out to vote for the president. Bourgeois representational politics can thus still mean something in certain conditions. But this is an exceptional case.

Thus one of the problems that we face as political activists is that the very idea of politics and political parties of all types is something from which many people feel alienated. Our particular concern is in terms of left or revolutionary organizations, which are the subject of the harshest criticism from activists in the social movements because it's precisely to those parties that they look to find support and allies in their different struggles. We have all in our different countries and in our different ways experienced these forms of criticism:

▶ that the party form as such, the idea of a political party that organizes at a national level around a general programme, is outdated because there can be no overall project for society as a whole any more, so that all we need is a network of local activists;

▶ that left political parties are out of date and boring because they talk about the working class, and either classes no longer exist (in the opinion of some), or "the working class" is not a revolutionary class; a process led by the working class cannot defend the interests of all, or speak for all because such a notion doesn't take into account the variety of experience of the oppressed and exploited;

▶ that left parties are elitist because they think that they represent or can have an idea about what are the best interests of the class; this is also sometimes considered as being vanguardist, inasmuch as these revolutionary parties think that they in and of themselves represent the class;

▶ that they are hierarchical, bureaucratized, or to put it another way, Leninist;

▶ that they're old-fashioned in their ways of being active, because they talk about strikes and demonstrations and selling newspapers and giving out leaflets, and what we should all be doing is sitting in front of computers sending e-mail all around the world, which is the new, modern way of doing politics.

There is one more criticism to which I'm going to pay the most attention: that we should do away with this sort of organization because it's simply masculine and has nothing to do with half of the population.

2. Remember the context

The first thing that we have to do is put this back in political context, which is as we all know post-1989. After the fall of the Berlin Wall, the collapse of Eastern Europe, the question is posed for many people: Is revolution still on the agenda? Is it possible still to have a project, a perspective of changing society? It's from this point of view that these questions about how you do it become important. Obviously the world has changed; there is a new world disorder; things are posed in a different way, and there is no revolution on the horizon just at the moment.

The example of Chiapas shows us that there can still be very important radical struggles, which are certainly different because they are in this new context. They're different because they come after a whole experience for example of the feminist movement and the gay and lesbian movement: think of some of the things that Marcos has been known to say. When we say there's no revolution on the horizon, it doesn't mean that there can't be very important struggles. But Chiapas is not something that can change the world relationship of forces at this point in time.

This new situation is forming new generations of political activists with a new outlook on the world. I'm a product of a generation for which it seemed that we could actually experience revolutions. On the European continent in the early 1970s, there was not only 1968 and what that represented, there was the beginning of the development of the revolution in Portugal; and there was the fight to overthrow Franco, the dictator in the Spanish state, with the whole question of what would that society become. So I came into politics with the idea that I would actually see a revolution on my continent in five or ten years.

Obviously that's not the case in general for young people today. Unless we bring into our organizations people who come with these new political experiences and this way of looking at the world that is formed by the political context of today, we're going to miss things. But despite the new world disorder, the revolutionary left's goal does still remain a radical transformation of society. We still want a democratic, self-managed society that defends the interests of all of us. I think, unlike some, that there are general interests for the whole of the human race.

On this point I will refer to an article by Norman Geras, a well–known Marxist writer who has written a lot about Rosa Luxemburg but also about Marx's conception of human nature: *"It's not on account of any special forms of acculturation, historically particular social structures or types of learned behaviour, that people generally do not want to die of starvation or disease, or to lose their loved ones in these ways, or to be cruelly humiliated, or to die, or be permanently damaged physically or emotionally at the hands of a torturer, or to be persecuted for what they are or what they believe, be forcibly confined for it or be violently destroyed."*[7]

Those are the values that we would say we're fighting for, of a just and equal society. Geras goes on to say, to put this in continuity with Marx: *"Could anyone familiar with his writings really be in two minds as to whether his project of emancipation—whatever else it might be held to be about—included the aim of meeting the basic needs of human beings for survival and healthy activity and of eliminating from the world these more terrible cruelties and oppressions?... The principle he espoused of distribution according to need was to cover at least those fundamental material needs consequent upon the common make-up of human beings."*

It's an important point in these post-modernist days to stress that we do have common goals and common interests.

To apply this more particularly to the question of women, I would say that, despite the differences in the social, cultural and economic position of women throughout the world, there is a common demand for all women, which is the right to control one's own body. It may be posed in very different ways, in terms of what that means about having children: whether the fight is for the right to have children in good conditions, or for the right to have access to contraception or to abortion. But without that basic right—the right to decide what you do with your own body or who you're going to have sexual relations with, the right not to be violently attacked—how can you possibly live in any sort of decent way? This is not something applicable only to Western Europe. It is a universal value for all women, wherever they are. So we can have general goals, goals that we can share, though we have to define them in a particular way in our different continents, countries and contexts.

---

[7] Norman Geras, "Human nature and progress", *New Left Review* no. 213, Sept/Oct. 1995, p. 153.

3. Development of collective consciousness, where and how?

But the problem is: how are we going to get there, and who is going to lead the struggle?

This brings us to a question that has been much discussed: Which is the revolutionary class? Is there a revolutionary class? Is the notion of a revolutionary class still applicable? The discussion is posed particularly in Latin America as the question of the "revolutionary subject", though not put in those terms in Europe. The Mexican revolutionary Sergio Rodriguez developed a useful distinction in the late 1980s, between the practical-political revolutionary subject and the theoretical-political revolutionary subject. He distinguishes, in other words, the subject likely to make a social revolution—the subject which has the social massivity to impose a change in the social relationship of forces—and the subject which is more involved in developing the social project which it will be possible to build after the revolution.[8]

Classical Marxist thinking on this question did not make this distinction. It assumed that the social force capable of transforming society would itself develop the consciousness necessary to elaborate the social project. Our appreciation of the role of forces such as the independent women's movement leads us nearer to the position developed by Rodriguez. However, while the political contribution of these forces may be crucial, it cannot substitute for the consciousness developed by the mass of the population that the current order is something they want to change. Our first concern is thus to understand how this initial consciousness can develop.

For people to decide to fight, to struggle against the society that they're living in and for something better, means that they have to become aware of the fact that they are suffering, or to put it another way, that they are being exploited and/or oppressed, and that something can actually be done about it. It isn't just natural, they have to realize. God didn't actually make it that way, with the rich and the poor, and it doesn't have to stay that way forever.

This was the work that Marx did in *Capital* and elsewhere. He studied how the society he lived in was organized, in what way people were exploited and oppressed, and therefore how their consciousness of being so would develop. We have to look at that again because we

---

[8] Sergio Rodríguez Lascano, Sujeto revolucionario, vanguardia y alianzas, IIRE *Working Paper* no. 30, Amsterdam, 1992.

know that society has changed. Let us study our society today in the way that Marx did to measure what has changed and what hasn't.

What is the "classical" Marxist appreciation of the formation of the working class as a subject with a "consciousness"? We can get a sense from some texts written by Ernest Mandel about twenty-five years ago.[9] In these texts, Mandel explains that the working class, the people who work, the people who are wage-labourers—who in the English translation are only ever "sons"—are first of all a category, and thus a social subject because they're a social group that exists. But if they begin to struggle and attain a certain level of organization, we can talk then about the development of a layer of "advanced workers", or a "broad vanguard"; and then as their understanding of how they are exploited and how they should be organized becomes more and more systematized, we can talk about the revolutionary vanguard and revolutionary organization.

Mandel explains that it's the workers in big factories, especially those with a big weight in the economy, who most easily become conscious that solutions can be found to social questions through collective activity, since this is less obvious to workers in smaller workplaces. Workers who live in big cities and those who are literate and educated also have greater possibilities of developing this consciousness. He emphasizes that developing consciousness is a product of actual activity and involvement in struggle, but also depends on an individual capacity to assimilate a systematic understanding of what's going on around you, and thus requires a certain level of education in order to become a revolutionary militant. This is the classic schema of the development of class consciousness. Mandel wrote this in 1971; in the following twenty-five years, his ideas presumably changed. In fact this is an inadequate way to explain how the collective consciousness that is the prerequisite to being a political or revolutionary subject can develop anywhere else than in a highly industrialized working class that works in big factories. If we take the Third World, where there's low industrialization and industrialization takes certain very specific forms—the *maquiladoras* of northern Mexico and the free-trade zones in parts of Asia, for example, where there may be quite large industrial plants but where workers may be living in barracks or in practically army-camp-type surroundings—this is not very conducive to the development of a real, political class consciousness.

Then there's the question of the development of class consciousness among those who are not wage workers, because the

---

[9] Ernest Mandel, *The Leninist Theory of Organization*, London, 1972.

majority of the population in many of those countries aren't wage workers. This is not just the traditional peasantry, which is important, but also the poor urban population, the shantytown-dwellers, the street-sellers. So this classic schema is, if not totally inoperative, not a very useful guide as it stands from that point of view.

In Western Europe itself, fewer and fewer workers are actually working in big steel mills or car factories. There are more and more who are working in the service sector, who are working in part-time and so-called "flexible" jobs. There are more and more young workers who have never had a job but remain part of the working class. There are more and more immigrant workers; when there still were car factories there were many immigrant workers in the big car factories of Western Europe, but the way they were inserted into this work force was specific.

And there are many women workers, working in different sectors, again in a specific way. The sex segregation of the work force is a constant that has been noted time and time again. It remains relatively invariable even when other factors, such as social rights, the percentage of women working, or even their place in political life, change. Women are also more likely to work part-time and to take career breaks, in general to give more attention to their family responsibilities when combining the two requires prioritizing one or the other.

So the working class and the mass of the population are changing. Either they are not made up of wage workers, or if they are made up of wage workers they do not fit in the classic schema. The traditional structures of the working class, the trade unions, the political parties, and even the actual communities that existed are also being broken up.

For example, one of the reasons why miners have so often been able to wage extremely determined struggles is that miners tend to live in mining villages, in specific communities around their mines. Coal mines are not normally in the middle of big cities; they tend to be in isolated areas. So people who work in a mine live around it and so do all their families. The community can see very clearly its dependence on the jobs in the mines and created by servicing the miners. Obviously with the closing down of the mines you no longer have the communities. So there is a total break-up of many of these traditional forms of organization.

4. Development of women's collective consciousness

Let's focus more specifically now on the question of the development of consciousness. In his 1971 text Mandel talks about many different factors that affect the way that people become conscious of where they are and what role they play; how they came to see that their situation is not an individual one but a collective one shared with other people. But he never mentions that one of the things that would determine this is the fact of being a woman.

Women in the work force tend not to be in the big factories, they tend to be in sectors with less economic weight. Although there has been a structural change with the entry of women into the work force, many women are actually excluded or confined, or their preoccupations centre on the domestic sphere even if they do go out to work. When we come to the individual capacity and level of education, certainly in a historical sense, women had less access to education, even though things have changed: now at university-entry level it's about half-and-half women and men in most of the Western European countries. But women really do not fit very easily into this classical schema of how class consciousness develops.

Does this mean that women haven't participated, didn't participate historically in revolutionary and radical struggles?

In general, women participated much more than we know about. One of the aspects of the work done by the feminist movement is the re-discovery of women's history and precisely women's involvement in many of the social movements of historical periods, which you would never have known about by reading traditional history books. We have to deduce that women participate in forms of collective activity which do permit them to develop a collective consciousness and therefore to become part of the group that will be a motor force in the struggle for change.

This can take place in different ways. It can be through participation in general struggles, struggles of a community, struggles of a sector of workers; and it can be in struggles that are more directly related to women's situation as women. This doesn't necessarily mean immediate struggles on specific questions related to women's oppression. Experiences in Latin America have often shown that because women are responsible for the home and the family, in the division of labour which is seen as natural in our societies, they are the ones who become involved in struggles for drainage, electricity or mains water in their communities, or as women peasants to be allowed themselves to cultivate the land or to have loans in their own names. There's a whole host of examples that can be cited where women struggle because of a specific situation they're in because they're women, but it is not posed as a challenge to women's oppression in the explicit way that the feminist movement would do so.

That's one example of the way that class consciousness, consciousness of oneself as part of a group suffering from a particular form of exploitation or oppression, can develop in all sorts of different contexts and through all sorts of different experiences of struggle. That is extremely important, because if we were to confine ourselves to thinking that only workers in big factories in the economically powerful sectors could develop class consciousness, the outlook today would be a little bleak.

Women can struggle in different ways on different questions and develop a consciousness, though the development of consciousness is uneven. You may first go into struggle because of your situation as a waged worker, or because of your situation as responsible for the family, or it may be that the spark will be your oppression as a woman: as a victim of sexual violence, for example, or, as was the case with a certain number of the movements in Western Europe, directly around questions like the right to abortion.

What's important is that usually, as consciousness develops, it becomes less unequal. When you struggle, for example, as a local resident around a question regarding your neighbourhood, problems can arise if you as a woman have family responsibilities in terms of the division of labour, or if the men in your family—husband, son, brother or father—think that you should be at home looking after those responsibilities rather than being out on the street petitioning or seeing the local representative. You may find that when you go as part of a delegation of women to meet whatever local elected representative, he listens and says, "But what do the men think?"

All of those sorts of experiences accumulate into an understanding that there is something about the fact of being a woman that means that you're taken less seriously. This can lead therefore to developing a consciousness of the actual oppression of women, what we call a feminist consciousness. This is not an unimportant question: that the development of consciousness of women through struggle becomes a feminist consciousness.

5. Role of the women's movement

We consider that a women's movement that openly challenges women's oppression has a strategic role to play in the revolutionary struggle itself, in the fight to build a new and better society, because women as a sex are oppressed. This doesn't mean that all women are equally oppressed. Your class, your age, your race, and which country or continent you're from affect the way that this oppression is experienced. We must be extremely careful of generalizations about exactly what women's oppression is and how it is experienced.

Let's look at the question of the family. We generally locate the organization of the sexual division of labour, which we feminists consider oppressive, within the family. This holds good. But we have to pay a lot more attention to looking at the family forms in different societies. These factors affect the way that women's oppression is experienced, but this oppression can't be separated from other forms of oppression and exploitation and must be fought at the same time.

People are people, with all the facets of their identity. They're women, they're workers, they're from a Third-World country, or not, or they're an immigrant worker in an imperialist country, or not. There is no way that a movement can say, We're going to fight to liberate that bit of you, but that aspect is going to have to wait. That's just not a realistic proposal to make to anybody about how you're going to help them change the situation that they're in. The fight against women's oppression has to be a fight for today, in the same way that the fight against racism is a fight for today, the fight against imperialism is a fight for today, and the fight against class exploitation is a fight for today. On the other hand, neither can you say you are a combination of this and that specific identity, so you are different from the person next to you who is a different combination, and therefore you can't join together because you only share one facet of your identity.

6. The Marxist tradition and women

The Marxist movement has traditionally defended women's rights. But when we make a balance sheet of the Marxist movement, we see that women remained oppressed in the countries where Communist parties were in power. They may have had all sorts of equal rights. There may have been an enormous percentage of women doctors in the Soviet Union, which when you compare it with other countries seems wonderful. But when we look at what doctors were paid and what the social status was of being a doctor or an engineer or any of those other jobs that were held up as being so wonderful for women in the Soviet Union, we see that there's a problem.

In general, we have had a rather mechanistic understanding of what we meant when we said that there is a historical materialist link between women's oppression and class society. That led to the idea that what we're doing is fighting for the socialist revolution, and it's the working class that fights for the socialist revolution, and then because we'll have abolished class society we'll have abolished women's oppression and everything will be okay. That's proved not to be true, because the transitional societies didn't seem to have solved the problem.

The other problem with this idea is that it totally ignored the anti-capitalist dynamic of women's struggles themselves. Worse, it was often accompanied by a totally false class characterization of those struggles on the basis of the social composition of the movements, which is not a historical materialist way of judging the importance of a political struggle. If we were to judge the Marxist movement then many of its most eminent representatives, starting with Marx and Engels, were not sociologically working-class.

It was also very clear from the struggles of the women's movement of the 1960s and 1970s that the anti-capitalist dynamic of these struggles brought many women to revolutionary politics. The experience of the 1970s brought into all the far-left organizations a new layer of women who had been radicalized through the women's movement. Through a fight on questions such as the question of the right to control one's own body they had come up against all the problems and seen that obtaining this right was impossible in capitalist society, and that therefore the only perspective was the revolutionary struggle. The fight was not only against the doctor who refused to perform an abortion, not only against the law, not only against those (men) who made the law, but against the system that allowed such laws to be made.

If we said that that's the reason why we support the women's movement, however, that would be a rather instrumentalist approach. We do want to recruit to and build revolutionary organizations. But we also want and have a duty to fight in the here and now to change things and improve things as far as possible. That's what trade unions do, that's what the other social movements do, and that is something therefore that we should do in relation to women's oppression, just as we build these other movements of the exploited and oppressed to take forward struggles in the best possible conditions. On this question as on others, if gains are won through collective struggle, this helps change the relationship of forces in general between the classes, and therefore is a contribution to strengthening all the struggles of the exploited and the oppressed.

7. The autonomy of the women's movement

Therefore a women's movement has a role now in the revolutionary struggle and will continue to have one even at the time when there is a revolution. Its role is to fight the manifestations of oppression, both now and in all the period leading up to the revolution: to create first the conditions for a revolution that will lay the material basis for eliminating women's oppression and second for a struggle that continues after the revolution. Women's oppression is certainly not simply a product of capitalism, possibly not simply of class society, so we have no absolute guarantee—indeed historical experience tends to demonstrate the contrary—that it will vanish. Thus the struggle will need to continue. But then the question is how the struggle can be carried on, and what the role of a women's movement is.

Women's interests have clearly not, in the historical balance sheet, been adequately defended by mixed organizations. Thus, a movement that takes as its starting point the intransigent defense of women's interests is a necessity. But to say that a movement has to take as its starting point intransigent defense of women's interests does not mean to say that somehow there is an apolitical way of defending women's interests. Any struggle around the interests of any group in society has a class character, because in the last analysis they're either pro-working class or pro-ruling class. And from what we understand of the inter-connection between women's oppression and class society, it's obvious that if we're going to intransigently defend the interests of the majority of women, that requires taking an anti-capitalist stance.

Thus we can't remain neutral on the politics of this movement. If we think that this movement is necessary, we have a responsibility to propose to it ways to take forward its struggle in the most effective way. That is not to say that we want to build a politically exclusive movement that requires that women first of all sign up and say that they're anti-capitalist before participating in a movement that defends their own interests. Because politicization, political understanding, and radicalization develop through participation in collective struggle; and because, to ensure that the defense of women's interests is primary in this movement, it has to be as broad, as large, as weighty as possible, with the most women possible involved in it, and not a movement that will accept that its interests come second to those of any political organization.

It may well be that such a movement would make an alliance with a political organization, with several political organizations, but on the basis of best defending women's interests. It's for this that the idea of a party-women's movement, such as the Communist Parties, particularly of the Third International, tended to have, does not seem to us an adequate tool for leading the best defense of women's interests. But the exact form of organization of a women's movement depends on circumstances.

During the 1980s there was a discussion about the women's movement in Nicaragua in the period of the revolution and after the revolution and its relationship with the FSLN. It was a specific circumstance where there had been a revolution and there was a revolutionary government. One opinion was that the women's movement should take a position in defense of the revolution but should not accept the FSLN as a political organization dictating (for example) who should be the leadership of this movement. This seems to me the best approximation you could have in that very particular situation of what we would mean by the autonomy or the independence of the women's movement.

But that's a very exceptional situation. Our general stance would be that the women's movement, the different groups that compose the women's movement, should be not linked to any political party. Obviously there are going to be women from political organizations who participate in the women's movement, who may be more or less organized in certain forms, and we would be against the exclusion of organized political women from the women's movement. But we do defend the right of the women's movement to decide independently on the way to take forward its struggle.

We should understand the women's movement, the organized, conscious movement, as part of what we call "the vanguard", that is: a conscious minority that has been developed through the experience of struggle and the development of a systematic understanding of what's at stake in that struggle. It thus acts as a leadership, on the one hand organizing the movement and on the other leading it forward into a confrontation with the system, in other words class society.

It's important to understand that, and to have that understanding of "the vanguard", because revolutionaries, as a force consciously intervening in the struggles that break out, are not usually in a position to directly address masses. Most of us don't have a mass party or organization. Revolutionaries in the PT in Brazil may, some revolutionaries in the Philippines may, but for most revolutionaries it's not the case. Therefore we have a special relationship with the vanguard that has been created through the experience of struggle. And to pretend that we can directly address the masses and that we are the vanguard, which can for example propose to the mass movement to call a general strike tomorrow, is ridiculous. We can argue in our trade unions or elsewhere that there should be a general strike, but for a small organization of several hundred or several thousand activists, anything that we propose has to be in a sense addressed to the natural and organic leadership of those movements.

8. The revolutionary party

Our organizations today, for most of us, are not "the revolutionary party" that we might think about in some abstract way. What do we mean when we say "revolutionary party"? The first thing to say is that sometimes in discussions there is a big thing made about the question of the word "party". For the average person, a party is a political formation which has a programme and which stands in elections. It's actually a very simple word to use. But the term "revolutionary party" means something else as well.

If the level of consciousness, of class consciousness, of some form of collective consciousness was just left as it develops spontaneously, you would have many different parties and movements, on a regional basis, on an ethnic basis, on a sectoral basis. And we need many of those movements. But to develop a general plan for how to change society, a general idea of where we should be going and what a new society should look like, how a new society could be organized that would eliminate all the material and objective bases of exploitation and oppression and therefore make it possible to begin to eliminate all the ideological remnants of such oppression, you need something more than the conjunction of a number of different sectoral movements, which could not themselves be representative of the whole.

So the first thing we mean when we talk about the revolutionary party is a formation open to all those who are ready to discuss within a common framework on the basis of common principles and therefore a common programme. That's a condition for democracy, to have common principles and a common programme, because if you're not even discussing in the same framework, then it's impossible to discuss and come to any conclusion. If the starting points are so wildly different that you haven't even agreed on whether or not you're for women's liberation, then you could never discuss and decide what to do together.

Therefore revolutionary organization is in fact just a practical application of our Marxist analysis—which is that the inherent contradictions of the capitalist system are going to take the form of struggles which have a revolutionary potential, that they could change how things are organized in a positive way, but that requires an active intervention by an organized force. We can change the course of history, there is a common interest of the exploited and oppressed which goes in one general direction, which is the elimination of class society, and it is possible to create a more equal and just society. Here we return to what you might call the moral or ethical aspect of Marxism: we don't want to change society for the sake of change, we want to change it to make it better; we want to change it to eliminate injustice and inequality.

In order to have an idea therefore about where we're going, how we intervene to take things even a tiny little step forward in that direction, we have to have a programme that is not simply a reflection of a whole number of different experiences but has tried to put them together in order to see where the possible contradictions—because there may be contradictions between different sectors of the exploited and oppressed, at least apparent contradictions—and to see what the overall best way is to propose for the organization of work, for the way that life should be organized, for ecological questions, and so forth. In other words we need to make what we call a synthesis of all those experiences.

When we make a synthesis, to come back to my main question, it has to include the needs of women, and the best way for women's interests to be defended in the new society we want to build, and therefore how are we going to take the struggle forward today. This is not a question of being nice to women, it's a very practical question. How could we possibly have the pretention that we could propose anything to anybody about how society could be better, if we don't take into account the experience of half of humanity? This is something that it has taken us a long time to learn. Even now I don't think that we are able to do it at all times; we're still inadequate on this point of analysis and understanding and integration. But it is something that is absolutely crucial.

How does this process of synthesis take place? How do we then put into practice what we might have decided about how we should intervene in the struggles that go on around us? Well the traditional answer is summed up in two words, which these days are generally considered rather badly: the words "democratic centralism" or "Leninism".

Before reacting let's look at what these words mean. If we want to act with the idea that we're going somewhere and not just on an immediate, localized basis, we have to have a programme, something that sets out an idea of where we're going, and to act within that framework. But how do we get such a programme, how do we make the synthesis that I talked about? For that we have to have a political centralization. It is impossible to synthesize anything, unless the information, the points of view, the analyses are centralized somewhere. And they have to be within a common framework we want to develop, a systematic understanding.

We also have to have an organizational centralization for a number of other reasons. Because we want to intervene: if there are big struggles, when the contradictions of the capitalist system do provoke major upheavals, unless we are able to act in a collective and therefore centralized way, our impact is not going to be felt. We have to act in the struggles, and we also have to act on every occasion we can to help develop consciousness, whether that's in a period of big struggles or in a more propagandist way in a different sort of political situation.

Left organizations also have to be ready to act in a centralized way to change when the situation changes: to change our orientation, to change what we have decided to do, because when the situation changes, then that has to be taken into account and we have to make adjustments. We also have to protect ourselves against repression. And there is the classical argument that's always given for centralization, which is: the day will come when we'll be preparing to take power against a centralized state apparatus. So we need a centralization in order to be effective.

But what we should never do is confuse that need for centralization with a vertical, hierarchical, command structure of a party. It's not the same thing. Democratic centralism—I'm going to talk about the democracy—was never conceived of by Lenin as a set of internal party rules. It was in fact in the Third International that what Lenin had insisted on, which was the need for centralization after a democratic discussion in order to be effective, became systematized after his death in what was known as the "Bolshevization of the party".

What is the democratic side of democratic centralism? Would it be the best democratic discussion here if everybody just talked when they felt like it? What would happen? We all know: those who talked loudest would be heard, those who don't like to shout and impose themselves wouldn't be heard.

So democracy is not just the free expression of all points of view at all time. This point is made in the article "The Tyranny of Structurelessness"[10]. This article is a product of the women's movement, a movement that from its very beginnings challenged traditional political organization, saying that it was hierarchical,

---

[10] Jo Freeman, "The tyranny of structurelessness", *Ms. Magazine*, July 1973.

bureaucratic and masculine, and that the way that things should be organized was locally, in small groups. But the balance sheet drawn in this article, which dates from very early in the women's movement, was that if you don't have any organization at all, if you just have anarchy in that sense, it is undemocratic. In order to ensure that everybody is heard, we have to organize that expression, and it has to take place in a democratic framework where there is a commonly agreed way of doing that. So the question of being centralized and being democratic is not a question of internal party rules or being administrative; it's a profoundly important political question in order to be able to do what we have set out to do.

But having said that, does that mean that there are no problems? If we say it doesn't mean internal party rules, but we're going to be centralized in order to be effective and we're going to be democratic, does that mean that there are no problems?

As Mandel said (and Lenin said first), there is a tendency to reproduce the social division of labour within the revolutionary organization. Now Lenin was talking about the social division of labour between intellectuals and workers, which undoubtedly exists also in left organizations. But what also very definitely has a tendency to exist in left organizations is the sexual division of labour. Women have also been oppressed within Marxist organizations in the sense of being excluded; not by rules that say 'We'll have no women' but by the fact in practice, there are few women in leadership positions. At least we have become conscious of that, and we know that simply having a revolutionary programme and a conception of democratic centralism which is not the Stalinist conception is not enough. We have to have, as Mandel says, counterweights or counter-tendencies.

The fact that the Fourth International, for example, has at least partly understood the problems that are posed within its organizations in terms of the place of women and has corrected its position in relation to the importance and strategic role of the women's movement since 1979 is in itself a proof of the effectiveness of this type of organization. Why in fact did the Fourth International take these positions? Because the women in its ranks fought for them; because there was a collective weight, a collective voice, an activity, that had an effect. The fact that there was an international experience was extremely important: this enabled people to see that there was a new rise of the women's movement which was taking a particular form and was expressing a certain balance sheet of what the past, including the revolutionary Marxist movement's past, had been and the way in which it fought women's oppression.

People had international experiences with the problems of the women within their parties, which made it obvious that it was not simply a question that this or that organization was working in very difficult conditions of clandestinity which therefore made it difficult to integrate women, or that another organization was very specific because it was very rooted in the industrial working class which is overwhelmingly male. The existence of an international structure made it easier to see that in all the organizations, whatever their situation, there were common problems being faced, and therefore this was a general feature that had to be dealt with. Obviously this was based on the classic programmatic positions of the Marxist movement. But women's experience and women's collective voice were necessary to solve the problems. This is again a demonstration that an active and militant party is the best guarantee against inner–party distortions.

9. Why is it so difficult for revolutionary parties to recruit and integrate women?

If we say that revolutionary parties are fighting for the interests of all the exploited and the oppressed, we would expect to see the exploited and the oppressed if anything over-represented in their ranks. Women for example have a particular interest in this fight, so that's where we should be.

The first thing we have to be clear on is the general dynamic in this society, which is a dynamic of exclusion of women from the political process. The political process is something that takes place in the public arena, outside the home; and the sexual division of labour in society makes the home and the family women's concerns and work and politics men's affairs. This is something that continues to exist even where majority of women work, are educated and have equal political rights. There are only five percent women in the French National Assembly despite the high level of participation of women in the workforce. This is so widely true today that even many bourgeois forces are becoming preoccupied about it. The United Nations produces reports on women's situations which tell us that women are discriminated against and only earn two-thirds of the male average wage. Also increasingly underlined is the lack of women in public affairs and in the decision-making process of societies in general.

This general process of political exclusion is reinforced because politics was traditionally organized in the place where class consciousness was seen to develop, and we have seen the classical understanding of that process. Politics was organized through the workplace and the relationship between the workplace and the outside, so women were not involved in that. In terms of women's involvement in revolutionary politics we should also take into account the time needed to study in order to become a revolutionary militant. It's necessary to make a conscious effort to understand in a systematic way. This is something that's difficult for women, not just because of exclusion from the formal education system but because women, either for reasons of family responsibility or for other, more internalized psychological reasons, often individually give less time to study. They feel that they should be doing something rather than taking the time to study.

This may seem an extraordinary generalization. But I know of at least one revolutionary party in a Third-World country where a few years ago there were no women among the party's formal members. There were women in the broad layer of sympathizers, but the comrades demanded a level of political education in order to be a party member which they felt that none of the women comrades had attained. There was a problem in the way that they presented this—I think they had a mistaken idea of what level of education one should demand from somebody who's joining the organization—but there was also a problem in the fact that women spontaneously didn't feel it was important to spend their time studying the Marxist classics. It was important for this party to discuss how the question of education should be posed, and how education should be organized so that the women comrades would feel that they were able to participate.

A second question is the general dynamic of reproducing the dominant ideology and the sexual division of labour. The sexual division of labour is reflected in our organizations, with women tending to take on more administrative and technical tasks. It is relatively easy to say: this is absolutely unacceptable, the women comrades are doing all the typing, so we should make an effort and women should be given political responsibilities. But you should also see what happens when women are given political responsibilities. All of a sudden the post of (let's say) trade-union organizer, which when it was a post held by a male comrade required analyzing what was going on in the working class, in the trade-union movement, elaborating political perspectives—a very important political role—is no longer that when it becomes a role held by a woman. All at once the important thing is to make sure that this woman has sent out the letters that call people to the meetings and that the documents have all been reproduced in advance so people will have them, and that everything is well-organized.

Both the women and the men tend to have that conception of what is the important part of any particular responsibility, depending on whether it's undertaken by a man or a woman—obviously for different reasons. Why do women internalize that aspect? Because it's safer. You know that you can send out the letters on time and do the photocopying. It's a much more difficult thing to write an analysis of what's going on in the working-class movement in your country and therefore how you should propose that the trade unions recompose and fuse. It is surprising how many men do really think that they're capable of doing that. That's one way in which the division of labour also affects what happens in left organizations in a less obvious way than simply who's doing the typing.

There's also the political process among women and the way in which that is devalued. It is astonishing that leaders of women's movement work who have led mass movements fighting for women's rights, mass movements that have been able to create alliances with the trade union movement, with political parties, with a whole range of people; leaders of women's work who are engaged in educational work where they explain and make a critical balance sheet of Marx and Engels and place them in their context and explain historical materialism, what it really means and how you can use it to understand women's oppression, are consistently seen and treated as just specialists of women's work. You may understand historical materialism sufficiently to be able to make a critical balance sheet of how Engels applied it to the family, but nonetheless you're just a specialist of women's work. No one suggests that these skills could be applied to any other sector.

On the other hand, the young male comrade who has just been a leader of a student struggle and has shown his capacities to be a leader of the mass movement, is a leader; now he's stopped being a student he must immediately be put somewhere else so that he can lead some other area of work and use those leadership capacities he developed in two or three years of student politics.

I hope that this is a caricature; but I have seen all these things happen. We could go on.

Many women have noticed this, for example: you're in a discussion, and you say something—you give an opinion or you make a proposal—and the discussion goes on, and then somebody else makes more or less the same proposal, gives the same opinion. From that moment on, all we hear is everybody saying: Oh yes, he was right, he was right, I agree with him. Of course, you never said it. There's a Greek legend about a certain King Midas: everything he touched turned to gold. Sometimes women think that it's the reverse for us: everything we touch turns to something much less important than it used to be when a man was doing it.

Another problem that exists in left organizations is at the level of the individual relationships between men and women comrades. Because there is an unequal power relationship in what sometimes we call the real world, and because we are affected by the society that we're in, that unequal power relationship exists also within our organizations, and at the level of individual relations between one male comrade and one female comrade. I'm not talking about acts of violence which can happen, but just the way that people relate to each other in a normal way: the assumptions with which a woman goes into a political discussion and a man goes into a political discussion; the way in which what might be exactly the same behaviour takes on a totally different meaning when it's between two men or between a man and a woman.

When you have one of those passionate political discussions that we all love so much and everybody gets excited and raises their voice, it's one thing when it's between two men. But it is another thing when it's between a man and a woman, because it takes on an aspect of power and authoritarianism, which isn't meant but is there because of what we've all internalized from the society that we live in. And it can seem totally unbearable to be the object of that. There is the other alternative, which is that women in order to survive learn to give as good as we get. I can shout and bang my fist on the table too. But it's not a very pleasant way to have to discuss.

It's astonishing to what extent this can even be true of young comrades—I'm no longer very young and I do have a certain amount of experience —with their, I'm sure quite unconscious, arrogance. A few years ago at a youth camp, I did a report on the origins of women's oppression, in which I put forward the opinion that men derive certain privileges from women's oppression. A young comrade with a particular point of view came up to me and said, "You said that men have these privileges, well, I think you expressed yourself badly." I replied, "Well no, that's what I meant to say. I meant to say men have privileges, because that's what I think." And he said, "But you're wrong. You haven't understood." So I said, "Excuse me, but I have been discussing these questions for twenty years. You may disagree, but it's not I haven't understood." This unconscious arrogance came from somebody who must have been practically young enough to be my son. I heard: You expressed yourself badly, and then, You haven't understood about women's oppression: rather than, "I disagree", which is what he really meant.

Another problem that we face in left organizations is the difficulties that men have in looking at women as political individuals. For example, if there's a very lively discussion about something in a meeting, when you leave the room normally everybody continues the discussion. But it is extraordinary: at least 50 percent of the time, if as we go out of the meeting a male comrade speaks to a female comrade, the discussion will almost immediately turn to something quite different, not political, something more personal. They'll either begin to tell you about the latest exploits of their children or their new job. But to continue to treat you, once you're outside the meeting, as a political being is quite rare. This is something that women have noticed sufficiently in our different countries to feel that once again it's a sign that women as political beings still, even in revolutionary movements, are under-valued because our opinion isn't given the same importance. When people want to know, Oh, you didn't speak in the meeting, what do you think?, the question is very rarely addressed to a woman comrade.

10. Changing the power relations

So the question is now: What do we do about it? First, this is not going to be some sort of natural process. The fact that we discuss the problems of women's oppression and how to fight for women's liberation does not mean that we can easily and naturally solve all these problems. As Mandel said, living in bourgeois society cannot be a school for how to be a proletarian revolutionary, that is to absorb and assimilate into our own consciousness a different way of behaving. We need counter-tendencies, counterweights to the prevailing division of labour and power relationships. Obviously there are no precise remedies that are going to be applicable in all places, at all times, and in all different forms of organizations. The answers will depend on the general evolution and political history, on the different periods and circumstances in which we are active. Many different ideas have been developed and tried, and we can learn from them, both from what has worked and what hasn't.

We can have some general ideas. The first one is that we should have organized feminist work. This is not easy in a period like today, when in many countries the feminist movement is either at its first stages of development or is in some sort of retreat. But we don't give up our other areas of political work because there aren't big struggles going on. We wouldn't dream of doing that for trade-union work, or work in the peasant movement, or any other form of movement.

We also have to have consistent education on these questions, and it should always be part of the education that we give in our organizations. In particular we have to pay attention to the demands of women comrades for organized education. That has to be seen as a party task, because of the internalized feeling that so many women have that we should be always doing something practical. Women are less ready to say, No, I am going to take the time to do it for myself. So we have to organize it.

We also have to pay great attention to our organizations' image and profile. What symbols do we use? Who are our spokespersons? Who do we send to meet other organizations? Comrades from some Third-World countries in particular say that this is a real problem. Sometimes when an organization wants to send a delegation to meet representatives of another party or of a social movement, there's a pressure to send men because otherwise the delegation may not be taken seriously. We have to make a conscious effort to combat that, and say, We think that our women comrades can speak for us, and that they are just as capable as male comrades of doing so.

This question of party image and profile may seem only to have a symbolic value. But symbolism is important. It can seem that it's most natural to put male comrades forward as spokespersons and representatives. But the more we fall into that "natural" way of acting, the less our organizations will be attractive to women, and we won't have the conditions for changing our organizations because we won't be attracting and recruiting women. We also have to change our inner-party functioning. We should rethink what democratic centralism means. When we talk about democratic centralism, we want on the one hand the expression of different points of view and experiences, and we want to be effective when we act. But if we want to ensure expression of points of view, then we have to ensure that women's voices, which are so often not heard, are heard. This is not a natural process. We will have to do what may seem to be artificial things, because the "natural" is the exclusion of women: not to hear women's voices, not to give the space to women to express themselves.

To take an illustration from the history of the Fourth International: in 1979, when we discussed and adopted in our World Congress a very important document on the struggle for women's liberation and socialist revolution, as an appendix to that document we took a position, which I disagreed with at the time and still disagree with, that meetings of women within the party were anti-Leninist. The argument was that women's-only meetings were meetings of a biological sector of the organization, not on a political basis or on the basis of involvement in an area of work but on the basis of the fact that women were women. The argument was in my opinion totally mistaken, even from the point of view of wanting to be a functioning democratic-centralist organization, precisely because it didn't understand the need for special measures to ensure that women's experience is heard.

True, left organizations are not federations of the different sectors of the exploited and oppressed; women in our organizations are not representative of all women. But overcoming the obstacles to women's expression and participation is an important question for democracy in our organizations; and if this requires a special measure such as having women's meetings within the organization, then we should do it. At the same time, because we also want to be politically centralized, that experience has to come back into the organization as a whole. Such questions should not only be discussed among women, nor should women decide without them. Organizations have to decide collectively how to solve the problems that have been pointed out.

One of the problems that's often raised by women is precisely the way in which discussions often take place. Often people are expected to come into a discussion with a set position; you have to go in and defend that position in a very polemical way. Not all organizations necessarily have the same tradition, but often there is a tendency to have tendencies and have discussions that are posed in that way. This means that you have to have a complete alternative in order to contribute to a discussion. It even seems as if you have to be absolutely convinced that what you're saying is right and that what everybody else is saying is wrong, and fight for it in that way. If we just look at some of the vocabulary that is often used in organizational discussions, we can see this.

To tell another story, I was once discussing with a male comrade and asked, But why do you always have to attack when you want to give your point of view? Why can't we just put forward a point of view and have an exchange? He said to me, But you have to understand, when I'm convinced that I'm right, then I think that if the position I disagree with is adopted, it's going to destroy the organization. So I have to smash my opponents, because I don't want this organization to be destroyed. This is a conception that every political position can make or break an organization. That is a way that men are in general more likely to act than women are.

When women begin to discuss the questions of inner-party functioning, they raise the problem of how we can work in a more collective way. This can go from very basic practical questions—such as, if everybody had the documents in advance, and everybody had a chance to read them, then you would be able to have a discussion where everybody could contribute—to styles of speaking. Women more easily talk about themselves and raise their own feelings of personal inadequacy. They are more ready to say, I'm not sure, or I don't know much about this. Anybody who has looked at the actual functioning inside an organization will see that. So it does have an effect to change the composition of for example leadership bodies and to have more women in them.

This is not an automatic process, because a certain amount of informal discussion—the discussions that take place after the meeting, outside in the corridors—tends still to go on among the men. But putting more women in leadership creates a pressure to change things in a way that can make the functioning more democratic and more collective. Of course this doesn't mean, and we have to be careful about this, that women are naturally better and more collective. Anybody who has been active in a women's group knows that women can also have bad ways of functioning. For one thing, many of the women who have spent some time already as political militants have had to learn to become aggressive in self-defense. So an organization cannot resolve all its problems simply by putting a lot of women in its leadership.

These problems of functioning are not just something that affects women. There is a whole problem of the relationship between those who are seen as leaders and those who are seen as rank-and-file militants, including among male comrades. Younger comrades feel this also, in the way that discussions are carried out with them. It's not just a problem for women: we very often have a problem in organizations of extending the leadership beyond the initial core. Many of the organizations that I know best were essentially rebuilt through the 1968 period, that experience and that political generation. What's incredible is that so many of the people who were formed through that experience, and therefore were very young at the time, are still there twenty-five years later. The core of the leaderships of a whole series of left organizations are still the same people. Now there's an objective reason for that, which is that the 1968 generation was formed through a very important political experience, at least for the Europeans. It was a period when revolutions seemed on the horizon, when there were whole new vistas opening up, and a generation was formed that had the self-confidence that they were going to make the revolution; and they came and they took the leadership. No generation since then has had a sufficiently strong experience to form a strong enough generation to say, OK, you lot, you're all now over forty, get out of the way and make room for us.

But we're not interested in just seeing what the objective or the natural process is. We want to do something consciously to change our organizations to make them as adequate as possible. We have to extend that initial core of our leadership. We have to extend it to women, to younger generations, to immigrants and so forth. We have to have to have a conscious plan for changing our leaderships, and have to have a conscious look at how we select leaders, what criteria we use. Do we use an individual star system? Does each and every individual person have to be brilliant at everything—very few people are brilliant at anything at all—or is our goal to build a collective team that within it combines all the different strengths that we have and that are necessary for the leadership of an organization?

Once we try to develop a conscious plan, the much-discussed question of quotas for women or other forms of positive action comes up. If we go with the flow, if we go with what's natural, then we're going to continue reproducing what is such a heavy burden on us: the ideology and the division of labour that exist in society as a whole. Many left organizations have discussed this. There's been a very strong contribution for example from the Brazilian PT. These things are difficult, because we have to be prepared to take measures that might seem to be "artificial".

11. Party responsibility for private life and individual behaviour

But this is not half as difficult as the question of the "private life" of comrades. We have another responsibility in revolutionary organizations, when we consider that we can contribute to taking struggles in a good direction. We have to have militants who have credibility, who have prestige in their political work. This means that they have to act at all times, if such a thing is possible, in a way that's in keeping with our programme. So a party has a responsibility for the behaviour and also for the well-being of comrades.

We have to create the best conditions we can for comrades to carry out the tasks that we give them, and ensure that there is no discrimination on the basis of material factors when we ask comrades to take different tasks and different responsibilities. For example, in a situation of clandestinity and repression an organization has a responsibility to do what it can to ensure its members' protection. If an organization asks comrades to work full-time, we have to guarantee that they are able to do that without materially suffering from it.

Another question is very often raised when women discuss the obstacles to participation in an organization: organizations have to take responsibility for childcare. If comrades are asked to do party tasks, they have to be able to do so in relation to their family responsibilities. Of course, there are just as many fathers if not more in left organizations than there are mothers. But because of the way the sexual division of labour works, it's very much more frequent that women comrades when they have children begin to drop out of political activity because it is so difficult. This is something that we have to take seriously.

Two points should be made about this. The first is that very often when we discuss the position of women and the obstacles to their participation, childcare becomes the major question that is discussed. But it is not having children that makes women oppressed or makes difficulties for women participating in political organizations. There is a general dynamic that applies to all women whether or not they have children that tends to exclude them. The question of childcare is important. We have to apply to it the same criteria, making it possible for women comrades to carry out party tasks. But we also have to take into account what burden can be put on other comrades in terms of their time or the financial responsibility if the organization has to finance childcare.

Second, we need to ask: Are we putting our comrades in a privileged situation compared to other women with whom they are active in the mass movements? Do we fight for collective childcare organized in the case of meetings of the mass movements, or do we simply deal with our own comrades? Are we substituting for what should be state or local government or something provision? The question of childcare is not something that we can simply resolve for our own comrades within our own situation without looking at it also in relation to what do we do to help all women who have the problem of childcare responsibilities. This general statement is of little help with the very difficult problems of when you're a woman in the underground, in clandestinity, and you have responsibility for children. That is a particularly difficult question because it also involves the feelings of women (and men) as parents and the difficulties of being separated from their children for a long period of time.

All these things will of course depend on what our organizations are able to do. They depends on the size and resources of our organizations.

Left organizations also have a responsibility for their members' behaviour, because organizations will be ineffective if our comrades' behaviour is in contradiction with what we say we stand for. We cannot allow comrades to have behaviour that puts the organization in danger in any irresponsible way.

Once again, this is a very difficult problem of different cultures. To take just one example, a revolutionary organization in India has a code of conduct in which they state that religious belief is in contradiction with their programme and therefore incompatible with membership. This issue is posed in a different way in countries or regions where there is a very strong progressive, radical religious movement like liberation theology, as is the case in parts of Latin America. It may well be that in those countries comrades feel that it is perfectly natural and logical that people who do have a professed religious belief should be part of revolutionary organizations, once there is agreement with them on the tasks and the programme. That's just one example of how this question is posed differently in different countries.

However there is one aspect of behaviour about which in my opinion we certainly cannot say: This is a cultural difference. Our programme commits us to fighting all forms of women's oppression. Therefore we have to say that sexist behaviour is in contradiction with that programme. Here I agree with what the PRT (Revolutionary Workers' Party) decided in Mexico: we have to take sanctions against sexual violence and sexist harassment, not because we're going to be able to solve the problem of oppression within our organization, but because we have to have that as a minimum for collective functioning in our organization[11]. How could our women comrades participate in an organization where there are not sanctions against such behaviour?

Now, although we can't accept that some cultures have more machismo than others and therefore it's all a cultural question and we don't have to apply the same standards, there are difficulties. Violence and sexual violence are clear: it's clear when a case of violence has taken place, and there have to be sanctions for that. The question of what constitutes sexist harassment is more difficult to determine. It's more difficult for women to raise, and it may be more difficult for other people to understand. But the point of view that we have developed in terms of for example the workplace is that when women say that there has been a case of sexist harassment, then we take her word for it, because she's the one who is suffering and who

---

[11] "Política de sanciones en un partido feminista", *Bandiera Socialista* no. 402, Dec. 1989.

feels her ability to function is harmed. I don't think that there can be a different criterion inside left parties.

If we want to have democratic parties, if we want to have politically effective parties where women participate, then we have to ensure that women can act politically in confidence and work with male comrades without feeling that they are going to be treated in a sexist way that makes them feel uncomfortable, excluded, or devalued.

In at least one left organization that I know of, there have been cases of extreme sexual harassment: women comrades felt that they were obliged to have sexual relations with certain of the male leaders, because these male leaders used their authority in a way that made it impossible to refuse, without there necessarily being an actual violent act. When this was finally raised in this particular organization, the men concerned either resigned or were in fact expelled. But the women comrades still didn't feel that enough had been done. The attitude taken was that this was an individual problem of some men who were perhaps drunk at the time. The women didn't feel that the organization had recognized that there was such a situation of inequality, of unequal power, in the organization, that had made it possible for this to happen and had made it so difficult for the women comrades to raise it. There was no collective responsibility taken by the organization that said: We allowed a situation to exist in this organization that meant that male comrades felt that they could use their authority as leaders in this way.

We have a collective responsibility to take sanctions; at the same time there is an individual responsibility as well, to understand what your behaviour is and how it affects others. This in no way means creating some sort of anti-sexist police force, or resorting to the sort of revolutionary-puritanical tradition that has existed in some movements, for example in clandestinity when people were involved in guerrilla fighting, where the camps were separated between women and men. That is not solving the problem, it's just trying to avoid it. It's not confronting the reality that we are not liberated human beings even if we belong to revolutionary, feminist organizations. We do suffer from our conditioning, all of us, and male comrades have a special responsibility because of their position of power in relation to women, which can be reflected in their individual behaviour.

In our fight for a new and better society, where the whole relationship between the two genders are revolutionized, it's going to be difficult and probably painful. It's certainly going to require a big effort. Certainly no one is protected from being sexist, having (to put it mildly) inappropriate not to say incorrect behaviour, by joining a revolutionary organization that has the fight for women's liberation in its programme. But no one ever said that making a revolution was going to be easy, so that shouldn't be any surprise.

Conclusion: a short balance sheet

The left has made some progress over the past twenty years. We have made progress collectively through bringing together our experience, particularly by recognizing the role of the independent women's movement, which was a very important step.

Everything is always partial: there's combined and uneven development. We can be critical of our first steps now as we look back at them. We generalized from West European and North American experience as to how women's movements would develop, for example. A very important contribution has subsequently been made by comrades in Latin America. They have explained that through other forms of movements in which women get involved because of their social situation as women, without the starting point being a challenge to women's oppression, an understanding of gender oppression can develop. That was an important contribution.

There are many questions that we still have not sufficiently discussed: for example, the question of the rise of religious fundamentalist movements today. We can all agree here that all forms of religious fundamentalism, whether Christian, Islamic or Hindu, are contrary to women's interests. On the other hand, in many countries, women are very active in religious fundamentalist movements. The Islamic fundamentalists of Algeria have mobilized women massively. This is a whole area that we have yet to develop fully.

We have made advances. In general, those segments of the left that have made a contribution on this question have been able to because we have been permeable to what is going on outside. This is a class society, with a sexist ideology, but there have also been big struggles, there's been the development of the women's movement, and the left has also—unevenly—been affected by that. The real world outside has helped us to change, and we were able to take that experience and to synthesize it and develop our programme.

That's really the concluding point that I want to make: unless we are open to learning from the struggles and from the movements that develop around us, we will not move forward. We will stay stuck somewhere, and we won't be able to do what is the job of revolutionaries, which is to intervene to take the general struggles and the general movements forwards.

Notebooks for Study and Research

- 27/28 Fatherland or Mother Earth? Essays on the National Question , Michael Löwy   (108 pp., €16, £10.99, $16)
- 29/30 Understanding the Nazi Genocide: Marxism after Auschwitz, Enzo Traverso   (154 pp. €19.20, £13, $19.)
- 31/32 Globalization: Neoliberal Challenge, Radical Responses, Robert Went   (170 pp, €21, £14, $21)
- 33/34 The Clash of Barbarisms: September 11 & the Making of the New World Disorder, Gilbert Achcar (128 pp. €15, £10, $16)
- 35/36 The Porto Alegre Alternative: Direct Democracy in Action, Iain Bruce ed.   (162 pp. €19, £13, $23.50)
- 37/38 Take the Power to Change the World, Phil Hearse ed.
          (144 pp. €9, £6, $12)
- 39/40 Socialists and the Capitalist Recession (with Ernest Mandel's 'Basic Theories of Karl Marx') Raphie De Santos, Michel Husson, Claudio Katz   (196 pp., €9, £7, $12)
- 41 Living Internationalism: The IIRE's history, Murray Smith and Joost Kircz eds.   (104pp, €5)
- 42/43 Strategies of Resistance & 'Who Are the Trotskyists' Daniel Bensaïd   (196pp. €8, £6, $10)
- 44/45 Building Unity Against Fascism: Classic Marxist Writings, Leon Trotsky, Daniel Guérin, Ted Grant   (164pp. €8, £6, $10)
- 46 October Readings: The development of the concept of Permanent Revolution, D. R. O'Connor Lysaght ed.   (110pp, €5)
- 47 The Long March of the Trotskyists: Contributions to the history of the International, Pierre Frank   (168pp. €8, £6, $10)
- 48 Women's Liberation & Socialist Revolution: Documents of the Fourth International, Penelope Duggan ed.   (224pp. €8, £7, $11)
- 49 Revolution and Counter-revolution in Europe, Pierre Frank (280pp. €10, £9, $14)

Forthcoming

- Dangerous relationships, Marriage and divorces between Marxism and feminism, Cinzia Arruzza
- Marxism and Anarchism, Marx, Lenin, Trotsky et al.
- Returns of Marxism, Sara Farris and Antonio Carmona Baez eds.
- The conflict in Palestine, Cinzia Nachira ed.
- Towards a New Left: experiences from Europe, Bertil Videt et al.
- Women and the Crisis, Terry Conway ed.

Subscribe online at: http://bit.ly/NSRsub

To order, email iire@iire.org or write to International Institute for Research and Education, Lombokstraat 40, NL-1094, Amsterdam.

Women's Lives in the New Global Economy

Penelope Duggan & Heather Dashner (editors)

IIRE Notebook for Study and Research no. 22 (68 pp. €5)

Women's Lives in the New Global Economy links together transformations that are affecting women in factories and farms, as peddlers and professionals, as neighbours, mothers and wives, in old age and even in the womb.

Twelve feminist activists and scholars on five continents describe sweeping changes that are being brought about by the growth of world trade, regional economic integration (EU/NAFTA/ MERCOSUR) and austerity policies that respond to pressures for 'competitiveness'.

Focusing sometimes on working conditions, sometimes on family life, sometimes on the interaction of gender, class, race and caste, they show how much capital's projects for economic reorganization depend on women's cheap labour in the Third World, 'flexible' labour in advanced capitalist countries and unpaid labour in homes everywhere. And they show how from Sweden to Malaysia new forms of women's oppression are stimulating new forms of women's resistance.

These contributions are the product of several years of sessions at the IIRE devoted to examining women's place in society. In all their diversity, they illustrate how activists collaborating within a shared frame of reference can use their different experiences to develop a truly international analysis of the processes at work today.

————

Also available in French as *Les femmes dans la nouvelle économie mondiale*, Penny Duggan & Heather Dashner (72p. € 5.00)

To order, email iire@iire.org or write to International Institute for Research and Education, Lombokstraat 40, NL-1094, Amsterdam.

www.ingramcontent.com/pod-product-compliance
Lightning Source LLC
Chambersburg PA
CBHW021902020426
42334CB00013B/443